STEPHEN MAXWELL was born in Edinburgh in 1942 to a Scottish medical family. He grew up in Yorkshire and was educated there before winning a scholarship to St John's College Cambridge, where he read Moral Sciences. This was followed by three years at the London School of Economics studying International Politics. Attracted by stirrings of Scottish Nationalism, he joined the London branch of the SNP in 1967. He worked as a research associate for the International Institute for Strategic Studies in London and a Lecturer in International Affairs at the University of Sussex. In 1970 he returned to Scotland as Chatham House Research Fellow at the University of Edinburgh. He was a frequent contributor to the cultural and political journals from *Scottish International Review* through *Question* to *Radical Scotland*, which fertilised the Scottish debate from the 1970s to the 1990s. From 1973 to 1978 he was the SNP's National Press Officer and was director of the SNP's 1979 campaign in the Scottish Assembly Referendum. He was an SNP councilor on Lothian Regional Council 1975–78 before serving as SNP Vice Chair, successively for Publicity, Policy and Local Government. From the mid-1980s, he worked in the voluntary sector, initially with Scottish Education and Action for Development (SEAD) and then for the Scottish Council for Voluntary Organisations (SCVO). He retired in 2009. He was the founding chair of a Scottish charitable company which today provides support to enable 600 vulnerable people to live in the community. He contributed to numerous collections of essays on Scotland's future, most recently *The Modern SNP: from Protest to Power* (ed Hassan, EUP, 2009), *Nation in a State* (ed Brown, Ten Book Press, 2007) and *A Nation Again* (ed Henderson Scott, Luath Press, 2011). He died in April 2012.

Luath Press is an independently owned and managed book publishing company based in Scotland, and is not aligned to any political party or grouping. *Viewpoints* is an occasional series exploring issues of current and future relevance.

Praise for *Arguing for Independence* by Stephen Maxwell

A lifelong campaigner both for an independent Scotland, and for a socially just and peaceful one.
JOYCE MCMILLAN, Scotsman

An important book which deserves to be widely read by nationalists and unionists alike.
TOM DEVINE, Sunday Herald

A wonderful book... a great legacy for him to have left Scotland at this time.
ELAINE C SMITH, The Herald Books of the Year

A fine contribution by a fine man.
ALEX SALMOND, Scotland on Sunday Books of the Year

A book of astonishing clarity... beautifully written.
MARGO MACDONALD, Sunday Herald Books of the Year

[A] thoroughly integrated vision of this nation's next step (I hope).
PAT KANE, Sunday Herald Books of the Year

Truly original... his parting shot will make a huge contribution to the end game.
MICHAEL RUSSELL, Scottish Review of Books

The Case for
Left Wing Nationalism

Essays and Articles

STEPHEN MAXWELL

Luath Press Limited
EDINBURGH
www.luath.co.uk

First published 2013

ISBN: 978-1-908373-87-8

The paper used in this book is recyclable. It is made from
low chlorine pulps produced in a low energy, low emissions manner
from renewable forests.

Printed and bound by
Martins the Printers, Berwick upon Tweed

Typeset in 11 point Sabon

Contents

Acknowledgements

There are a number of people I'd like to thank. Gavin MacDougall and everyone at Luath Press have been endlessly supportive, as have Luke and Lisa, Katie and Chris, and my mum Sally (together with the extended family in England and New Zealand). Emma Burns, Pete Ramand, Scott Lavery, Callum McCormick, Andrew Smith and Bryan Connolly have all, in different ways and at different times, been a source of great encouragement. Dan Paris provided some useful editorial advice. Harry McGrath and Owen Dudley Edwards were invaluable every step of the way. Above all, though, I'd like to thank my dad for leaving me / us / Scotland with these wonderful essays – and so much else besides. You were a gem.

Editor's Note

'Beyond Social Democracy', from April 1976, is the earliest of the pieces here. But it is perhaps the densest and most challenging. For that reason I have decided to start the collection off with three shorter, punchier articles – 'Can Scotland's Political Myths Be Broken?' (November 1976), 'Scottish Radicalism' (May 1976) and 'Scotland's Foreign Policy' (September 1976). From 'The Double-Edged Referendum' (January 1977) onwards, the essays follow a strictly chronological order. For the sake of clarity, I have included the original introductory notes to 'Scottish Radicalism' and 'The '79 Group: A Critical Retrospect'.

Foreword
A Nation's Blueprint?

NOTHING WILL MAKE UP for Stephen Maxwell's disappearance, it goes without saying. However, there remain some consolations, very important both to those who knew him and to those who will learn more about him from this book. He lived to perceive the political dawn coming, and in his final collection of texts this quiet man summed up much of what that should stand for. With good luck, his nation will come to embody it in due time, as a more distinct identity in the wider political world. I can't think of any other country – new or renewed – whose formation has benefited so much in this way, or in such a timely fashion.

I also have the strongest personal reasons for welcoming this posthumous contribution. It was Stephen who put me right about both the cases and the likely character of Scottish nationalism, in a period when I remained over-attached to the fossilised remains of 'Internationalism'. Like many others I had imagined direct transitions from a personal level of faith on to the overarching sky of totality, whether represented by capital-letter Socialism or Communism (philosophically hallowed by Marxism). And in this imagined passage, nationality was somehow bypassed, or treated as a hereditary accident – more likely to impede than assist individual progress towards humanity's capital-letter plane. In that sense, secular internationalists had simply taken over the deeper framework of so many religions: Hegel's 'Absolute' in 200 or so assorted tongues and disguises. Readers will find the episode referred to below, in typically forgiving style.

Nationality can't be glossed over or occluded, was the Maxwell message. It has to be incorporated into the contemporary, forward-looking mode of sociality. I think this is the sense of 'left wing' in his unceasing struggle to redefine Scotland's identity and its place in the post-Cold War world. He wasn't hoping to reanimate Soviet or other phantasies, or to reinvent Socialism. The struggle for Social Democracy in Scotland has been 'belated', inevitably. However, such a situation has advantages, too: the belated may be intertwined with the novel, the onset of a different age. The circumstances of 'globality' grow daily more distinct from those of 18th to 20th century industrialisation. The latter was a competitive and militarised transformation which had demanded everywhere what one might call 'high-pressure' identification. This demanded an over-intense devotion to the peculiar features and needs of each competitor: 'ethnicity', as it came to be labelled. Life-or-death turned into part of a deal from which escape was impossible, leading to incessant warfare – of which the 'Cold War' was the protracted but (one hopes) concluding episode.

Personally, Stephen would have laughed at the notion of being a 'prophet'. Nor was this just a matter of temperament. The prophetic period of Scottish nationalism came earlier, between the two World Wars, most famously in the work of C.M. Grieve ('Hugh MacDiarmid'), whose Drunk Man contemplated a Thistle persisting against all odds, and needing a violent revolution to evolve more freely. The Maxwell equivalent is non-violent, and democratic: a kind of 'Yes' to our collective being, and a restoration of the latter's self-confidence — what Carol Craig has called *The Scots' Crisis of Self-Confidence* (2003) in one notable survey of the terrain. However, there is surely something more deeply prophetic about the Maxwell oeuvre – expressed in works like *Arguing for Independence: Evidence, Risks and the Wicked Issues* (Luath Press, 2012). The wicked issue is of course straightforward resumption of national statehood: a 'Union' originally opposed by so many, who are now given their chance to affirm a different course.

Such affirmation will be peaceful, and uncontaminated by inherited hatred or resentment. What was wrong wasn't 'the English', but the 'Great Britain' which an early 18th-century elite had signed up for, in pursuit of both industrial development and natural resources to be derived from more successful colonisation. The contrary of that union might of course be a differently articulated association, some kind of 'confederation' along Swiss lines. But any such reform would itself demand that 'sovereignty' be first relocated and diversified, among Scotland, Wales, Northern Ireland and a restored 'Little England'. This return of statehood would not be an impossible backward plunge into the epoch of extinct '-isms'. We can't help inheriting ideologies from the past; but 'nationalism' in that time-bound sense will itself alter and adapt, to confront the novel circumstances of 'globalisation'. Sovereignty means having the final word; but also, seeking more freely for the new words urgently needed, in such rapidly shifting times.

The prospective alteration has been underway for long enough. As well as Stephen's own *Arguing for Independence*, the academic W. Elliot Bulmer has produced *A Model Constitution for Scotland: Making Democracy Work* (Luath Press, 2011). A little later, *Scotland's Choices: the Referendum and What Happens Afterwards*, by Iain McLean, Jim Gallagher and Guy Lodge (Edinburgh University Press) appeared, as did *A Nation Again: Why Independence will be good for Scotland (and England too)*, edited by Paul Henderson Scott (Luath Press). There are already many forerunners of what will be a year's debate on the resumption of our country's updated statehood, considering the process in much detail. However, vision matters even more than the realism imposed by an oncoming age. And I doubt if anything more telling on the spirit of this coming moment will be published than the essays here, from the great thinker (and activist) who worked so long and determinedly towards his country's re-established independence.

The most recent addition to new nationalism's title list has been Lesley Riddoch's *Blossom: What Scotland Needs to Flourish* (Luath Press, 2013). All classical theories of nationalism, like those of Ernest Gellner (*Nations and Nationalism*, Blackwell's second edition, 2006) and Liah Greenfeld's *Nationalism: Five Roads to Modernity* (Harvard, 1993), indicate nation-state formation as always arising from an alliance between popular restlessness and an evolving intelligentsia, inclining towards separate and independent development. 'Among ordinary Scots… the process has already begun', observes Riddoch, and 'the task is to let that flower blossom – to weed out the negativity and self-doubt' deposited by the half-history of an anachronistic Union. At the end of his *Scotland the Brief: Short History of a Nation* (Argyll Publishing, 2010) Christopher Harvie noted that 'a confederal covenant within the islands would be valuable', and the most obvious next step, if only the negativity could be got rid of. Stephen Maxwell's positivity is surely the answer, for dismissing 'the last enchantments of imperialism', and convincing the English majority of their own need to 'blossom' independently.

'Yes' is about the conditions required for such advance, which can't be 'cultural' or emerge from civil society alone. Scots invented 'civil society' in the 19th century as an alternative to the loss of statehood, but in the 21st century it's no longer sufficient. The prolonged recession between 2008 and the present has underlined the need for more political diversity, for new ways to tackle a 'cosmopolitan' capitalism no longer able to guarantee reasonable development and prosperity. Of course independence 'by itself' won't generate miracles; but the point is, surely, that no society is any longer 'on its own', and will only be able to contribute to a broader 'Common Weal' with the means to act, experiment, and be different. Independence was never a sufficient condition of societal success; but does it not remain a necessary condition of tolerable change and bearable identity?

Tom Nairn, October 2013

Preface

'THE CASE FOR LEFT WING NATIONALISM' was originally published, as a pamphlet, in 1981. My father, who was Chair of the '79 Group at the time, wanted to challenge the view held by SNP traditionalists that a shared sense of Scottish identity would be sufficient to build a majority for independence. Instead, he argued, nationalists needed to 'disregard romantic [conceptions] of nationhood' and make an 'unsentimental [appeal to] the social and economic interests of the Scottish people'. Specifically, he believed the SNP should develop policies attractive to those most exposed to the effects of British economic decline – Scotland's industrial working class. He was confident of Scottish workers' radical constitutional instincts: two years earlier, in the first referendum on devolution, most working class Scots had voted in favour of home rule, while wealthier Scots had voted overwhelmingly against.

How does this (crudely surmised) analysis fare today, 32 years later, in a Scotland less than 12 months away from a vote on independence?

Well, my dad was right about working class attitudes to constitutional change. In 1997, 91 per cent of working class voters supported the creation of the Scottish Parliament compared to 69 per cent of middle class voters. A similar pattern emerges when it comes to independence. Last year, Ipsos MORI published a poll showing that 58 per cent of people living in the most deprived areas of Scotland backed independence compared to 27 per cent of people in the most affluent areas. There is a clear class dynamic to the constitutional debate in Scotland.

My dad was also right about the limits of what Neil McCormick called 'existentialist nationalism' – the belief that a nation should be independent simply because it is a nation. Such logic is an intellectual dead-end which, thankfully, few in the SNP subscribe to these days. Its opposite is national sovereignty as the basis of social, economic and cultural change.

This is the thread that binds the essays here, from the first published in the mid-1970s, when my dad was working in various capacities for the SNP, to the last published in late 2011, roughly six months before his death from cancer at the age of 69. Not all the pieces are polemical. They offer a wide-ranging, nuanced analysis of contemporary Scottish history and culture, although usually with a political dimension. Almost all refer in one manner or another to Scotland's changing economic landscape. My dad's academic training, at Cambridge and the LSE, was in political theory and that inevitably informed his writing and thinking.

Not long after 'The Case for Left Wing Nationalism' was published my dad was expelled from the SNP, alongside Alex Salmond, Kenny McAskill and others, for his membership of the '79 Group. He was readmitted a few years later but I'm not sure his relationship to the party ever fully recovered. He had, at any rate, always lived at something of an angle to it. For someone with such a gentle personality, he was surprisingly rebellious. His commitment to independent, critical thought – evident on every page of this book – never sat comfortably with the requirements of party discipline.

Jamie Maxwell, October 2013, London

Can Scotland's Political Myths Be Broken?

Question Magazine, November 1976

PROVINCIAL SCOTLAND, denied the opportunity of defining its sense of national identity through the exercise of self-government, drugged itself with consoling myths. Even today, when Scotland is arduously working provincialism out of its system, there are few sections of the Scottish community which do not require a regular fix of their particular apologetic myth.

Indeed, in the present transitional state of Scottish consciousness, Scotland's dependence on myth is perhaps greater than ever. As old myths lose their potency, new ones are sought in their place. At a time of nationalist revival it is not only the Nationalists who see in the manipulation of national myths a powerful instrument of propaganda. In Scotland today, no political interest can expect to be allowed a monopoly of myth-making and propagating.

Scotland's recent cultural history provides extreme examples of the different roles myth-making can play: on the one hand, the mythical Scotland of Harry Lauder and the Alexander Brothers supplying whisky flavoured opium for the bruised Scottish ego; on the other, the ferocious myth-making of Hugh MacDiarmid intended to recreate a complex, dialectically vigorous Scottish culture as a weapon of social and national revolution.

As the focus of Scottish interest has switched from cultural to political revival, Scottish national politics has proved itself as prolific a breeding ground of myth as Scottish cultural politics once was.

The unionist myths are the most banal. They range from the myth of the Scot as the loyal North Briton and warrant officer of Empire through to the concept of the Scot as a hard-nosed, self-interested grafter – the target, presumably, of Sir Alec Douglas-Home's notorious 'buttered bread' appeal in New York – to the demonological myth of the Scot as the natural Bolshevik, the eternal barrack room lawyer or garrulous but inarticulate union agitator.

Defensive

Among unionist interests, it is the Scottish Left, the interest most directly threatened by political nationalism, which has equipped itself with the most impressive array of national myths. Given the Left's present defensive posture, it is not surprising that most of its myth-making has a conservative purpose. Perhaps the dominant Left-wing myth is of a Scotland that has lived – and continues to live – precariously on the verge of political and social reaction. It finds its historical references in the repressive nature of Scottish Presbyterianism and the religious intolerance of 17th-century Scotland, in the authoritarian and punitive values embodied in the Scottish Poor Law and Scottish education, and in the brutalities of Scottish capitalism. Its symbolic figures could be drawn from a gallery which included Lord Braxfield, Burns on the cutty stool, a tawse-swinging dominie, and Andrew Carnegie with John Pinkerton at his elbow. The myth is all the more potent for the support it draws from that strain of Marxist theorising which sees bourgeois nationalism as necessarily reactionary, in line with recent examples of European nationalism.

Conservative

The historical accuracy of a myth is, in this context, less interesting than the political use to which it is put. The Left's favourite myth yields an obvious anti-nationalist conclusion. The only force which contains the Scotsman's Calvinist genius for social reaction is England's benign and progressive influence and the main obstacle to political reaction in Scotland is the united British labour movement.

   As a conservative myth this suffers from the basic flaw that it depends on a continuity of experience which is itself under challenge from the changes the myth is designed to prevent. It ignores for example the possibility, if not the probability, that the influence of traditional religious institutions will be eroded, not strengthened, as rival institutions emerge to challenge their claims. What price the General Assembly's boast that it is Scotland's parliament when there is a real Scottish parliament? It ignores the possibility that bourgeois nationalism may attract back into Scotland's public life those radical middle class elements who have been conspicuously absent over the last several decades and who are likely to be the most hostile to the ethos of provincial Scotland. It ignores the probability that a new political status for Scotland would create a new responsiveness to international influence.

This myth of black, Calvinist Scotland has coexisted on the Left with another superficially antipathetic myth – the myth that the Scottish working class has an instinct for radical if not revolutionary socialism lacking in its Sassenach counterpart. Although this myth can draw on a formidable roll call of heroes – embracing names like Maclean, Gallagher, Maxton and McShane – its political impact is ambiguous. Its chief role seems to be not to act as a spur to radical action by the Scottish Left but to console it for the bleakness of its own vision of Calvinist Scotland. That the myth contains great potency in this role is suggested by the current fashion for political theatre based on this period of Scottish labour history, and by the fatalistic, self-lacerating Connolly cult. As the perspective of change widens for Scotland, the Scottish Left perversely hugs closer to itself its bittersweet images of defeat.

Scottish nationalism is if anything even more fertile in myth than Scottish socialism. Nationalism after all has experienced a far longer gestation period in which the moulding and remoulding of national myth was its only sustenance. For many Nationalists, the constitutional objective of independence has itself acquired an almost mythical quality, dragging in its train all manner of social and political glories.

To many Nationalists, Scotland's claim to a distinctive history rests on the grand myth of Scottish democracy. Its historical sources are suitably eclectic, embracing Celtic tribal democracy, Wallace's popular struggle against the English, and the Presbyterianism radicalism of the Reformers, and extending to cover the Reform agitation, the 1820 Rising and the Home Rule days of Scottish socialism before achieving its apotheosis in Scottish nationalism.

Alien Import

The idea that Scottish society is egalitarian is central to the myth of Scottish democracy. In its strong nationalist version, class division is held to be an alien importation from England. In the weaker version it describes the wider opportunity for social mobility in Scotland as illustrated in the 'lad o' pairts' tradition.

Education has played such an important part in the survival of Scotland's sense of her own identity that it has developed its own distinct mythology. The parochial school, in which the children of the Laird, the doctor, the grieve and the farm labourer unselfconsciously rubbed shoulders; the belief that the Scottish working class was the most literate if not literary working class in Europe; the fancy that every ploughboy has a poet's pen in his knapsack; the conviction that Scottish education was not only more democratic but also of a higher quality than that available elsewhere – this whole 'literature and oatmeal' tradition has played a key part in moulding Scotland's image of itself as a democratic society.

Another element in the democratic myth popular with Nationalists is the idea that Scotland is politically a more open, less centralised society than England.

Although Scotland could not escape all the centralising consequences of the English form of parliamentary government, Scottish political opinion never embraced the doctrine of parliamentary sovereignty preferring the more radical doctrine of popular sovereignty. Complementing this, the long history of conflict between the claims of religious organisations and the claims of the executive in the form of a remote English authority implanted in the Scottish soul a sense of being permanently 'agin the government'. Even Scotland's regional differentiation, and the role of Glasgow, Edinburgh and Aberdeen as distinctive centres, is interpreted as a form of social and cultural federation.

These myths have served a valuable role in mobilising Scottish energies to attack a failed status quo. But as the formative ideas of a party now challenging for political power they contain great dangers. The myths of Scottish democracy have too often served to justify an uncritical acceptance of nationalism's claim to be a decentralising, anti-bureaucratic force. They have given support to the denunciation of class-based politics and the collective wishing away of class issues which is a well-established SNP ritual. They condone the facile assumption that independence will automatically release a flood of reforming energy to wash away Scotland's social ills.

It must recognise first of all that Scotland is a class society, not only in the sense that substantial inequalities exist (one in five of Scotland's population live on the official poverty line and wealth is overall more unevenly distributed than in England) but also in the sense that it is, relatively, both a socially stagnant and a segregated society. What other northern European democracy has so high a proportion of its population living in physically isolated single-class housing estates? In the first three-quarters of the 20th century, Scotland's political leadership included a large number of working class representatives. In the final quarter it is increasingly middle class. The SNP leadership itself, notwithstanding its official 'classless' ideology and its evident ability to win working class votes, fits the classic model of bourgeois nationalism.

Poor Education

Contemporary Scotland's education system is neither democratic nor of a particularly high quality. Recruitment to the universities is probably more limited socially than it was for a period in the mid-19th century, and opportunities for post-school education outwith the universities are more restricted than in England. Scottish authoritarian attitudes too often combine with the general philistinism and provincialism of Scottish society to undermine both the intellectual and the emotional confidence of young Scots as illustrated (albeit summarily) in the recent 'Euroscot' report.

The anti-bureaucratic, decentralising role claimed for nationalism faces a formidable challenge if independence is achieved.

Scotland's social problems, as well as the economic problems caused by the dominance of foreign capital, will necessitate strong and sustained action by the Scottish state, and the resources will be available in the form of oil revenues to meet the need. Without determined corrective action, an independent Scotland could develop into the most 'statist' society outside Eastern Europe.

Threats

Nationalism's further claim to be the agent through which the value of 'community' and 'fraternity' will be restored to Scottish life will be threatened by the increase in competitive bargaining between economic interest groups, which is likely if SNP's promised economic miracle materialises. The economically weak may prove early victims of the 'revolution of rising expectations' which the SNP is preparing.

To criticise the cherished nationalist myths of Scottish democracy is not to deny them all significance. They reflect real, though partial, elements in Scottish society which in the past probably has been more democratic than English society and which even today has a more democratic ethos. A political programme for an independent Scotland must, however, be built on a more substantial base than that which the dream of Scottish democracy provides.

Scottish Radicalism

Question Magazine, May 1976

Taking up Christopher Harvie's article in last month's 'Q' on radicalism, Stephen Maxwell argues that radicalism in Scotland today is specifically Scottish and not just the vanguard of a British movement.

THE MAJORITY OF activists in the Scottish National Party assume that they are participating in a genuine Nationalist movement. They would be surprised to learn that many academic commentators dispute the SNP's Nationalist credentials. Although electoral developments have forced these commentators to refer to 'Scottish Nationalism', they use the words merely as shorthand. In their analyses they seek to provide the SNP with a familiar British habitation and a name.

In this spirit, the SNP has been variously identified by British commentators as the North British manifestation of the protest vote against the two-party system; as a regional variation of a general British reaction against bureaucracy and over-centralisation; and as a protest against relative economic deprivation.

The latest example of this intellectual conservatism is Christopher Harvie's article –

> 'The Road from 1885' – in last month's *Question*. 'Devolution,' writes Harvie, 'is not fundamentally about Welsh or Scottish nationalism, but about the political feelings of the people as a whole ... Our salvation (if such there be) may well lie in returning to the politics of 1885 – replacing the politics of economic manipulation, patronage and welfare with a politics which is about identification, participation and responsibility – with the radical future that Gladstone stole.'

That 'radical future' was Joseph Chamberlain's 'unauthorised' radical programme of 1885, embracing manhood suffrage and an end to plural voting, direct working class representation in Parliament, free elementary education, an element of 'social' taxation and a programme of decentralisation to strengthened local authorities.

Decentralisation was Chamberlain's alternative to Gladstone's cherished policy of Irish Home Rule. By insisting on Home Rule for Ireland,

Gladstone forced Chamberlain out of the Liberal Party and into a stormy alliance with the Conservatives. Without Chamberlain's radicalism the Liberals served merely as a 'pusillanimous prelude' to Keir Hardie, the Labour Party and the 'politics of manipulation, patronage and welfare'. In Harvie's scenario the significance of the SNP is as a catalyst to the recovery of a lost British radicalism.

Harvie thus appears to strip Scottish politics of both its chief contemporary interest – the emergence of a politically effective nationalism – and one of its proudest traditions: its distinctive radicalism.

Reductionist

The flaws in Harvie's description of the choices facing Britain at the end of the 19th century reflect flaws in his understanding of contemporary Scotland. Chamberlain's programme depended on a reductionist analysis of Irish nationalism in the 19th century as Harvie's own prescription depends on a reductionist analysis of Scottish nationalism in the 20th.

Chamberlain held to the Unionist belief that the Irish problem was basically a 'knife and fork' one to be met by social amelioration and reform. But his proposals for a Central Board with legislative powers on education and communication would not have proved acceptable to Irish opinion. As the history of 'constructive Unionism' under Balfour demonstrated, the brave 'radical future' in Ireland would have likely proved a bloody one.

Chamberlain's reductionist view of Irish nationalism was somewhat paradoxically combined with a conviction that Home Rule would lead to separation. His fears on this score were reinforced by the equivocal stance adopted by Parnell, whose Parliamentary avowals that Home Rule would satisfy his ambition for Ireland had to be discounted against his famous Dublin statement at the beginning of 1885.

Imperialism

'No man has a right to set a boundary to the onward march of a nation. No man has the right to say: 'This far shalt thou go and no further'. Such sentiments presented a direct challenge to Chamberlain's developing imperialism: to an Irishman the 'identification' which Harvie picks out as one of the values asserted in Chamberlain's programme was to be enforced identification with the metropolitan heart of imperial Britain.

Many of the proposals in Chamberlain's 1885 programme were, of course, part of the common radical currency of the time. Indeed, Chamberlain's programme was trumped by the Liberals' Newcastle programme of 1891 which so affronted Gladstone and Morley. Chamberlain's advocacy of social reform, however, had sinister overtones absent from the proposals of the Liberal or socialist radicals. Chamberlain saw constitutional and social reform as a way of mobilising Britain's human and moral resources for imperial purposes. As a recent historian of the period has put it, where the Liberal Party remained a party of liberty and liberties, Chamberlain sought a party that would uphold the claims of the state. The line of development represented by Keir Hardie and the radical Liberals did indeed mature in the mid-20th century into something akin to a corporate state. But there is more than one way to corporatism and Joseph Chamberlain's way, with its Bismarckian references, would have posed graver dangers to liberal democracy.

Of course, Chamberlain appeared to pose a far more serious threat to the British Establishment in 1885 than Hardie did as the victor of West Ham in 1892. Chamberlain propounded his radical programme from an established position in British politics. Hardie, by contrast, was almost as much of a political eccentricity in 1892 as Winnie Ewing was as the victor of Hamilton in 1967. But 'Queer Hardie' of the yellow tweed trousers, the serge jacket and vest and the soft tweed cap had gained a secure position in the demonology of late Victorian middle class Britain, as a socialist agitator and fomenter of class hatred, at a time when Chamberlain was a Cabinet colleague of no less an establishment grandee than Lord Salisbury.

The personal history of Keir Hardie, as of many of his International Labour Party (ILP) colleagues, illustrates the difficulty of dividing the radical men from the reformist boys. Kenneth O. Morgan's recent biography – *Keir Hardie: Radical and Socialist* – emphasises Hardie's deep roots in late Victorian radicalism. With fellow ILP pioneers Bruce Glasier and Ramsay MacDonald, Hardie drew his socialism not from the Methodist or Baptist chapel culture of most of his English and Welsh colleagues but from headier, more eclectic sources – from Scottish democracy and from anti-Calvinism, from the legends of Wallace and the poems of Burns, from

Carlyle and Ruskin, Morris, Emerson *et al.* Hardie was tireless in the work of building bridges to the trades unions but nevertheless found, or made, time to give active support to a wide range of radical causes – pacifism, feminism, anti-colonialism, inter-nationalism – which most of his trade union colleagues understood little.

Hardie's View on Home Rule

Hardie's radicalism also embraced a concern for 'identification, participation and responsibility'. His views on home rule are well known. As the Member for Merthyr Tydfil, he learned to sing the national anthem of his adopted country in Welsh. He had a clear view of the choices facing Welsh nationalism, as other nationalist movements, and warned against the advances of rich Liberals like the industrialist Sir Alfred Mood:

> The Nationalist Party I have in mind is this – the people of Wales fighting to recover possession of the land of Wales... that is the kind of nationalism that will be emblazoned on the red flag of socialism.

Hardie's concern for participation and responsibility was evident, too, in his view of socialist society. Although he was notoriously vague about the details of that society, he knew what he didn't want – on the one hand, the state socialism of the German Social Democrats, on the other, any version of anarcho-syndicalism.

Unlike many socialists, Hardie took local government seriously, on a theoretical level perhaps as seriously as did Chamberlain. It was one area in which his usually woolly socialism took on a reasonably concrete form. Municipal socialism, in addition to laying the foundations for communal ownership at a national level, would help to restore a sense of civic pride and public involvement. Municipal socialism in Hardie's vision was not to be restricted to the trams and electricity. The management of a nationalised coal industry, for example, should be undertaken by county councils.

Hardie's aversion to anarchism and syndicalism sprang from the same civic roots. Like Ramsay MacDonald, he was opposed to a division of political power on the basis of economic or social function. He acknowledged the fact and the political potency of class interest while insisting that it must be subordinated to a wider political and civic community.

The home rule sympathies of Hardie, MacDonald and Glasier followed naturally from their shared Scottish background. It is perhaps less obvious that their wider concern for constitutional action, political community and civic identity owed anything of significance to that background.

Although neither Hardie nor MacDonald were brought up in a conventional Presbyterian environment, they were unavoidably exposed to the political and social ethos of Presbyterianism. The fundamental democracy of Calvinist theology was reflected in the tendency to the formation of schismatic groups (like the Morisonians to which Hardie himself adhered), often with a more thoroughly democratic policy than the established Church. Presbyterian policy itself, however much amended and qualified, never lost contact with the principles of popular election and lay participation, and so provided a practical education in democratic politics as well as a potent constitutional model. The importance attached to an educated laity added a social dimension to the constitutional scheme.

Inheritance

Hardie's inheritance of political radicalism was absorbed in, and partly nullified by, the centralised welfare state which developed to meet the claims of his social radicalism. He himself would not have been too dismayed at the antimonies which history has thus uncovered in his radical-socialism. As a gradualist he rejected the apocalyptic Marxist view that socialism would spring fully armed from a resolution caused by the progressive 'immiseration' of the working class. He welcomed the improvement in living standards enjoyed by the working class in the 19th century, holding to the characteristic radical view that socialism was more likely to be built by an economically confident working class than by a crushed and demoralised proletariat. In the same spirit he would surely have seized on the current reaction against over centralisation and consensus politics as an opportunity of injecting an energising dose of political radicalism into the lethargic body of the welfare state.

As an organised political force the Scottish radicalism of Keir Hardie did not survive the decline of the political party he founded. But its continuing vitality as a moral and intellectual force was attested, in distinctive forms, in the thought and works of three leading and neglected Scots of the mid-20th century – John Grierson, John Reith and A. D. Lindsay.

Indeed, in some ways their response to the claims of political and civic community in a managed industrial society owed more to Presbyterianism than did Keir Hardie's response 40 years or so earlier to the political and social challenges of his time. Perhaps the political and social legacy of Presbyterianism, made the more mellow and humane by further secularisation, will prove one of the most valuable assets Scottish radicalism will carry into independence.

Scotland's Foreign Policy

Question Magazine, September 1976

DEBATE ON SCOTLAND's future as an independent country swings between the banal and the melodramatic. The conventional Nationalist account of a douce nation, making a dignified progress to independence and then calmly, even complacently, ordering its affairs like any self-respecting social democracy, is countered by melodramatic predictions of civil strife on an Ulster scale, of rampant xenophobia, of social reaction cheered on by religious bigotry.

In the field of external affairs, the most distinctive counterpoint to the theme of a Scotland easily accepted into full membership of the international community and calmly deliberating its international options before proceeding to a dispassionate choice between them comes from the left. Scotland will win her independence – if at all – against the opposition of powerful external forces and once independent will find herself permanently besieged by them. The struggle first for existence, then for survival, will leave no room for diplomatic explorations nor for public deliberation leading to the luxury of open, democratic decision-making.

In his contribution to *The Red Paper*, John McGrath, in a paper entitled 'Scotland: Up Against It', uncovers the 'grim international reality behind the strategy of [the SNP's] bid for 'freedom''. The State Department, the multi-national corporations, the US military's arm in Europe – NATO – not to mention the CIA, will not tolerate the prospect of a Western European nation that is not very firmly subordinated to the demands of international capital and its imperialistic logic. And when that combination of forces, plus the entire apparatus of the British state is lined up against you, you take a look at Vietnam, Chile and what remains of Cuba's hopes and modify your stance. No nation of five million people will alone defeat that imperialist machine, or defy its wishes, without heroic sacrifice and the risk of total destruction.

McGrath's purple passage deserves a place in Grimm's anthology of political scare-stories alongside Professor John Erickson's dark hints that Kalashnikov rifles lie buried beneath the rose bushes in Princes Street Gardens waiting to arm the 'internal' enemies of the new Scottish state.

But unlike the Professor's imaginings, John McGrath's warnings enjoy a degree of intellectual support in the shape of fashionable neo-colonialist theory portraying United States' imperialist ambitions operating through American economic dominance and various forms of covert intervention backed up by diplomatic bluster, blackmail and blunder in the style of Dr Kissinger.

To bring the danger closer to home, Italy can now be added to the list of victims of US neo-colonialist efforts. The moral is clear: unless Scotland arms herself with the institutions and revolutionary faith of a Socialist Workers' Republic, independence will be no more than a constitutional facade concealing the continuation, even the intensification, of neo-colonialist exploitation.

Heavy Investment

In this ideological perspective, Scotland does indeed appear a likely target. Even before the wave of American oil investment, Scotland's economy, with the highest per capita level of US dollar investment outside Canada, was thoroughly penetrated by US capital. Scotland's oil is a potentially important factor in the political economy of the West, while her location in the North-East Atlantic gives her a key role in Atlantic security, symbolised to Scottish opinion, albeit misleadingly, by the US Polaris base at Holy Loch.

The extent of the United States' interest in Scotland is, therefore, obvious. What is not so obvious is that the US, with or without the help of her allies, possesses either the will or the appropriate means to enforce that interest.

On this point, the Left is not specific. Rather than attempting to assess the complex factors which will determine the extent and the *modus operandi* of US influence on Scottish policy-making, it resorts to the well-thumbed checklist of victims of US imperialism, from Cuba to Chile, and leaves imagination to do the rest.

A Manichean theory of history requires a strong devil if it is to carry any conviction. The trouble with the fashionable neo-colonialist theory is that it is by no means obvious that the United States and its multi-national allies possess the required political and economic muscle. The fate of Western oil companies in Libya and other Middle East countries suggests that within the restraints imposed by the present global balance and patterns of economic dependence, US power is severely limited even in respect of small Third World countries. Certainly Dr Kissinger's recent threats of military action against the more militant oil producers created more embarrassment in Washington than fear in the Arab world.

When the United States has swallowed the nationalisation of US assets in Libya and limited its response to Norway's tough oil policy to some discreet diplomatic grumbling, it is difficult to see why it should suddenly turn nasty on Scotland. If it did, it would find Scotland a far tougher proposition than most of the other intended victims of post-war US imperialism. Scotland, with her diverse exports, is no 'one-crop' economy dangerously dependent on restricted markets. An investment strike by US companies could certainly prove troublesome, but there is evidence that for reasons unconnected with Scottish nationalism, US companies are already losing interest in Scotland as a location for major investment projects.

Anyway, US multi-nationals are by no means tame followers of the State Department, and investment capital will be a commodity in abundant supply in a Scotland controlling her own oil revenues.

Different

Scotland should also prove stony ground for US covert operations. No politically significant section of Scottish society will feel its interests so threatened by independence or by the foreseeable actions of a Scottish government as to seek the serious patronage of external interests. It is hardly necessary to stress that as a country with a long democratic tradition Scotland has a political culture very different from that of the classic victims of US neo-colonialism.

If it is unlikely that Scottish opinion will have been rendered impregnable to US subversion by a militant people's socialism, a confident and assertive nationalism will provide an adequate (and perhaps less selective) substitute.

Although the United States is usually cast as the neo-colonialist villain, England's major oil and security interests establish her as a strong claimant to the role in Scotland.

Unlike the United States, England through her control of the physical power of the British state and of the symbols of its political legitimacy might appear to have the means to abort the very emergence of an independent Scotland. In fact, England's power is less than it seems. The legitimacy of the British state could not survive the persistent denial of the basic right of self-determination to a constituent part whose constitutional identity is formally acknowledged by the state itself and whose historical and cultural identity has never been challenged. In terms of *realpolitik*, the constitutional crisis which would result from such a denial would destroy what remains of the international confidence on which sterling and the United Kingdom economy now so precariously depend. A choice between constitutional crisis and economic collapse on the one hand and a negotiated transition to independence with agreement on English access to the international benefits of Scotland's oil on the other would leave London with no choice at all. The inevitable settlement will presage a pattern of interdependence between the two countries far more advantageous to Scotland than the bare differences between the size of their populations and economies would suggest.

This is not to argue that the United States and England will not seek to influence Scottish policy, nor that they will forswear all forms of interference and coercion. What is being argued is that their relations with an independent Scotland will be more like their relations with other Northern European democracies than like the political protection racket pictured in left wing melodrama. The banal truth is that Scotland's foreign policy – like her domestic policy – will be determined more by the natural conservatism of the voter and the received wisdom about the context of decisions, than by specific pressures, overt or covert, exerted by large neighbours or dubious allies.

Diverse Influences

Scotland's international context is dominated by influences emanating from England and the Common Market, from North America, from the Nordic countries and from the Soviet Union. The fact that Scotland stands at a point where such diverse influences converge immediately distinguishes her position from that of the small Benelux countries whose location and pattern of commercial dependence subject them to the overriding influence of continental developments as mediated through the EEC and the wider Atlantic influence as mediated through NATO. Scotland's situation is closer to Norway's, with whom she shares a scope for diplomatic manoeuvre (and the accompanying risks of miscalculation) denied to the Benelux countries.

England's influence will naturally be the most pervasive. But because it will be mainly economic and Scotland enjoys some important economic advantages, it need not be unduly restrictive. Although England takes a higher proportion of Scotland's exports than vice versa, Scotland is even now England's biggest export market. As oil-financed expansion makes Scotland into one of the fastest growing markets in the world, England can expect to increase her already substantial trading surplus with Scotland – at a time when her global balance of payments will have been further weakened by her surrender of oil rights.

This balance of commercial advantage will ensure England's support for a free trade agreement without Scotland having to deploy the bargaining strength represented by her foreign currency oil earnings. It is worth noting that the exceedingly favourable trading balance England can expect on (non-oil) Anglo-Scottish trade – contrasted with the massive deficit in her trade with her EEC partners – makes Scotland in some ways a more valuable trading partner than the EEC.

England's security interest is subsumed in the wider Western interest. It follows that English policy towards Scotland will be subject to strong US pressure, if not veto. Although the adoption by Scotland of a policy of 'non-nuclear' membership of NATO would, in strictly military terms, be more embarrassing to England with her lack of convenient alternative bases for her nuclear-armed submarines than to the United States, the latter would seek to obstruct any English response which might induce Scottish opinion to look for alternative security policies based on Nordic examples outwith NATO.

The Nordic option is the most intriguing aspect of Scotland's international situation, if only because it is the least explored. It does not rest on any alleged similarity between Scottish and Scandinavian society. Incontrovertibly, Scotland's social and economic structure is far closer to that of England than to that of the Scandinavian countries. For that reason Scotland's membership of the Nordic Council, a body directed towards harmonisation of social and economic affairs, will be no more than an interesting possibility, whereas membership of some form of association of states within the British Isles, having aims and structures similar to the Nordic Council, will be an important requirement.

The Nordic option derives instead from Scotland's entanglement in a web of shared and complementary foreign policy interests, embracing extended fishing limits within an Exclusive Economic Zone, oil development issues, control of the complex of civil activities in the Norwegian Sea and, as peripheral countries, a common concern for the North-East Atlantic sector of the East-West balance and for the economic and political direction taken by the Common Market.

Similar Resources

The significance of this 'opening to the north' is that it offers an opportunity of co-operation with a group of countries, ecologically favoured and relatively rich in basic resources like Scotland, to counter-balance the influence of the much larger but ecologically unbalanced and relatively resource-poor England and the Common Market to the south. By virtue of the same relative wealth of resources, it also represents an international grouping through which Scotland, as a developed country which is also an important raw material producer, might contribute positively to the emergence of the 'new international economic order'.

Although the Common Market will be of economic importance to Scotland as an export market its political significance, at least on present trends, will be modest. As trading access is not dependent on membership, Scotland's political options remain open. Most of the Nationalists who in a post-referendum *crise de nerfs* claimed Market membership as the decisive reply to the separatist charge quickly recovered, and now only the Scottish Labour Party continues to use that intellectual crutch as it hurtles towards independence. Among EEC members only Ireland, with her fishing interests and oil ambitions, emerged as a possible ally for Scotland. France will fear the influence of the Scottish example on her regionalist movements while the Benelux countries share West Germany's interest in common energy, monetary and other policies hostile to Scotland. While Scotland has a duty to proclaim the rights of cultural minorities – and an even stronger duty to advance them in Scotland – the linguistic-ethnic base, poor electoral prospects and federalist ambitions of most of the continental regionalist movements separate them fundamentally from contemporary Scottish nationalism.

In short, the Left-wing vision of an independent Scotland besieged and coerced by hostile forces has little substance. Scotland's capacity for independent decision-making will be comparable to that of other small European democracies, with Norway providing perhaps the closest parallel. Her situation may lack material for political melodrama but it will present many challenges to the statesmanship of a newly independent country.

Beyond Social Democracy

The Radical Approach (ed. Gavin Kennedy),
April 1976

THE SCOTTISH NATIONAL PARTY has traditionally rejected any ideological label which would fix its position on the conventional Left-Right spectrum. The reasons are partly opportunistic and partly a matter of principle. In the Party's early years, a strong body of opinion argued that the SNP's role should be to act as an umbrella under which all who believed in Scotland's independence, whatever their social or economic convictions, could unite. The implication was that the Party would dissolve on the attainment of independence, freeing its members to rejoin the political organisation of their ideological choice. By the early 1960s, the gestation period of the modern SNP, this position was a minority one within the Party, although the acute SNP listener may still detect echoes of the argument today.

A second and perhaps more important reason behind the SNP's rejection of a conventional ideological label was a belief that the SNP represented a distinctive Scottish way in politics. It can be identified in the occasional writings and the recorded speeches of SNP activists over the last several decades. Its point of departure is the myth of Scottish democracy, which is seen as rejecting class theories of politics, as being anti-bureaucratic and egalitarian with strong populist overtones and placing great emphasis on the value of local and community identity. To some extent, indeed, it reflects the small-town ethos of the pioneers of the SNP. In recent years it has been mixed, rather uncertainly, with more fashionable ideas of decentralisation, the value of what is small in scale, a belief in the need to restore *communitas* as an antidote to the alienation created by mass industrial society and even with conservational ideas.

As the SNP's electoral support and its prospect of governmental responsibility have grown, the Party has felt impelled to define more closely its position on a wide range of social and economic issues. In the process it has explicitly rejected an umbrella role. It has stated its ambition to provide not merely a vehicle for a broad movement for independence, but to form the future government of an independent Scotland. At the same time, it has relaxed its opposition to conventional political labelling. Following the February 1974 general election, some SNP spokesmen for the first time publicly identified the SNP as a social democratic party and the Party's October 1974 election manifesto claimed to outline a comprehensive programme of 'social democracy'. Since October 1974, the SNP's social democratic claims have been restated in public by leading SNP members and have been the subject of discussion within the Party.

Why has the social democratic label proved acceptable to large section of a party that has traditionally rejected ideological labels? Social democracy is consistent with the SNP's non-ideological tradition only to the extent that in its contemporary meaning it implies a rejection of the ideological stereotypes of socialism and *laissez-faire* capitalism. Partly for that reason it carries a public relations gloss of moderation and even of conservatism which is convenient to a party proposing a major constitutional upheaval. It also sounds Scandinavian and SNP opinion is agreed on the merit of things Scandinavian. Critics may suspect that its acceptability is further enhanced by its vagueness. Certainly none of those within the SNP who have declared themselves social democrats have yet offered a systematic account of what they understand by the phrase.

What is Social Democracy?

Generically, social democracy denotes a belief that social and economic justice should be pursued within a framework of democracy, liberty and the rule of law. Such a belief, however, fails to distinguish the social democrat from the democratic socialist or the Liberal or even the progressive Tory. Historically, social democracy describes the democratic parliamentary road to socialism advocated by 19th-century German Marxist revisionists like Edward Bernstein. In the 20th century, however, social democracy has been drained of much of its socialist content until today the most ardent socialists use the label 'social democrat' to abuse the right wing of the Labour movement.

The main area of disagreement between socialist and social democrat concerns the role of public ownership of the means of production. Anthony Crosland considers public ownership – which he sees exclusively in terms of nationalisation – as no more than 'one of the instruments available to government to deal with excessive monopoly power, or consistent under-investment or (as in the case of oil or minerals or development land) a failure to plan a natural resource in the interests of the community'. He congratulates the Swedish, West German and Austrian social democratic parties for their ideological indifference to the issue of public ownership.

In upholding the case for the mixed economy, social democrats intend a challenge to the traditional socialist belief that public ownership is the key to the achievement of such socialist objectives as equality, full employment and the elimination of poverty. In their view, these objectives can be achieved through a combination of social legislation, public expenditure and the use by the state of its powers of control over the private sector. Consistent with this they evince little interest in exploring alternatives to the state corporation model of public or social ownership. A commitment to industrial democracy is usually all that remains of the classic socialist aim of the elimination of private ownership.

The social democratic belief in the virtues of the mixed economy is accompanied by a commitment to public expenditure through the welfare state as the chief instrument for the achievement of social objectives. In health and education the social democratic welfare state embraces the socialist principle of universal flat rate benefits. In the case of personal income support and family welfare, however, the welfare state in its British form offers a mixture of universal, selective and graduated benefits. Universal flat rate family allowance exist side by side with selective, means-tested free school meals and supplementary benefits, and with graduated unemployment and retirement benefits.

Since the 1930s, social democracy has been virtually synonymous with Keynesian economics. Keynesian theories of economic management had the great attraction to social democrats of offering an alternative to public ownership as a way of combating the recurring crises of capitalism and of ensuring full employment and steady economic growth.

The final tenet of social democracy is equality. Indeed, today's social democrats seek to establish a rhetorical commitment to equality as the touchstone of socialism in place of the traditional commitment to public ownership. Anthony Crosland has written:

> By equality we mean more than a meritocratic society of equal opportunities in which unequal rewards would be distributed to those most fortunate in their genetic endowments or family background. We also mean more than a simple redistribution of income. We want a wider

social equality embracing the distribution of property, the educational system, social class relationships, power and privilege – indeed all that is enshrined in the age-old socialist dream of a 'classless society'.

Contemporary social democracy rests therefore on five tenets – political liberalism, the mixed economy, the welfare state, Keynesian economics and a belief in equality.

The Corporate State

As an organised and effective political force social democracy was largely the product of the Labour movement. The aims pursued by Labour's political wing – the improvement of the social conditions of the working class, the defence of the legal rights of trade unions and the creation of economic conditions which supported the bargaining power of labour against capital – were initially seen as steps *towards* socialism. But as the industrial and political pressure exerted by the Labour movement forced the state to recognise its claims, the movement began to distinguish its sectional interest from its universalist aims. It became, in brief, more 'labourist' and less socialist and was confirmed in this tendency by the unsuspected capacity of the state, under the influence of social democratic ideas, to develop new means of meeting its demands.

Partly in response to continued pressure from the labour movement, partly in response to broader electoral pressures, the initial achievements of the state generated the demand for further extensions of the state's role. The state's power to plan the economy was consolidated by the national-isation of strategic industries. The need to limit the cost to the community of sustaining full employment drove the state to seek improvements in industrial productivity and efficiency through the elaboration of a range of state agencies and financial incentives designed to encourage rational-isation and restructuring. Having weakened, if not eliminated, the harsh discipline of the market by social democratic economic management, the state sought to substitute the gentler discipline of state sponsored incomes' policies. To meet the escalating administrative demands imposed by the growth in its responsibilities, the state spawned a bureaucracy whose power grew in proportion to the range and complexity of the tasks assigned to it, until it became a dominant – perhaps *the* dominant – political feature of the social democratic state.

The growth in the economic bargaining power and political influence of organised labour, and the extension of the state's role in the economy and society which it stimulated, provoked other interests to organise themselves in order to impress their sectional views on the attention of the state. The private sector of industry, which was anyway undergoing a secular process of concentration, had the most obvious incentive to deploy a countervailing influence on the state, but other interests, from the British Medical Association and the National Farmers' Union to the self-employed, sought likewise to maximise their influence on state decisions. And while the labour movement preserved its institutional solidarity, the broadening of its membership, in an increasingly specialised economy, to include large sections of non-manual and even middle class groups, served to emphasise the fact that the movement contained different, potentially rival, interests. Paradoxically, the social democratic state, built on the principle of society's collective responsibility for the welfare of the individual, has come to preside over a society of competing sectional interest groups.

Decisive power in the democratic state, however, lies with a triad of interests: a trade union movement which owes much of its power to the state while reserving an ultimate independence from it; a concentration of financial and industrial interests which has learned to see the state as a source of potential support in times of crisis, as well as a constant supervisory presence in normal times; and the state itself, acting in its administrative capacity with all strength of an extensive and often impenetrable bureaucracy.

In its representative role, the state, although in democratic theory the instrument of the collective will of this sectionalised society, has been forced to acknowledge severe limitations to its power. Sometimes it has been limited to holding the ring while competing interests bargained to determine their share of society's resources: sometimes it has accepted the role of *primus inter pares*, treating sectional interests at one moment as rivals in a hard bargaining process, at another as partners. The close relationship which has developed between the executive and bureaucratic organs of the state and the leadership of the major sectional interests, above all the labour movement forms the skeleton of the corporate state.

Compounding these corporatist tendencies, social democratic orthodoxy has tended to pursue political integration alongside economic integration. It has been an axiom of social democracy that whatever is bigger is best. For example, support for rationalism in the economic field has been paralleled in the political field by the reform of local government to create larger and putatively more efficient units and by advocacy of political integration at the level of the EEC. In the UK, EEC membership has the support of virtually all leading social democrats. In the Scandinavian countries, opposition to the EEC has come from populist and parochial interests, and dissident intellectual groups, outwith the consensus built around Labour/social democratic parties and the trade union establishment.

Failures of Social Democracy

Today, both the doctrines of social democracy and the structure of power characteristic of the social democratic state are under attack. The assumptions and techniques of centralised Keynesian economic management are proving incapable of reconciling full employment with price stability. The introduction of incomes' policies represents the social democratic state's response to the dilemma, but while statutory policies have proved ineffectual due to union opposition, voluntary agreements have still to prove themselves.

The reduction in the rate of wage increases in the United Kingdom under the present Labour government's incomes' policy may be due more to the insecurity generated by the exceptional levels of unemployment than to trade union support for the policy on its merits. The real test of such voluntary agreements will come when the developed countries move out of recession into the next boom.

The social democratic state has also failed to eliminate poverty. In the United Kingdom, according to one estimate, some ten million people live on or close to the official poverty line as defined by the qualifying level for supplementary benefits. In West Germany a pilot research project in Dortmund has revealed the existence of a significant amount of submerged poverty. A commentator on the 'Level of Living' studies being carried out in the Nordic countries has concluded that 'fairly substantial groups – in particular in new urban residential areas and among the old – are unable to meet every day needs even with apparently reasonable incomes.' Moreover, in spite of the survival of poverty in the growth years of the 1950s and the early 1960s, and the doubtful prospects for sustained growth in the immediate future, many social democrats remain committed to the view that resources needed for the elimination of poverty can come only from economic growth.

Social democracy is nowhere more ambivalent than in the way it interprets its much advertised commitment to equality. The social democrat's tolerance of a private sector of education alongside a comprehensive state system may be understood as his proper homage to liberalism. But the persistent reluctance to take action deliberately to reduce differences of income and of wealth beyond certain generous limits cannot be explained so conveniently by a tension between different values within the social democratic credo. Fourteen years of social democratic government since the war have left the United Kingdom still a notably unequal and class-ridden society. Indeed Denis Healey, social democratic Chancellor of the Exchequer, apparently believes that even the present range of inequalities of income, and the even greater differences in standards of living, gives an inadequate incentive to the middle class.

In most social democracies the balance between the public sector and the private sector in the economy has been eroded by the continued expansion of public sector employment and by the increasing proportion of national income going on public expenditure. Some social democrats now believe that further increases in the share of national income going to public expenditure will seriously endanger the individual's freedom of economic choice, but as long as this simplistic view is held it will serve to restrain the growth of expenditure in many areas in which social democracy has patently failed to achieve its social objectives.

Although social democracy officially endorses the claims of political liberalism, it has not been conspicuously fertile in ideas for curtailing the growth in state power or for protecting the citizen against its misuse. Anti-discrimination legislation apart, social democratic concern for individual rights has been concentrated on the rights of employees in respect of their employers and has tended to relapse into ambivalence on the issue of the individual's rights in respect of the collective power of his trade unions. Social democracy typically identifies the balance between private economic power on the one hand and individual rights or public power on the other as the crucial political relationship. The balance between central and local power, or individual rights (beyond the basic democratic freedoms) and state power, has been regarded as of secondary importance, with initiatives often depending on a leading politician's personal commitment or on acute electoral pressure.

Social democracy has, further, inherited from its trade union origins an instinct to concentrate its strength and to avoid particularist division, while the adoption of Keynesian techniques of aggregate economic management has served to reinforce the dominant role of a powerful central state, as illustrated by the fact that social democracy's endorsement of regional policy has been firmly posited on the need for central administration. Further support for these centralist tendencies has come in the United Kingdom, from the fact that the political leaders of social democracy have been drawn increasingly from an English middle class nurtured on the peculiarly English doctrine of parliamentary sovereignty.

Social democracy's tattered record provides an ironic commentary on the claim that the SNP represents a new form of politics: 'a contemporary social democracy… the realignment of all good Central/Left men which the trendy leader writers keep calling for'. An examination of the problems which will face an independent Scotland confirms that social democracy, at least as conventionally practiced and preached in the United Kingdom, will prove an unreliable and even dangerous guide for Scottish legislators.

Scotland's Industrial Crisis

Scotland faces an industrial crisis composed of three main elements – an overdependence on traditional industries now in decline, an inadequate level of new investment and an exceptionally high level of foreign ownership. While independence will create an opportunity for sustained economic growth denied to Scotland as part of the United Kingdom, such growth will not by itself solve these structural weaknesses.

In recognition of this the SNP has accepted the need for wide ranging state intervention in the Scottish economy supported by a massive programme of public sector investment through a possible doubling of overall public expenditure in real terms over a five year period. To implement this policy the SNP has proposed a range of state agencies from Scottish boards for existing nationalised industries to a Scottish Industrial Development Corporation and State Holding Companies operating under a Ministry of Development and Industry.

Scotland's long-term economic prospects cannot be made secure while the present degree of external control exists. (Only 41 per cent of Scotland's manufacturing labour force is employed by Scottish controlled firms.) The SNP has advocated a more selective attitude to the award of development incentives to foreign capital and the introduction of a system for monitoring threatened foreign takeovers of Scottish firms as of other forms of proposed foreign investment. But foreign capital is already so dominant in many key industries that direct intervention will be required if the Scottish economy is to develop a self-renewing base. The most direct form of intervention would be for a Scottish government to take a share in existing foreign-owned firms or to purchase them outright. Given the abundance of liquid finance available to a Scottish government in the form of oil revenues, a systematic policy of repatriation of industrial control would pose no financial problem, though other considerations would dictate a gradual and selective approach.

These three key developments – a massive programme of public sector investment, the elaboration of new agencies of state intervention and the direct state purchase of foreign-controlled assets – measure in the industrial field the extent of the swing towards state dominance of the economy which must be expected in an independent Scotland in the absence of corrective policies.

Oil and the Mixed Economy

The accretion of power to a Scottish state is further illustrated by the financial implications of Scottish oil. In the United Kingdom at present, public expenditure represents some 60 per cent of gross domestic product, which according to one leading English social democrat is the maximum compatible with reserving to the individual a proper freedom of choice. Public expenditure, in Scotland, however, represents no less than 66 per cent of Scotland's Gross Domestic Product. At an annual production of 100 million tons, oil will be contributing some 36 per cent of Scotland's total GDP in 1980, assuming an annual 2.4 per cent growth in non-oil GDP. If a Scottish government continued the present level of public expenditure and added to it the revenues yielded even by the London government's modest 66 per cent tax on the gross value of the oil, the resulting public expenditure, at 66 per cent of total GDP, would represent no less than 90.5 per cent of the non-oil GDP. If public expenditure was increased by the revenues yielded by, say, a 75 per cent tax on the oil (in line with SNP plans), then it would represent close to 70 per cent of total GDP (and 94 per cent of the non-oil GDP).

Of course, the Scottish economy's limited capacity to absorb new resources means that a Scottish government would not wish to increase annual public expenditure by anything like the £3bn plus which oil taxation would yield. On different – and more realistic – assumptions, embracing an annual nine per cent growth in non-oil GDP from 1980, an end to deficit financing and a lightening of the tax burden, the level of public expenditure could be reduced to 55 per cent of non-oil GDP by 1985 *while still allowing for a doubling of public expenditure in real terms.* While this reduction would meet the fears of some social democrats of the growth in public expenditure, both the extent and the manner of the reduction would be at the state's discretion, the reduction in effect being a substitution of oil financed expenditure for non-oil financed expenditure. At the same time, the scope for increased public expenditure would continue to pose a threat to the industrial base of the mixed economy.

The task of sustaining a balance between the private and the public sectors of industry will be a difficult one for Scottish social democrats. The conventional instruments of development grants, tax incentives, the provision of infrastructure and of central research and advisory services, would almost certainly fail to overcome the exceptional weakness of the private sector. Native Scottish industry would be unable to absorb financial resources in the necessary volume or to compete successfully against foreign enterprises in exploiting the benefits of a higher rate of growth and of the new infrastructure. At the same time, social democracy's endorsement of economic integration within the Common Market would limit its ability to pursue the discriminatory measures which might redress the balance of advantage in favour of indigenous industries.

If, notwithstanding these obstacles, the new Scottish state were to persist in attempting to revive a large private sector through the lavish disbursement of public funds to private interests, it would be exposing politicians and administrators to the most intensive lobbying and pressure from the carpetbaggers, con men and speculators who would undoubtedly be attracted by the prospect of state hand-outs. The result would be a jerry-built private sector lacking sound foundations. In these circumstances social democracy could be expected to resort as a *pis aller* to the creation of more state corporations of a familiar kind so consolidating and intensifying the statist pattern of power which London control has already grafted on to Scottish society.

The Radical Alternative

The combination in an independent Scotland of a potentially overwhelming state power and a conspicuously weak private sector not only makes the social democratic model of a mixed economy dangerously inappropriate; it also challenges the SNP's commitment to the decentralisation of power. At the same time it creates an opportunity for a move towards a new pattern of economic power based on an alternative concept of the mixed economy. The social democratic concept describes a mix between centralised public ownership and a private sector which in practice is increasingly dominated by large corporations. The radical alternative is a mix between state corporations on the existing model and a combination of public ownership and decentralised social or employee control and ownership.

A variety of models of economic decentralisation, ranging from the conservative to the radical, offer themselves. The basic requirement, however, is that a Scottish government should make it a normal, if not necessarily an invariable, condition of any development grant, loan or tax concession that the favoured enterprise should be organised on democratic principles with decision making power lying either with employees or with employee representatives and representatives of public bodies, preferably local, acting together.

In the conservative model, new industries could be encouraged through a partnership of the state as the main source of capital, and workers' co-operatives. The state would have a share in control through a state holding company and its nominees on the board of the co-operative. The same formula of shared control could be applied to foreign firms bought back into Scottish control by the state and also, at local level, to democratically organised enterprises established by reformed and strengthened local authorities. A democratically organised industrial sector sponsored in this way by public bodies could co-exist with a private sector (and a nationalised sector), modified by whatever statutory forms of co-determination or employee participation might be considered appropriate. In an economy mixed in this way, some of the disadvantages which new, democratically organised enterprises might face in a market dominated by larger, often externally controlled, firms in the private sector could be reduced by fiscal and other measures favouring small firms. Legal provisions for the extension of employee control – and hence an element of local control – in all firms whose labour force exceeded a certain size could also be made available.

The radical model of economic decentralisation is built on the transformation of private ownership and control into employee control through the statutory transfer of the voting rights of shareholders to the employees. Share ownership where relevant could continue to draw an economic reward in the form of a dividend (or even of capital appreciation) but would no longer constitute a claim to a share in the collective decisions of the enterprise. The assets of enterprises might be entirely held by outside shareholders or they might be owned on co-operative principles by the employees themselves. Clearly this model assumes the continuation of a private capital market, which could be supplemented by state banks offering loans either at commercial interest rates or, in the case of venture capital or enterprises in development areas, at subsidised interest rates.

The case for employee sovereignty has recently been advocated as part of a strategy to restore to the market the central role in the allocation of resources denied it by social democratic economic management. In this strategy, democratically organised units of production would compete for markets and investment in an economy in which the expansion of the money supply would be as large as – and no larger than – the growth in productive capacity warranted. Increases in money wages would not automatically be covered by inflationary increases in the money supply as the politically expedient short-term alternative to unemployment, and workers' control and ownership would impose a new sense of economic responsibility on the labour force.

As an alternative to the looming corporate state this picture of employee and consumer sovereignty has its attractions. But it assumes that the centralised bargaining power of the trade unions would be broken up by the spread of dispersed centres of employee control and that elected government would withstand the inevitable electoral pressures to accommodate their economic policies to premature or excessive demands for sectional increases in living standards. Both these assumptions are problematic. Whatever new economic policy options decentralisation of industrial control might uncover, it should be pursued in an independent Scotland in the first instance with the aim of limiting the growth of state power.

Redistribution of Wealth

The problem of poverty in Scotland poses an equally serious challenge to social democratic orthodoxy. The SNP's early estimate that one and a quarter million Scots were living on or close to the poverty line has been supported by subsequent academic research. An increased rate of economic growth, although it will certainly reduce poverty related to unemployment, will not by itself improve the situation of the majority of those living in poverty – those dependent on state support and the lower wage earners who often lack economic bargaining power even at times of economic expansion. Nor can it be assumed that the increased revenues available to a Scottish government as a result of the oil and a high rate of economic growth will allow a painless redistribution of wealth on the classic social democratic model. In the growth years of the 1950s and early 1960s, the poor in the United Kingdom were denied an adequate share of the increasing wealth because more powerful interests pressed their own claims in the form of higher personal incomes or of increased public expenditure of which they were themselves often the chief beneficiaries.

The expanding wealth of an independent Scotland will be no less subject to competing claims. The demands for increased industrial investment have already been noted and if the movement for independence does indeed represent a 'revolution of rising expectations', as some commentators plausibly suggest, independence can be expected to release an enormous pent-up demand for the higher standard of living of the south-east of England, or the even higher ones of Scandinavia or Switzerland, which SNP propaganda has encouraged them to anticipate. Even if the social democratic consensus were to prove itself capable of securing, against the competing claims of powerfully organised sectional interests, the volume of resources required to eliminate poverty, the welfare state has been shown to be an imperfect instrument for distributing resources to those most in need. It may prove particularly ill-equipped to meet the problem of the relative poverty which will be constantly recreated in the dynamic, expanding economy of an independent Scotland.

The best hope of eliminating poverty in Scotland lies not in any selective attempt to repair the many holes in the welfare state net, but in a combination of an expanded programme of environmental improvement, including housing, and the introduction of a national minimum income or social dividend set at a generous proportion of the median wage. Automatic entitlement on a non-contributory basis would extend to pensioners, the disabled, the unemployed and to all those of working age who are excluded from the labour market by responsibility for dependants. Single parents, those engaged in the full-time private care of the elderly and infirm and whichever partner accepted primary responsibility for the home and care of children would all thus be eligible. Such a reform would dramatically strengthen the economic position of women by removing the mother's dependence on a breadwinner, and would thus contribute more to women's liberation than volumes of anti-discrimination legislation. The eventual extension of a guaranteed basic income to those who chose to opt out of the labour market for no other reason than to do their own thing would mark a further step towards a libertarian civilised society.

The raising of Scotland's 'forgotten fifth' out of poverty through a guaranteed income would not transform Scotland into an egalitarian society. Although differences of income are slightly less marked in Scotland than in England, this is due mainly to the under representation of Scots in the senior executive and managerial groups, a state of affairs which the economic consequences of independence could be expected to correct.

A recent report by the Royal Commission on the Distribution of Income and Wealth has confirmed that personal wealth is to a significant degree more unevenly distributed in Scotland than in England. The wealthiest one per cent own 27.6 per cent of personal wealth in England and Wales, but 32.2 per cent in Scotland, while the top five per cent own 62.8 per cent in Scotland against 50.4 per cent in England. Such inequality, however much it may be condemned in the official rhetoric of social democracy, does not appear to be intolerably offensive to social democrats in government. It remains to be seen whether, in response to the new political opportunities of independence, the egalitarianism which is one element in the myth of Scottish democracy will inspire a radical attack on such inequalities.

Sectional Demands

In the determination of this issue, as of the minimum income guarantee and the overall social and economic prospects of an independent Scotland, the role of the more powerful sectional interests will be as crucial as it is to the current prospects of the United Kingdom. It promises to be no less problematical. Even with oil the resources of an independent Scotland will be under serious strain. The massively increased programmed of industrial investment and the lightening of the tax burden will make heavy demands on economic capacity, while the increased rate of economic growth will generate its own upward pull on incomes. If, in addition, a minimum income guarantee were introduced, it would not only represent a further demand on resources but would threaten the traditional range of income differentials in one of its most sensitive areas – where the skilled worker compares his reward to that of the unskilled worker or the non-worker. If powerful sectional interests set themselves the target of preserving the full range of differentials on the higher base of the guaranteed minimum income, the resulting inflationary pressure added to the other pressures could destroy the opportunity of steady and sustained growth which independence will offer.

The danger of intense sectional competition for resources in an expanding Scottish economy will be increased by the greater proportionate power which employee organisations are likely to enjoy in Scotland. Given the dominant role of the state, it is likely that an even higher proportion of the Scottish labour force than at present will be employed in the public sector (currently about 33 per cent of the Scottish labour force compared to about 30 per cent in the United Kingdom as a whole), where market discipline is non-existent and where, as a result, employee militancy, particularly among the higher paid sections, has recently been on the increase.

A Scottish government's greatest asset in dealing with these problems will be its ability to offer a credible prospect of rising real standards of living. Its second most important asset will be fear of the destruction of that prospect. But these intangible assets have to be turned into specific policies, and no technical economic or institutional device can protect a democratic government from sectional or popular pressure to pursue misguided economic policies. Workers' control will certainly put the responsibility for decision-taking in the given circumstances on the employees. But the government can change circumstances – or at least some of them – and the public can change the government.

The success of offering tax reductions or increases in the social wage in return for union support for an incomes' policy will depend on the unions' own assessment of the opportunities for advancing their sectional interest which they will sacrifice by acceptance. The Government could certainly include in its package an offer of action to reduce the grosser inequalities of wealth. But, regrettably, this demand has not been high on the unions' shopping list in their recent bargaining with the London Government.

It is probable that observed differences of income generate more resentment, insecurity and competitiveness among sectional groups than veiled differences of wealth. And in their post-socialist manifestation, the success of organised sectional groups, and above all of their professional leadership, is measured precisely by the spirit of competitiveness they display in defending, or improving, their position on the incomes' ladder. Social democracy, born from a universalist inspiration out of the needs of one broad, majority interest, seems now to be tied to a Procrustean bed of competing sectional interests.

Scottish Radical Democracy

Radical measures of economic equalisation may have to wait on the outcome of efforts to inculcate in the competing interests a new sense of community and democratic responsibility. While an independent Scotland is unlikely to prove more sympathetic than other industrialised societies to efforts to restore a traditional *communitas*, independence will offer an opportunity of testing the strength of the radical aspirations which support the myth of Scottish democracy.

Among the elements of a revived Scottish democracy should be a Bill of Rights embracing, among the familiar individual, religious and political rights, a Freedom of Press Act on the Swedish model: the introduction of proportional representation; provision for referenda, including initiative referenda; a radical decentralisation of power within Scotland to all-purpose local authorities possessing a wider and more elastic tax base than is afforded by the present rating system, as well as powers of industrial initiative; the development of a system of specialist committees in the Scottish legislature; the broadcasting of the Scottish parliament; measures facilitating the creation of new Scottish based newspapers and journals organised on workers' control principles; public participation in the control of broadcasting media, perhaps through some version of the Dutch Television Foundation; and the establishment of a system of Neighbourhood Law Centres, with salaried staff, to extend the individual's ability to enjoy his statutory rights.

These political reforms contemplating the measures of decentralisation and democratisation in the industrial field, would provide the institutional framework for a democratic Scottish society.

The priority in the educational field should be the extension of the comprehensive principle to post-school education, replacing the present system which reserves higher education to a selected minority usually at one period of their lives, with a system designed to give the citizen non-selective access to further and higher education in the form of accumulated entitlements to day and period release and sabbaticals, throughout his life. The extension of educational provision in this way would help to lift the incubus of examinations from Scottish schools and give substance to the alluring vision of Scotland as an educated democracy, the true home of the democratic intellect.

In the social field a nationwide network of paid, part-time, neighbourhood social workers should be established to act as a community based source of help and channel of liaison with the professional social work services. This would provide a local complement to the national strategy for welfare based on a guaranteed minimum income and on environmental improvement.

A programme of radical democracy in political institutions, industry, welfare and education is consistent with the generic definition of social democracy as the pursuit of social justice within a liberal framework. But it directly challenges today's received social democratic orthodoxy – which too easily accepts the centralisation of power even to the point of legitimising the corporate state; which supports a mixed economy even when the mix is increasingly one between centralised state and private corporation; which has made a dogma out of rationalisation and integration; which has tolerated large scale poverty in the midst of affluence in the complacent hope that economic growth would open the way to a politically painless redistribution of wealth; which has failed to seek new forms of democratic community to moderate the rivalries of competing sectional interests; and which has allowed a concept of politics as a manipulative exercise undertaken to create and maintain a compliant consensus to smother the radical ideal of politics as a central activity in a socially responsible arid vigorously self-critical culture.

The dogmatic political realist will of course discount this vision of a radical alternative to social democracy against its lack of any strong interest group support. In so doing, he runs the risk of underestimating the extent to which nationalism – by publicising old ideals and proclaiming new standards, by accelerating the rate of social and economic change and by uniting different sectional groups behind a common aim – can open up new political perspectives.

The historical sources of radicalism in Scotland are diverse, not to say disparate. Although the claim that class division is a wicked English import must be dismissed, the ethos of Scottish society is more egalitarian than that of English society. This egalitarianism, in part the legacy of Calvinist radicalism, in part of a romantic and selective retrospect of Scottish history, has survived the decline in the national role of the Protestant churches and the universities which once gave it institutional expression, albeit incomplete. The legend of Red Clydeside, and the popular myth – which owes more to the idiosyncrasies of the British electoral system than to anything else – that Scotland is a socialist country, may perhaps be taken as testifying to an unsatisfied political idealism.

More substantial is the radical tradition in Scottish politics, which found expression through the Liberal Party in the nineteenth century, then, as the industrial crisis deepened and the influence of religion waned, through the Labour Party, and is now finding expression, as the British idea declines, through the Scottish National Party. Consistent with that tradition there is among many Scottish intellectuals a gratifying suspicion of the doctrine of parliamentary sovereignty as an alien and stultifying dogma, and an acceptance of the politically more suggestive doctrine of popular sovereignty, claimed as a distinctive theme in Scottish history.

The contemporary sources of radicalism are no less disparate. The circumstances facing an independent Scotland will, it has been argued, dictate an economic radicalism which will not easily be contained within the bounds of conventional social democracy. The rhetoric of the Nationalist movement will have created high expectations of social reform in an independent Scotland. As a genuine nationalism (cf. John Mackintosh and others who persist in seeing Scotland as a 'quasi-nation' presumably incapable of nurturing a mature nationalism) the independence movement is likely to demonstrate a specific hostility to the integrationist and federalist aims of most social democrats. As Scotland's cultural, linguistic and regional complexity enhances the movement's role as a vehicle for the general reaction against over-centralisation, so Scotland's inherited sense of being 'agin the government' adds strength to the reaction against bureaucratic, 'closed' government.

The post-imperial rediscovery of Scotland's identity as a small European nation has produced a welcome readiness to seek in the experience of other small democratic countries – particularly Norway – political, social and economic lessons for Scotland. Likewise, the discovery of Scotland's wealth of energy resources – at a time of near panic about future supplies of all basic resources – has reinforced a concern for man's relationship with his environment and for a proper balance between population and resources which was first stimulated among Scottish intellectuals in the mid-war period as they assessed Scotland's experience of industrialisation.

Whatever its historical role, the social democracy preached today in the United Kingdom represents a stale conventional wisdom which too often serves as an apology for conservatism. In the approach to independence, the SNP must strive to synthesise disparate pressures and ideals into an alternative programme of radical democracy.

The Double-Edged Referendum

Question Magazine, January 1977

THE OPENING OF the debate on the 'Scotland and Wales' Bill, with its four hundred or more amendments and the endless scope it affords for procedural wrangling, marks the onset of the bleak midwinter of Scottish politics. Even aficionados will seek relief from this prospect. Amongst the grey fogs and wintry longueurs of the devolution debate, that relief will be found in speculation and argument about the shape, content, outcome and constitutional implications of the referendum that will follow the Bill's successful passage through Parliament.

It is assumed that the referendum was the payment exacted by the moderate anti-devolutionists among Labours backbenchers for their compliance with the Government's policy. But even without pressure from its backbench the Government must have been tempted by the thought of a referendum. The division of public opinion revealed in the polls with approximately 20 per cent support for independence and for the status quo, and 60 per cent for some form of devolution, offered the Government the prospect of winning a convincing endorsement of its own policy while at the same time inflicting on the SNP its first major defeat since the 1970 general election.

Either a three-option choice – between status quo, devolution and independence – or a two-option choice – between devolution and independence – appears to contain the promise of securing that objective.

On closer examination, however, the referendum is revealed as more problematic. The Government's desire to humiliate the SNP may conflict with its need to win popular endorsement of its devolution proposals.

Little Enthusiasm

Government planners must be uneasily aware of the problems which the conduct of a referendum campaign will pose. In spite of the general support for devolution revealed in the opinion polls, the cause excites little enthusiasm. In a campaign the devolution cause will have plenty of Government chiefs but it will be emphatically lacking in constituency Indians.

In contrast, Nationalist activists could be expected to respond with an explosion of enthusiasm to the challenge of a referendum on independence. For the first time in its history the SNP would be fighting directly on the issue which is its *raison d'etre*. The challenge could mobilise all those elements of the SNP which lead many observers to describe it as a movement rather than an orthodox political party – its talent for touching the anti-establishment, 'agin the government' instincts of the Scottish people, its single-mindedness, its brash publicity, its populist street campaigning.

Of course, the devolution lobby would have powerful allies. The Government itself can command formidable publicity, through its official information services and through the news value to the Scottish media of senior cabinet members involving themselves in a Scottish political issue in a way previously unknown in the political history of the Union. A referendum on independence would, further, put those Scottish newspapers which have given the SNP sympathetic coverage while disavowing independence under pressure to turn their energies against the SNP as by far the biggest vehicle of the independence cause. The STUC would presumably stand shoulder to shoulder with the Scottish CBI and the other rather hollow voices of the Scottish industrial establishment in damning the independence option.

Yet, the very unanimity of the Scottish establishment against independence might feed a populist campaign in its favour. The reputation of the establishment is indelibly tarnished by Scotland's long record of social and economic failure, painfully brought home to many Scottish voters by the exceptionally high unemployment and declining living standards of the years immediately preceding the referendum. A referendum on independence might be seized by younger Scots at least as an opportunity of casting the ultimate protest vote, not against a government merely but against the whole ethos of defeat which permeates provincial Scotland.

EEC *Referendum*

The EEC referendum provides little guidance as to the course and outcome of an independence referendum. The SNP will not be handicapped, as was the anti-Market campaign, by the presence of prominent co-campaigners easily typecast by the press as dangerous extremists. It must certainly be expected that the conservative instinct for the status quo which operated in favour of continued UK membership of the EEC will operate against independence. But the UK was popularly believed to be making her choice in the EEC referendum from a position of exceptional economic weakness. Only the result of an independence referendum will reveal how far the SNP's propaganda campaign on Scotland's oil has succeeded in creating a mood of economic confidence impervious to the inevitable scare stories and to the threats of withdrawal which must be expected from some of the more reckless foreign employers in Scotland.

An independence referendum will give the SNP an opportunity to recharge its oil campaign. It will be able to challenge Westminster through the person of the Prime Minister to confirm that a majority vote for Scotland's independence would confer on a Scottish government the same rights over Scotland's resources, including oil, as other independent countries possess. Confirmation would dramatically validate the SNP's case on oil. Denial would cast doubt on Westminster's sincerity in sponsoring the referendum, or at the very least would force it into some shameless special pleading.

The precise formulation of the independence option on the ballot paper is probably less important than its popularity as an issue of debate suggests. Opinion polls show impressively little variation in the level of support for 'separatist' formulations as against 'independence' formulations. The 'independence' formulations are nevertheless to be preferred on the grounds that independence (*pace* Mr Buchan) has a specific constitutional meaning where separation or separatism does not. (As has been aptly pointed out, the Americans have just finished celebrating the bicentenary of their Declaration of Independence, not of Separation.)

If Westminster insists on the separatist formulation the SNP can officially recommend its supporters to abstain or even to vote for devolution. If the separatist option nevertheless attracted a respectable vote, the SNP could re-enter the field to invite its opponents to consider what the 'separatist' vote might have been with official SNP support.

The Government's referendum planning is further complicated by developments in the Conservative Party. Although the official Conservative voice will no doubt continue to proclaim its devotion while criticising the particular form of devolution proposed by the Government, its demotic voice will be speaking in the unmistakable dialect of Cathcart unionism. The appeal that voice could exert if it is used to expound a message combining unionism and traditional Tory populism cannot be lightly dismissed.

The Government also faces the problem of defining exactly what would constitute defeat for the SNP in an independence referendum. The psychological benefit to the Government of a minority vote for independence would be eroded as the vote rose above the 20 per cent which opinion polls reveal as the existing level of support for independence. A vote of 30 per cent or more would embolden the SNP to claim a moral victory and would indisputably place independence at the top of Scotland's political agenda thereafter.

Depending on Others

These uncertainties about the level of support which the independence option might attract combine with the Government's need to win popular endorsement for devolution to preclude a referendum on independence. The lack of a ready-made popular constituency for devolution as such and the possibility of a vigorous rear-guard action by unionists mean that the Government may have to depend on the campaigning efforts of Nationalists to produce a convincing majority for its own policy, and the requisite Nationalist efforts on behalf of devolution will be forthcoming if independence is excluded as an option from the ballot paper.

Quite apart from the result, a referendum on independence has constitutional implications which will not find favour with Westminster. It would signify Westminster's acceptance of the principle that the future of Scotland must be determined by the people of Scotland – i.e. that sovereignty is popular rather than parliamentary. It would create a precedent which a Scottish assembly could invoke to hold subsequent referenda on the extension of the assembly's powers to cover oil, industry and the economy, or to complete independence. Resort to a referendum would, moreover, mark the formal acceptance by English opinion that there is a constitutional way to dissolve the Union of the English and Scottish parliaments.

The time for an independence referendum has not yet come. Westminster will hold such a referendum in reserve as the Union's final line of defence. It will be deployed only when the SNP wins a majority of Scotland's parliamentary seats on a minority of Scottish votes. Aficionados will have to seek consolation meantime in a referendum offering only the options of devolution and the status quo, and the prospect of more challenging times to come.

The Trouble with John P. Mackintosh

Question Magazine, March 1977

NO MP CONTRIBUTES so consistently and so notably to the Scottish debate as John Mackintosh. No other commentator is so readily accepted as an authoritative voice on Scottish developments by the Scottish media.

Yet, the somewhat plaintive tone which informs this acknowledgement of the growing autonomy of Scottish political debate illustrates an ambivalence which runs through John Mackintosh's prolific pronouncements on the state of Scottish politics. He is by no means the only Scottish MP to display such ambivalence. Indeed some of his colleagues – Norman Buchan and Denis Canavan spring to mind – display raging schizophrenia. But he is by far the most prominent, and he is certainly the one most respected by the Scottish establishment.

Track Record

Mackintosh's ambivalence may be due partly to that sense of isolation from the crowding events of Scottish politics to which many Scottish MPs in their enforced weekday exile in London testify. But it is surely also due in some measure to the peculiar role he plays in Scottish politics. No other Scottish MP or political pundit can boast a consistent level of support for devolution in some form or other going back to 1957. Yet, his contributions to the debate have always been made from the margin, as a gifted commentator, not as a man of power or a maker of policy. He has been right about Scottish politics more often than any other Scottish MP yet he has lacked the gift of identifying with any of the distinctive currents of Scottish opinions which intellectually more fallible politicians such as Norman Buchan, Jim Sillars, and even Willie Ross have displayed. Lacking a political base in either the Labour Party or in an identifiable popular constituency of the sort cultivated by Teddy Taylor, Mackintosh has found both his political allies and his intellectual peers in English politics, among the now dwindling ranks of Labour's social democrats. Similarly, as a political commentator he has found his most sympathetic and responsive audience among the readers of *The Observer, The Guardian*, the *New Statesman* (in its long decline from the nonconformist radicalism of Kingsley Martin) and of specialist periodicals like *Political Quarterly*. The high regard in which the English liberal establishment holds John Mackintosh as a political writer and analyst has undoubtedly increased his attractions as a political pundit to those still numerous managers of the Scottish media who crave metropolitan approval for their editorial decisions. But it serves, incidentally, to obstruct Mackintosh's influence among the new political public in Scotland, for it presents him, not entirely unfairly, as we shall see, as a symbol of Scotland's continuing cultural dependence on England.

The source of Mackintosh's ambivalence is most clearly revealed in his own considered contributions to the Scottish debate. These are at once superbly lucid and hopelessly flawed in their assessment of Scottish nationalism. Although Mackintosh has been ahead of opinion in both England and Scotland in interpreting Scottish developments, his interpretations have usually been couched in terms which are familiar and reassuring to conventional wisdom. In the shock of the SNP's Hamilton by-election victory, Mackintosh warned Labour's social democrats through the *Socialist Commentary* that the result was not a fluke, nor merely a mid-term protest against the economic failures of the Labour government. Behind all this, he revealed, was the 'elusive feeling that modern government is too complex, too remote'. He recommended that the Secretary of State for Scotland should exercise more leadership in electoral matters, that the extent of administrative devolution to Scotland should be more vigorously publicised and that a Scottish council or parliament should be set up to undertake the more local government functions and some of the central government duties devolved to the Scottish Office.

With some modest amendments, these remained the chief elements of John Mackintosh's diagnosis and of his prognosis until 1974. In the *Devolution of Power*, published in 1968, he joined his analysis of Scottish developments to a general account of the weaknesses of British government. He repeated his warning that nationalism was not purely, or even mainly, about economic deprivation. Many of the voters who supported the SNP belonged to a generation which had known only prosperity. Their concern was more with the quality of life and with their capacity to influence a system of government which too often presented itself as remote, indifferent and hopelessly complex. As part of a scheme of elected regional councils throughout the United Kingdom he recommended the creation of Scottish and Welsh assemblies, in the Scottish case with additional powers over the legal system, the Courts and other Home Office functions. Even in *The Government and Politics of Britain*, published in 1974, Mackintosh attributed nationalism to dissatisfaction with remote bureaucracy and with the poor economic performance of London governments.

Mackintosh's consistency in analysing Scottish nationalism as a precocious reaction, or overreaction, to general defects of the British system has been watched by his constituency in denying it the status of a genuine nationalism. To Mackintosh, Scottish nationalism has been 'neo-nationalism', a response to problems Britain shares with other highly developed political systems, but sharpened by Britain's peculiar post-war economic history and by a residual sense of Scottish identity preserved in the traditional Scottish institutions of law, church, education and local government.

Cultural Failings

The reason for Mackintosh's refusal to admit Scottish nationalism to the company of the classic European nationalist movements appears to be his belief that it lacks a foundation of cultural nationalism. One must be cautious here for Mackintosh has never claimed to be a cultural historian and his references to Scottish culture – or to culture of any sort – are invariably brief. If, however, he intends to draw attention to the lack of a literary-cultural base for contemporary Scottish nationalism of the sort which sustained the Nationalist movements of the 19th century, he is undoubtedly correct. (The nature of the relationship between the literary nationalism of the 1920s and 1930s in Scotland and contemporary political nationalism is a complex question so far almost untouched by Scottish historians.) And in the absence of a vital literary nationalism, Mackintosh is right to refuse to be impressed by whatever claims might be made for Scotland's traditional institutions as untapped reservoirs of cultural energy.

Yet, his implicit definitions of culture may be too restrictive. Cultural identity need not depend on literary culture alone. It can draw sustenance from other areas of culture, from social institutions or even, as the case of Switzerland demonstrates, from 'distinctive political ethos or institutions'.

As a political intellectual John Mackintosh might be expected to be alert to the possibility of just such an alternative cultural base for Scottish nationalism. Indeed, in an article in the *New Statesman* at the beginning of last year he hints at the emergence of a distinctive Scottish political culture. What blocks Mackintosh's vision is a quite explicit belief that the Scots have a dual identity – that they are both Scots and British – and that this is demonstrated above all in their political attitudes.

His pamphlet *A Parliament for Scotland*, published in 1976 by the East Lothian Constituency Association, includes one of his rare attempts to argue this thesis. He identifies the parliamentary tradition as 'purely British', cites the rejection by a majority of the Scottish public of the 'It's Scotland's Oil' slogan in favour of sharing with the rest of Britain and the SNP's failure to persuade Scotland to cast a tactical 'No' vote in the EEC referendum. He concludes by quoting opinion polls showing a large majority in favour of Scotland remaining part of the United Kingdom. Such flimsy evidence will appear less than convincing to those whose political formation and commitments are less directly British than those of Mackintosh. He offers no defence against the obvious response that these attitudes are the residue of a rapidly wasting sense of British identity. Even a brief excursion into Scottish cultural history would suggest to him that his British political identity would draw little support from the general culture. If such a hybrid as British culture ever existed it was surely only in the 19th century through such Anglo-Scottish figures as the Mills, Macaulay, Carlyle and Ruskin, before it guttered to an inglorious end with Robertson Nicol and *The British Weekly*.

Equally lacking from Mackintosh's assessment is a developed appreci-ation of the historical conditions making for a revived sense of Scottish identity. On rare occasions he has himself hinted at the possibility that the parallel decline in traditional Scottish inhibitions and the prestige of British political institutions has released the ambition to establish new – or rediscover old – reference points for Scotland. In a *New Statesman* article in 1974 called 'The New Appeal of Nationalism' he acknowledged that Scots might feel more at home in Oslo or Copenhagen than in London and recounts how, when invited to comment at a European conference on the shameless special pleading of a British Minister, he declined with the words: 'I am from Scotland and I must dissociate myself from all that you have just heard'. But he concludes the article by reasserting, if less confidently than usual, Britain's claim.

> Only one thing will halt or reverse the onward march of the SNP – a period of government in London which is really successful so that it ends with a satisfied electorate eager to vote positively for a country that once again restored the feeling that Britain is a successful, worthwhile country to belong to...

The absence of any suspicion that such long-term – and irreversible – changes as the abandonment of empire may be the crucial factors, as opposed to short-term changes in governmental performance, is entirely characteristic.

Even if Mackintosh is right in arguing for the dominance of a British identity, that identity would not necessarily provide a secure date for the continuation of the United Kingdom. The Scandinavian example demonstrated that some sense of common identity, even common political identity, can co-exist with constitutional separation.

Trudeau

Mackintosh's intellectual position in a Britain facing the problem of Scottish and Welsh nationalism perhaps bears comparison with that of Pierre Trudeau facing the challenge of Quebec separation. Like Trudeau, Mackintosh represented a new, reformist element in his immediate provincial context. Mr Trudeau believed that Quebecers should adapt themselves to the role of French Canadians, Mackintosh believes that Scots have a dual Scottish-British identity. As Trudeau sought to reform federal attitudes to accommodate Quebec's non-separatist ambitions, so Mackintosh has laboured nobly to instruct English political opinion in the new Scottish realities as he saw them. As Trudeau began by patronising the Quebec separatists as narrow-minded chauvinists only to learn that they had as keen a sense of the international context in which both Quebec and Canada must operate as he himself, so John Mackintosh once scorned the nationalists as political kailyarders only to learn that even if they were not familiar faces at Konigswinter conferences and the other gathering places of the new self-regarding European elite, they had their own, perhaps more Catholic, view of Scotland's international links.

The comparison takes added point from the fact that it is not long since Mackintosh was prepared to cite Quebec's role in Canada as a reassuring example of the viability of federal systems. Perhaps over the next few years Mackintosh and Trudeau will be witnesses of a practical demonstration that in an interdependent world of multinational corporations and international competition for natural resources, neither the economic nor the cultural survival of small societies can be secured within the political limits imposed by the classic federal division of powers.

Review: The Break-up of Britain

Question Magazine, June 1977

POLITICAL DEBATE IN Britain has not been distinguished for its theoretical content. There has been a disconcerting conceptual gap between the frequently avowed intimations of impending crisis and the scope of both the diagnoses and the prognoses which have been offered. Conventional wisdom has claimed to locate the remedies in marginal adjustments to the economic growth rate or to the degree of social mobility. In place of a structural analysis of Britain's problems, the interested public has been asked to accept short-term criticisms of dominant British institutions followed by proposals for adjusting the balance between legislature and executive or for widening recruitment of the Civil Service or for state encouragement of new techniques of business management or labour relations. The dominant assumptions have been ameliorist and gradualist, enlivened only by occasional blasts of moralising, formerly from the angry young, more recently, in the persons of Paul Johnson or Bernard Levin, from the middle-aged of a petulant English middle class. The radical humanist tradition of social criticism articulated briefly in post-war Britain by Richard Hoggart and Raymond Williams seems to have run dry. Mainstream left wing thinking lies under the blight of social democracy.

The monotony of the intellectual landscape of British politics has been relieved over the last 10 or 15 years only by the Marxist *New Left Review* (NLR) and the coterie of writers associated with it. They alone have brought to the analysis of British society a theoretical equipment adapted from the continental tradition. Now one of the editors of, and leading contributors to, the NLR has produced an analysis of Britain's post-imperial crisis which focuses on the new-nationalist movements in Wales and Scotland. In its intellectual vigour and sustained passion, Tom Nairn's *The Break-up of Britain* exemplifies that *perfaevidum ingentium* which Scots have been vain enough to claim as a national characteristic.

The development of Nairn's views on Scottish nationalism has something of an epic quality. The saga began with an essay called 'The Three Dreams of Scottish nationalism', published in the NLR in 1968 and brought to the notice of a wider Scottish public through its inclusion, in amended form, in Karl Miller's collection of essays, *Memoirs of a Modern Scotland*, published in 1970. Written under the shock of SNP victories at Hamilton in 1967 and in the local elections in the spring of 1968, it represented the first attempt at a serious analysis of the nationalist phenomenon from a Marxist standpoint. Its perversity and wilful pessimism (combined with the unaccountable refusal of the editors of the *Review* to print a reasoned rejoinder) provoked at least one reader who had subscribed to the *Review* since its days as the *Universities and Left Review* to terminate his subscription in despair.

'The Three Dreams' helps to identify the continuities and innovations in Nairn's thinking. Its thesis was that modern nationalism represented the third of three historical ideas which, because of the circumstances of Scotland's history, had established a dominance over the Scottish imagination out of phase with the social and economic developments which would have given them the progressive role they played elsewhere. The first of these ideas was the Reformation, which struck Scotland centuries before the process of capital accumulation which in Weber's or Tawney's thesis should have corresponded to it. Because, as a result, the Reformation could not be the 'veiled ideology' of a class, it was fated to become an 'abstract, millennial dream – in effect, a desperate effort at escape from history, rather than a logical chapter in its unfolding'. It was an attempt to translate 'theology into social relations without mediation', and even today Scotland is paying the price for the degree of success which the attempt enjoyed. Just as the Reformation was denied a role as the 'veiled ideology' of a native mercantile capitalist class, the second historic idea, Romanticism, was denied its role as the ideology of a nationalist movement in 19th century Scotland.

> No revolution against the humiliation of the Union, no Scottish 1848, was to furnish a historical counterpart to Robert Burns and Sir Walter Scott. The romantic consciousness too, therefore, could only be an absolute dream to the Scots,

a dream that became a 'possessing demon' in the hideously distorted form of the Kailyard. True to Scottish form, the third historic idea, nationalism, came to Scotland when it could no longer perform the functions of sweeping away outdated social forms and mobilising the population for socio-economic development, which it had performed in 19th century Europe. Nationalism was, in Nairn's eyes, the appointed vehicle of a reactionary bourgeoisie represented by John Gourlay (from George Douglas Brown's *The House with the Green Shutters*), where 'rough-hewn sadism would surely be present in whatever junta of corporal punishers and kirk-going cheese-parers Mrs Ewing might preside over one day in Edinburgh'. Against this nightmare, Nairn as an avowed nationalist could pit only a desperate declaration of faith:

> In the same years in which nationalism again became a force in Scotland, the Western world was shaken by the first tremors of a new social revolution, from San Francisco to Prague. I will not admit that the great dreams of May 1968 are foreign to us, the great words on the Sorbonne walls would not be at home on the walls of Aberdeen or St Andrews, or that Linwood and Dundee could not be Flins or Nantes.

Readers of the NLR over the past five years will be familiar with at least some of the stages of Nairn's reassessment. The emergence of nationalist movements elsewhere in Europe has forced him to discard his view of Scottish experience as a pathological deviation and to develop a general theory to integrate Scotland's history as far as possible with international experience.

Nairn's analysis explains nationalism as a response to the unequal development of capitalism in its industrial phase. As industrialisation spread outwards from the established states of 19th century Europe it faced politically subordinate societies with a choice between being ground under foot or fighting back. Nationalism was the product of the fight back by the bourgeoisies of at least the more resilient submerged societies. The intelligentsia created out of the available historical and ethnographical data the 'myth' of a continuing nationality which served as the ideological instrument through which the middle class mobilised the working class in its support. The nationalism was, in Nairn's phrase, 'Janus faced'. It put the past to work for the future. It translated a passive sense of 'organic community' into an urgent populist nationalism which mobilised popular energies in readiness for the ordeal of industrialisation under local leadership.

The most fascinating section of Nairn's book is composed of the chapters in which he turns his general theory to the task of explaining why Scotland avoided this process in the 19th century only to undergo a comparable experience in the later 20th century. The reasons are discovered in Scotland's economic backwardness in the pre-Union era and in the effects of the Union itself. After the Darien catastrophe had demonstrated its weakness, the only recourse of the Scottish bourgeoisie was union with England. Union satisfied the economic interests of the bourgeoisie by offering access to the English market and it met the interests of other sections of Scottish society by offering guarantees for the continuance of a comprehensive range of Scottish institutions. Of crucial importance in Nairn's account is the fact that the Union created a partnership which within decades was to emerge as the world's first industrial society. As such the spread of industrialisation internally was 'spontaneous' contrasting with the 'forced' industrialisation which Britain's continental rivals had to impose on themselves in the 19th century as they struggled to break Britain's industrial hegemony. In these uniquely favourable circumstances, Scotland was able to develop an autonomous industrial base, under native control, which was as advanced as England's and which enjoyed equality of access to the world markets which were the reward of the leadership Britain enjoyed in the process of industrialisation.

When in the 19th century, Scots became sensitive to the erosion of Scottish nationality, a self-confident, successful Scottish bourgeoisie, unlike its counterpart in societies whose cultural situation was comparable, was not in the market for an ideology of resistance. Its industrial revolution was complete. The Romantic impulse of the early 19th century, denied its ideological role or indeed any significant interaction with political or social reality, curdled into the mawkish sentimentality of the Kailyard.

Twentieth-century Scottish nationalism, like 19th century continental nationalism, is a response to the uneven development of capitalism. However, the catalyst provided in the 19th century by the impact of externally controlled industrialisation is now provided by the impact of multi-national capitalism, most effectively in Scotland in the form of American oil companies. Scotland's position differs from that of most of its 19th-century precursors in two vital ways. By virtue of her oil if not of other economic factors, Scotland stands in a favoured relationship to the declining metropolitan economy. In this her position resembles most closely that of Catalonia and Euzkadi as advanced industrial enclaves in a mainly agricultural land-mass. No less important, Scotland, by virtue of the Union, has retained an abnormally wide range of native institutions – its separate legal system, a substantial middle class, a separate educational system, a separate church, an administrative apparatus which has evolved over a century, almost all the elements of modern statehood, in fact, except political institutions. The wealth of this institutional inheritance gives Scotland a status as the most advanced example of an 'historic nation', compared to the 'non-historic' nations – those 'ruins of peoples' in Engels's phrase – who, lacking the institutional reality of nationality, can maintain their sense of identity only through imagining an ideal community.

This summary of Nairn's thesis does little credit to the way it is articulated through a wealth of references to English, Northern Irish and other European experiences. But it may succeed in giving an impression of its effectiveness as an antidote to naïve idealist theories of nationalism.

At the same time his very theoretical rigour may have obstructed his judgment of the balance between cultural and material factors. For example, although he disavows reductionism, his superficial dismissal of Edwin Muir's analysis of Scotland's cultural dilemma in *Scott and Scotland* raises questions about the adequacy of his concept of culture. Of course he is right to reject Muir's argument that the linguistic and cultural effects of the Reformation and the Union of the Crowns add up to a 'metaphysical disaster one must despair over'. But Muir's insights into the consequences of the split between demotic and official language deserve more respect than Nairn gives them. He seems unwilling to acknowledge that the cultural defeats – or adaptations, to use a neutral words – contributed in any significant way to the cultural catastrophe of late nineteenth century Scotland.

Nairn's determined 'cosmopolitanism' is obviously a crucial factor here. In his account the Enlightenment represents the high point of Scottish culture, the moment when Scotland made its seminal contribution to mainstream European thought. He defends the Scottish philosophes against charges of cultural apostasy. They simply belonged to a unique, pre-nationalist stage of socio-economic expansion. Concentrated in such a small area and time, in a land transported so incredibly quickly out of barbarity into civility, they were the chief exemplars of the European Enlightenment's vision of progress. The philosophes are not the only figures Nairn is prepared to take so readily at their own valuation. To insist that the age of the philosophes was lacking in one dimension of mature culture – the dimension inadequately described as 'imaginative literature' – is not to belittle the achievement of the Enlightenment, nor to despair over the loss of a mythical 'organic culture'. But it is to insist that Burns in the 18th century and MacDiarmid in the 20th both grappled with the same cultural dilemma whose causes predate the peculiar tensions created in the Scottish imagination by the abortive cultural nationalism of the 19th century.

The exclusion from *The Break-Up of Britain* of any serious examination of Scotland's pre-Union experience is significant. Perhaps he was aware that recent investigations by such historians as David Stevenson and Ian and Edward Cowan into the political impact of Presbyterianism made his simplistic account in 'The Three Dreams' hard to sustain. A similar failure of historical imagination perhaps accounts for the lack of attention given to the Scottish working class. It appears only in the role of Cinderella waiting for the kiss of a bourgeois intellectual Prince Charming to arouse its populist nationalist energies. The possibility that the Scottish working class as a component of an advanced 'historic nation' might have possessed a concept of political nationalism along with sentimental nationalism seems not to have been considered.

The challenges posed by *The Break-Up of Britain* simply outreach the scope of an 'instant review'. Its overall impact can perhaps best be illustrated by outlining a possibility implicit in Nairn's elaboration of Scotland's status as the most advanced example of an 'historic' nation – the possibility of a nationalism that discards nationalist myth. To put the point briefly: where such a wealth of evidence of nationality, ranging from the Scottish legal system to the Scottish football league, from the STUC and the Scottish National Orchestra to Andy Stewart, exists, the elaboration of myths about Wallace and Bruce is superfluous. A case for independence can be constructed which owes nothing to any of the traditional Nationalist categories, but which relies instead on a reasoned conviction that independence is as necessary to realise the full potential of Scotland in the latter part of the twentieth century as perhaps the Union – its problems and subsequent trauma notwithstanding – was to realising Scotland's potential in the eighteenth century. Such a view would frankly accept the problematic character of Scotland's cultural inheritance, but place it in the context of the general crisis of Western culture. The case for independence then becomes the demand to give Scots the fullest opportunity to articulate their own sense of crisis as a contribution to an international debate.

Tom Nairn's book will set the standard for debate on nationalism, in the different forms it is assuming in the different parts of the United Kingdom, for many years. We should be grateful it sets a standard of such excellence.

Scotland and the British Crisis

The Bulletin of Scottish Politics, Autumn 1980

IT IS PART OF Britain's crisis that the mood of crisis is so elusive. For a period a problem is caught in the public spotlight. A series of confrontations on the picket lines challenges the authority of Parliament. A race riot uncovers the social pressures building up in English cities. Law and order staggers under the impact of a wave of violence and police corruption. The British Constitution itself appears on the point of yielding to the assaults of devolutionists, champions of a Bill of Rights and assorted populists. Each New Year record unemployment figures announce the imminence of economic collapse. But, as regularly, before the resolve to find a solution has crystallised, the sense of continuity in British life, the desire for normalcy, reasserts itself. The crisis is absorbed, domesticated.

Politicians who exploit the rhetoric of crisis for electoral purposes can be misled. The Tories were returned to power last May after an election in which they had insistently proclaimed the existence of a British crisis requiring radical solutions. But the speed with which their popularity declined when they began to demonstrate in office that they meant what they had been saying suggests that the voters in the Midlands and the south east who abandoned Labour may have been moved more by the prospect of income tax cuts than by a desire to restore market forces, more by a vague resentment against the unions for the inconveniences of the preceding winter than by any urge to adjust the balance of economic power between capital and labour.

However, if the public's sense of crisis is fitful, its demand for improved living standards is constant. The existence of a British crisis is registered most insistently in the increasingly desperate efforts of British politicians to trim that pressure to fit Britain's economic capacity.

The facts are well-enough known. In 1955, the United Kingdom was fifth in the world league of income per head. Today she is not even in the top twenty. In the mid-1950s the United Kingdom contributed 20 per cent of world exports. Today she contributes eight per cent. Productivity per man in the manufacturing industry is between 30 to 50 per cent lower than in her main competitors. Industrial investment runs at half their rate.

The British domestic market now suffers a higher rate of import penetration than the domestic market of any of her competitors. The balance of trade has steadily deteriorated to the point at which, even with a £4–5bn boost from Scottish oil, it was over £1bn in deficit in 1979. 'Deindustrialisation' has contributed to a meteoric rise in unemployment. Like unemployment, inflation now fluctuates around a base level three times higher than in the 1950s.

Under the pressures generated by this decline, the consensus which has dominated British politics since the creation of the welfare state by the post-war Labour government has broken down. Since 1955 Labour and Conservative governments between them have worked through an impressive range of options within the consensus. Deflation, reflation, the devaluation and 'floating' of sterling, withdrawal from East of Suez, defence cuts, the 'white heat' of the technological revolution, industrial rationalisation, regional development, incomes policies (both voluntary and statutory), prices policies, the Common Market. All have been tried in the effort to reverse Britain's decline. All have failed.

The first sign that the consensus was beginning to fall apart was the 'Selsdon' programme on which Edward Heath fought and won the 1970 election. But in government Selsdon Man's nerves proved too weak to persist in a policy which threatened the destruction of whole sectors of British industry. The real break came nine years after the appearance of 'Selsdon Man' with the advent to power of Tory hard-liners armed with the ideological apparatus of monetarism.

Monetarism is an inaccurate, or at least an incomplete, description of the economic policy of the present Tory Government. Professor Friedman himself insists that monetarism restricts itself to the technical economic claim that the rate of inflation is determined by the rate of growth of the money supply. It offers no advice about the optimum level of public expenditure, or the distribution of the tax burden between income and expenditure, or the legal status of trade unions. The Tory Government has indeed been influenced by Professor Friedman's views on these and other issues of political economy. But its policy should be called Friedmanism, rather than monetarism.

As applied by the Tory Government, Friedmanism aims at the restoration of market discipline through monetary control and cuts in public expenditure, an increase in incentives through the creation of greater social and economic inequalities – as in the massive tax hand-outs to the one per cent of highest income earners, the cuts in unemployment benefits and the subsidies to private schools – and a shift of the balance of economic power from labour to capital, to be achieved by restoring capital's freedom of international movement, restricting the rights of trade unions and imposing economic penalties on strikers.

It is important to see this policy in historical context. There are two interpretations. In one view, Britain's economic problems have been caused by the pre-emption by the welfare state and over-powerful trade unions of an excessive share of increased output. As a proportion of Gross National Product, incomes and salaries have increased from an average 65 per cent in 1946 – '59 to an average 70 per cent in 1974 – '79 while corporate profits have declined from 17–18 per cent to 10–13 per cent. As a result British industry has been starved of the capital required for modernization. When new investment has been made, the full potential of increased productivity has too often been lost by the conservatism of the labour force. The only chance of recovery lies in a simultaneous reduction in the share of the national wealth devoted to public expenditure and in the power of the trade unions. In this perspective Friedmanism represents an eleventh hour attempt by British industrial capitalism to restore its profit margins – and its managerial prerogatives – before it is finally overwhelmed by foreign competition.

The other interpretation focuses on the British economy's subordination to the interests of multinational capital. Historically, Britain has been a large exporter of investment capital, a fact reflected in the annual £1bn plus surplus she normally enjoys on transfers of private property incomes. This international role precludes controls on capital and imports, and increases in public expenditure, as responses to Britain's economic problems. The monetarism component of the Friedmanite alternative has particular attractions. The build-up of Britain's short-term reserves on the back of rising interest rates facilitates an increase in the exports of long-term private capital. In 1978, for example, the usual outflows of company capital were supplemented by a £1bn outflow of portfolio investment. On this interpretation, Tory Friedmanism is inspired more by the economic interests – not to say the social prejudices – of an English rentier upper class, whose antecedents long pre-date the industrial revolution, than by the needs of British manufacturing industry.

In either case Professor Friedman's invocation of the shining success of his prescriptions in West Germany, Japan, Singapore or wherever is grotesquely irrelevant. As applied in Britain by a Government of former public schoolboys led by a woman with the formidable social prejudices of the small-town English bourgeoisie, Friedmanism may succeed in cowing the labour force in the short-term, but only at the cost of reinforcing the social divisions which are a major cause of the economic rigidities Professor Friedman so deplores. It is doubtful whether the Professor appreciates the historical irony at work here.

Professor Donald MacKay has assured us that the effect of monetarism as such on Scotland would be neutral, by which he presumably means that Scotland would suffer proportionately to the rest of the United Kingdom during the shock treatment and eventually enjoy her due share of the benefits of restored economic health. The impact of Friedmanism, however, is far from neutral. By cutting back public expenditure in the interests of the private sector, it hits harder at the country with the weaker private sector and the more extensive public sector. By freeing capital movements it facilitates the export from Britain of the massive profits now accruing from the development of Scotland's natural resources, no doubt to the benefit of London's financial role but to the detriment of Scotland's prospects for economic revival. By cutting child benefits along with benefits for the unemployed and the disabled, and by raising prescription charges, it increases poverty in a country in which more than 30 per cent of the population is already living on or close to the official poverty line. By legislating to reduce the power of trade unions, it bears with particular severity on a labour force which because of its weak economic base is especially vulnerable. By subsidising private schools and giving tax hand-outs to the top one per cent of income earners, it reinforces the social and cultural dominance of the privileged south east of England. Most serious of all, by planning for increased unemployment, above even the level imposed by the previous Labour Government, Friedmanism reinforces the culture of social despair which decades of decline have imprinted on the industrial communities of the West of Scotland. The instincts of the Scottish voter were sound when he voted against Mrs Thatcher in 1979.

The Labour Party's response to the collapse of the post-war consensus has been slower and more tentative than the Tory response. Indeed it remains doubtful whether the Labour Party will in fact abandon the values around which the old consensus formed. Those values were, after all, largely Labour's own. They helped it to secure three periods of government which, for all their disappointments, erased the humiliation of the inter-war decades. Furthermore the main targets for Labour's electoral planners will not the bitter steelworkers of Port Talbot or Consett but those voters in the Midlands and the south east who at the last election were seduced by the prospect of Tory tax cuts. If Mrs Thatcher fails to reserve a share of the oil revenues to finance the cuts, disappointment may induce the defectors to turn to Labour again but it will not transform them into raging radicals. And for all the pyrotechnics in the National Executive Council, Labour contains great reservoirs of institutional inertia and social conservatism in the parliamentary Party and the trade unions.

Nevertheless, there is a more developed left wing alternative to social democracy within the Labour Party today than at any time since the War. It sees Britain's hope for economic recovery lying in a major increase of public expenditure – on both public services and direct industrial invest-ment – behind a protective barrier of import controls. The chief economic instruments of this alternative are to be the nationalisation of the financial institutions and the introduction of a system of compulsory planning agreements between the state and key companies. Its social component as outlined by Stuart Holland MP in *What Went Wrong?* includes the planned 'distribution' of scarce employment opportunities, an equalisation of personal incomes, an increase in social income through the extension of the principle of universal, non-charging public service to new areas like transport, an extension of social control (including workers' control) and 'open government', embracing the right of participation by the trade unions in Whitehall policy planning as well as freedom of information and 'open' access to the press and media.

This left wing alternative certainly offers more hope to Scotland than either the atavistic Friedmanism of the Tories or the discredited social democracy offered by Labour loyalists and Centre Party enthusiasts alike. But even judged on its own term – as a programme for radical social reform and economic reconstruction in Scotland as part of the United Kingdom – it is open to major objections.

To take the most practical objections first. The UK is probably too large a trading nation to be able to pursue protectionist commercial policies without provoking a response from her trading partners, and Scotland, with her high export dependence, would be particularly vulnerable to retaliation. Second, the extension of state control, in particular the nationalisation of the financial institutions, would provoke a fierce power struggle on both the domestic and international fronts. Even if a left wing Labour government retained the support of public opinion and the trade unions in the crucial stages of confrontation – and the most determined optimist would have to admit this is improbable – the British economy would pay a heavy price. Undoubtedly Scotland's natural resources, as major sources of revenue and of bargaining power, would carry a large share of the burden of the struggle, or the compromises with international interests which it would almost certainly involve, and of the financing of the government's expenditure plans. Scottish oil is a significant – in a Scottish context a potentially decisive – economic resource, but as Tory strategists seeking ways of financing tax cuts are beginning to appreciate, it is less than a panacea for all ills. At best, 'socialism under siege', British style, would yield uncertain benefits to Scotland; at worst, it would intensify the exploitation she suffers at the hands of the British state. But there is a prior objection to the programme of the Labour left. For all the discussion over the last ten years of the defects of state socialism, it remains essentially a statist strategy. As presented in *What Went Wrong?*, the main obstacles to radical change in Britain are found in the bureaucratic inertia and class bias of Whitehall and in the Labour government's traditional claim to executive independence. The solutions are obvious: the replacement of heads of department hostile to a left-wing government, and party control over the parliamentary Labour Party and the government. But if Westminster and Whitehall are to be given new masters by the left, they are to remain the main channels of state initiative. This is a narrow enough base from which to launch a campaign aimed at restructuring the power relationships in society.

Apart from the reforms in Whitehall and in the structure of the Labour Party, the left has few institutional reforms to recommend – freedom of information, perhaps a system of specialist Commons' committees. (It must be said that the left's approach to the reform of the Labour Party itself is highly selective – more control for Annual Conference and the general management committees, but perish the thought of primaries for the selection of parliamentary candidates or other forms of direct democracy.)

The case for more powers for local government, for political decentralisation, for electoral reform and direct democracy finds no place in the
left's strategy. Nor is there any recognition that the grassroots demand for
workers' control – almost non-existent today even as an emergency
measure to stave off closure – might draw strength from a more vigorous
and assertive civic and political culture. If the radical democratic ideas of
G.D.H. Cole are enjoying a revival, the left wing of the Labour Party
seems largely impervious to their influence.

The left's strategy is as unashamedly centralist in economic as in
institutional matters. Compulsory planning agreements and the other
favoured instruments of state intervention are likely to leave little room
for a significant contribution by Scottish Office planners or by the Scottish
Development Agency.

No more was to be expected from left wingers like Neil Kinnock and
Eric Heffer. But what throws the unreformed, statist nature of the left
wing strategy into sharpest focus for a Scottish public is the acquiescence
of the Scottish Left. By accepting the centralist approach the Scottish Left
is, at best, turning its back on the possibility of mobilizing behind the
cause of radical economic and social reform the frustrated energies of
which produced the 1972–1977 Upper Clyde Shipbuilders' campaign, the
STUC Assemblies on unemployment and the mass defections of Labour
voters to the SNP. At worst it is condoning a strategy which reinforces the
defensive and dependent mentality of Scotland's public culture. It is not
only cynics who will say that this has become the Labour Party's traditional role in Scotland and the foundation of its hegemony.

The Case for Left Wing Nationalism

The '79 Group Papers, 1981

Introduction

THE CASE FOR LEFT wing nationalism has been asserted more often than argued. This pamphlet seeks to correct the balance. It argues that the only nationalism with a serious chance of winning and keeping the level of electoral support required to carry Scotland to independence is a nationalism which, disregarding romantic concepts of nationhood, builds its appeal on an unsentimental view of the social and economic interests of the Scottish people.

This claim will offend and puzzle many Scottish Nationalists. Probably the majority of SNP activists believe that an appeal to a common feeling of Scottishness is the only way in which Scots of different social and economic interests can be united behind the demand for independence. The historically minded will point to successful Nationalist movements in history and ask if they were not built on a common sense of nationality.

Others may ask where the source of contemporary Catalan, Basque or Quebec nationalism lies if not in a distinctive feeling of nationality.

One – National Identity

The Nation in History

Henry Ford claimed that history was bunk. It can certainly be misleading. The leaders of the Nationalist movements of 19th-century Europe couched their appeals in an exalted language of patriotism. But behind the rhetoric powerful social forces were at work – new educated elites eager for bureaucratic jobs, ambitious manufacturers seeking protected markets for their products, peasants hungry for land.

The same is true of today's Nationalist movements. Quebec nationalism draws much of its energy from the social and economic ambitions of a new Francophone educated elite. Catalan nationalism expresses the impatience felt by a sophisticated, economically advanced middle class towards the conservative and underdeveloped Spanish hinterland. The Polish patriotism of Solidarity expresses the frustration of Polish workers with the economic failures of a corrupt and conservative Communist regime. Without these social pressures the nationalist rhetoric would be of little political account.

This does not mean that nationalism is nothing but camouflage for the social and economic interests of powerful groups or ambitious individuals. The sense of national identity can be a genuine bond between people of different social classes and economic interests and once aroused it can serve to crystallise social discontent into political action. But it is a mistake to think of the sense of nationality as a fixed quantity evenly divided among the nations and simply waiting to be exploded into action by the right nationalist slogan in the mouth of the right Nationalist leader. Its significance as a political factor depends on the total circumstances of the nation – its history, the balance of social and economic forces, its relations with its neighbours.

Thus the impact on Irish opinion of the execution in 1916 of Connolly, Pearse and other leaders of the Easter Rising was determined by the long history of Ireland's suppression by the English since at least the conquest by Henry VIII. The impact of Solidarity's appeal to Polish patriotism depends on the anti-Russian feeling bred in the Poles by 200 years of struggle against the Czars. The sympathy which Gwynfor Evans' hunger strike for a Welsh language channel attracted even beyond the Welsh speaking community in Wales had its roots in a historical memory of the English suppression of the Welsh language as well as in more immediate anger at the effect in Wales of Mrs Thatcher's economic policies. Therefore, to assess the political potential of an appeal to a sense of Scottish nationality we must examine Scotland's history and circumstances.

Political Identity

Scotland's early history offers abundant material for the fashioning of Nationalist myths. Scotland had to assert her political independence by the sword in the 13th and 14th centuries and defend her territorial integrity against periodic English incursions for the next two centuries. But even during those centuries of national assertion forces were working to erode a distinctive Scottish identity.

For one thing, Scotland's political identity rested on insecure foundations. One factor was the weakness of the Scottish monarchy, hence of Scotland's central political authority, relative to the power of the Scots nobility. Another was the Scots' appreciation of their inferiority to England in respect of economic and military power. From at least the early 16th century there were Scots who argued that some form of political unity on the British mainland was inevitable if not desirable.

The manner in which political union with England came about made its own, somewhat ironic, contribution to eroding the Scots' sense of political identity. A political union imposed by a victorious army of occupation encourages succeeding generations to idealise the extinguished political institutions. By reaction it sharpens the sense of political identity. But a voluntary union created by dynastic succession and parliamentary agreement is a disabling legacy for a Nationalist movement. It gives little scope for the idealisation of the surrendered institutions and it permits no alibis. The loss of political identity cannot be dismissed as a brutal interruption of the nation's history: it has to be acknowledged as an integral part of it.

Of course the Scottish Parliament, as it debated the future relations of England and Scotland in the opening years of the 16th century, was aware of the possibility of armed intervention by England to impose a parliamentary union. But the majority of Scots parliamentarians had other reasons for wanting a union, not all of them to do with bribery or the hope of advancement at the court in London. The Union was a bargain between national elites – undoubtedly a hard bargain for Scotland but one which secured access for Scottish goods to the markets of England and her colonies, and consolidated the position of such national institutions as the Presbyterian Church and Scots law.

If political union in some form was a predictable consequence of Scotland's political and economic weakness, Scotland's experience as a junior partner in imperial Britain virtually extinguished her sense of political identity. Scotland's development into the industrial workshop of the world, her share in the international prestige which the English model of parliamentary government enjoyed in the 19th century, the career opportunities which the Empire offered to educated Scots, all seemed to provide an unchallengeable retrospective justification for the surrender of Scotland's nationhood. At the mid-century peak of British power and prestige a quintessential Scot like Thomas Carlyle could subsume 'Scotland' in 'England' in his writing without reproach or even comment from his Scottish contemporaries.

Meanwhile the social relations between Scots and English presented none of the obstacles to Scotland's assimilation to the more powerful partner that Anglo-Irish social relations presented in the assimilation of Ireland. After the 18th century, Scots in England were seldom the target of English chauvinism. Unlike Irish immigrants, Scots shared the religion of their host community. The Scots differed from the Irish again in escaping the social stereotyping which fed the racialism of the English response to mass Irish immigration during the 19th century. The professional classes were strongly represented among Scots immigrants and by virtue of their superior education Scottish working-class immigrants were socially mobile. Certainly some Scots (even educated ones) felt culturally and socially inferior in metropolitan English society and resented the condescension which they detected in English attitudes towards Scotland. But these were the responses of a provincialised not an oppressed culture.

The parallel development of the industrial revolution in the two countries was another factor which eroded the sense of a separate Scots political identity. Coinciding with the heyday of Empire, industrialisation created an area of common experience between Scots, English and Welsh which fed the growth of a united British labour movement.

Cultural Identity

A society may retain a strong sense of cultural identity even when it has lost its sense of political identity. In Scotland, however, the process of linguistic and cultural assimilation to southern models had begun even before the Wars of Independence of the 13th and 14th centuries. It was greatly accelerated by the adoption of English texts by the Scottish reformers of the 16th century and further reinforced by the removal of the Court to London on the accession of James VI to the English throne.

Although the centralisation of political power in London and the growing prestige of English cultural norms eroded the public status of Scots identity, a strong Scottish sentiment survived. Indeed the tension between the Scots' surrender to *force majeure* in political affairs and their continuing emotional attachment to their Scottish nationality is a constant theme of Scottish history from the 16th century to the present. Even while they acknowledged their ultimate dependence on English power, John Knox and succeeding generations of Scottish Reformers celebrated Scotland as a nation specially called by God to carry out His great work of reformation. David Hume, the star of Scotland's 16th-century Enlightenment, took elocution lessons to eliminate Scotticisms from his speech, while boasting that despite all their handicaps the Scots were 'the People most distinguish'd for Literature in Europe'.

The tension is shown at its sharpest and its most poignant as British power and prestige approached their 19th century climax. With one breath the Edinburgh Whig, Henry Cockburn, could praise the Reform Act of 1832 for giving Scotland a 'political constitution for the first time', while with the next he lamented the passing of distinctive Scottish manners. And from the Tory side Walter Scott defended the Union as the indispensable basis of Scotland's prosperity while deploring the destruction of Scottish tradition which it entailed.

The history of 19th-century Europe supplies many examples of societies, politically and culturally dependent, setting out to reconstruct a national identity from a cultural and linguistic base. In some cases, Norway and Czechoslovakia for example, the linguistic base had itself to be reconstructed by the labours of philologists and antiquarians. In different historical circumstances Scotland, herself one of the principal sources of the literary romanticism which fed 19th-century cultural nationalism, might have followed a similar road to national revival. But Scotland, unlike no other of Europe's 'submerged' nations, had to face a double ordeal. Its status as a junior partner in the Empire exposed the already attenuated sense of Scottish nationality to the full glamour of the British Idea at the zenith of its prestige. Simultaneously, the massive dislocation caused by industrialisation struck at the social base of Scottish cultural identity. It is not surprising that under such a battering Scottish nationality retreated to the twilight regions of the imagination where subsequent mutations bred the deformities of the kailyard and the Great Tartan Monster. Thus Scotland's cultural identity had been devastated even before its exposure in the twentieth century to the standardising impact of the mass media.

Cultural revival, even linguistic revival, must remain a major aim of Scottish nationalism. But cultural or linguistic revivalism on the 19th century model cannot provide a base for a popular Scottish nationalism in the closing decades of the twentieth.

As early as the 17th century, then, the pattern of Scotland's relationship with England had been established. Unlike Wales and Ireland, Scotland had had the strength to withstand the military challenge to her statehood. But she had neither the population nor the wealth to share the British Isles with England as a political and cultural equal. In an unequal compromise with her powerful neighbour, she sacrificed her political independence to her economic prosperity. Other key national institutions were spared, only to preside helplessly over the steady assimilation of the national culture to the English model.

Some Nationalists spend a lot of time wishing Scotland's history had been cast in a more melodramatic mould. If only Scotland had been the victim of English armed might as Ireland was. If only the Scots language and culture had been suppressed by the English in the way Welsh language and culture were suppressed. If only the Gaelic Scotland crushed by Cumberland had been the whole of Scotland and not just one part at war both with itself and with Lowland Scotland. If only history had treated Scotland with a less subtle cruelty, what a lion of a nation we might now be!

But nationalism must build on reality. Scots have little cause to be grateful to English governments but Westminster has not acted towards Scotland as a despotic colonial power. We may resent England but we do not hate it. To the great majority of Scots the English are not foreigners as Germans or French are foreigners. Most Scots think of themselves with little difficulty as both Scottish and British. Nationalist strategy must start by acknowledging that for easily understood reasons of history a sense of nationality exists in most Scots today only at a sentimental level remote from public affairs and political debate.

Two – Class

Class and Nation

Nationality and class are the two most powerful forces shaping political behaviour. When a vital sense of nationality combines with the interests of a powerful class, the nationalism which results is a formidable force. The paralysis of Scottish politics in face of the dual challenge of Britain's post-imperial decline and the oil-fired transformation of Scotland's economic potential is due to the fact that what remained of Scottish nationality by the end of the 19th century was strong enough to colour the ethos of Scotland's commitment to the emerging Labour Party but too weak to provide the basis for an alternative political strategy. The ironic result is that the Labour Party is better able to exploit the residual sense of nationality for its own conservative and defensive purposes than is the SNP for its radical purposes.

The task facing Nationalists is to challenge the unionist bias of Scottish class consciousness with a new sense of political nationality. Traditional Nationalists will look for this new nationality to rise, phoenix-like, from the remnants of the old, born upwards on the shoulders of Weelum Wallace, Rabbie Burns and the rest of MacDiarmid's 'heterogeneous hotch and rabble' of Scottish heroes.

Realists, on the other hand, will accept that the inspiration of a new Scottish nationality will not be found among the wreckage of Scotland's past but in the ambitions for Scotland's future.

Scottish Society

By the occupational categories used by the Registrar General, approximately 66 per cent of Scotland's male working population is in a manual occupation and 33 per cent in non-manual occupations [1971 Census Figures]. Refining the Registrar General's figures, David McCrone identified 54.5 per cent of Scottish male workers as being employed in manual occupations compared to 49.9 per cent in England and Wales; 21.2 per cent in lower non-manual occupations compared to 22.7 per cent in England and Wales; and 17.2 per cent in upper non-manual occupations (employers, managers, professional, farm owners or managers and own account workers) compared to 18.9 per cent in England and Wales. To call Scotland a 'class' society is, of course, to do more than point to a division of the labour force into occupational categories. It is to recognise that the 'life chances' of a Scottish child are determined to a significant extent by its father's occupation – that a Scottish doctor's son or daughter is far more likely to stay on at school beyond the statutory leaving age, to go to university, to earn a high income from a high prestige job, to enjoy good health and to have healthy children than the son of a local authority labourer or bus driver.

Jock Tamson's Bairns?

Since 1944 Scotland like other parts of the UK has had a system of universal free education, topped by the universities. Yet, only 29 per cent of Scottish school leavers in 1972 who went on to university were from working-class back grounds – i.e. had a father in a manual occupation (according to the Registrar-General's unrefined classification). Even more disturbing is the fact that between 1962 and 1972, the proportion of Scottish university students with a manual background declined by six per cent compared to a decline of 3.4 per cent in the proportion of manual workers in the labour force. There is no reason to believe that the trend has been reversed in the last nine years.

Students of working class background make up a higher proportion of the student population in other sectors of post-school education. One study estimates that 47 per cent of the 1972 school leavers who went to Colleges of Education were from working-class backgrounds, as were 43 per cent of those entering full-time courses in further education. But this is from an estimated 71 per cent working-class share of the comparable age group. The disparity in working and middle class education chances is measured by the fact that whereas 39 per cent of all middle class school leavers went on to higher or further education only nine per cent of working class children did so. With under 50 per cent of the Scottish school leavers receiving any form of post-school education Scotland lags behind most other developed countries including England. So much for the Democratic Intellect.

Of course, there is movement between occupations. Non-manual jobs have grown by over 33 per cent since 1921 and a significant proportion of these new jobs have been filled by people from manual backgrounds. Using a seven category occupational classification, one study has revealed that no less than 60 per cent of professional and administrative jobs (Class 1) are filled by individuals from lower occupational groupings, with the two lowest groups, the semi-skilled and the unskilled (Classes 6 and 7), contributing 20 per cent. But using slightly different categories the fact remains that 42 per cent of fathers in the professional and administrative group have sons working in their own top occupational group, compared to only nine per cent of skilled manual fathers and five per cent of semi-skilled and unskilled fathers. When the seven category classification is used, 42 per cent of the Scottish male working population is revealed as upwardly mobile, 27 per cent immobile and 30 per cent downwardly mobile. On a two category division between manual and non-manual, 65.7 per cent of the population is socially immobile, 23 per cent upwardly mobile and 11.3 per cent downwardly mobile. The authors of the study record their belief, based on circumstantial evidence, that social mobility is lower in Scotland than England.

The extent of social division is not determined by the degree of social mobility alone. The social 'distance' between occupational groups also depends on how sharply one group is separated from another by differences of income, wealth, values and attitudes. Some of the differences of income and wealth in Scottish society are described below. Attitudes and values are not open to such precise measurement but if, as some Nationalists claim, Scottish norms and values are less 'class-specific' than English – if Scotland is indeed a more open and democratic society than England – that can only be because England is one of the most class obsessed societies in the world. By less eccentric standards the gap between the lifestyles and values of the upper-middle and manual classes in Scotland is wide and has probably been little diminished by the increase in upward social mobility stimulated by the growth of professional and administrative employment.

Class and Health

The class into which a Scottish child is born determines his physical as well as his educational and economic 'life chances'. A recent study reports that in 1977 the infant mortality rate in the professional class was 9.2 per 1000 live births; in the clerical and skilled manual classes it was 14.2; in the semi-skilled manual classes it was 15.3; and in the unskilled manual class it was 21.5.

The inequality continues into adulthood. The incidence of lung cancer was 3.9 times higher among male manual workers than among male professional workers and 2.4 times higher among female manual workers than female professional workers (1972–74 figures). Post neo-natal mortality rates in the first year of life (excluding the first four weeks) – the period in which the child is most vulnerable to social and environmental hazards – were 2.8 times higher for the children of manual workers than for those of professional workers. The incidence of many other physical defects, from small stature to poor eyesight and poor dental health, confirms the importance of the social class into which the Scottish child is born. The study concludes that the social inequalities in health are not diminishing but may be increasing.

'A Man's a Man'

The distribution of wealth in Scotland is more unequal than south of the border. In 1975, according to the Royal Commission on the Distribution of Income and Wealth, the top one per cent of the population in England and Wales owned 22.9 per cent of personal wealth compared to a share of 27.3 per cent for the top one per cent of the Scottish population. The top ten per cent in England and Wales owned 61.6 per cent of personal wealth compared to 68 per cent in Scotland.

Nor is the English standard a demanding one. In the UK as a whole the distribution of personal wealth is more unequal than in most other Western countries, including the United States.

The difference between England and Scotland in the distribution of wealth is partly explained by the narrower spread of home ownership north of the border. Only 35 per cent of Scottish homes are owner-occupied compared to 55 per cent of English homes.

Another cause of the difference is the extreme concentration of land ownership in Scotland. A fraction of Scotland's population, 0.3 per cent, owns 63 per cent of Scotland's acreage. The UK imposes fewer statutory restraints on the size and use of land holdings than any other Western European country.

The great majority of Scots count their wealth in the form of income not capital. But income too is unequally distributed. In the United Kingdom as a whole the top 20 per cent of the population receives 42 per cent of the pre-tax income while the bottom 20 per cent receives only 6.2 per cent. The progressive character of the tax system has been so eroded that the distribution of post-tax income differs only slightly – the top 20 per cent receiving 39 per cent post-tax income and the bottom 20 per cent receiving only 7.5 per cent.

Again the Scottish pattern is more polarised than the UK pattern. In 1977/78 13.2 per cent of Scottish households had an income of £30 a week or less compared to 11.6 per cent of English households. At the other end of the income scale, 27 per cent of Scots households had a weekly income of £150 or more compared to 26.2 per cent of English households and 7 per cent had over £200 a week compared to 6.6 per cent of English households.

The high concentration of wealth and income is accompanied by what is by the standards of other developed countries an exceptionally large proportion of the population living in relative poverty. According to the Child Poverty Action Group's definition of poverty as the standard of living obtainable with an income below 140 per cent of supplementary benefit rates, at least one in five of the Scottish population is living in poverty. A former Depute Chairwoman of the Supplementary Benefits Commission has claimed that it could be as high as one in four.

Successive surveys, including the National Children's Bureau report, *Born to Fail* (1973) and the Department of the Environment's *Census Indicators of Multiple Deprivation* (1976), have established that Scotland's high incidence of income poverty is matched by an exceptional level of environmental poverty. Needless to say, it is manual workers, particularly unskilled manual workers, and their families who are the chief victims. The burden of Scotland's rising unemployment also falls quite disproportionately on manual workers, increasing yet further the gross inequalities which disfigure Scottish society.

Class and Power

The class-based inequalities of education, wealth and health, are paralleled by class-based inequalities of power. The 'superstructure' of Scottish society – those public institutions which take decisions on our behalf about the future of society and which mould its values – is dominated by the middle class. The senior civil servants in St Andrews House are predominantly middle class. The Scottish legal profession is overwhelmingly middle class. Cultural institutions like the Scottish Arts Council and BBC Scotland are dominated by middle class personnel and values. The staff of Scotland's universities and colleges are mostly middle class. The majority of school teachers are from middle class and lower-middle class rather than working class backgrounds.

Scotland's political parties are firmly bound into the class system. The

Conservatives, Liberals and SNP are almost exclusively middle class in their leadership and their MPs. Even in the Labour Party, two-thirds of the MPs are of obviously middle class background or occupation and in the last ten years middle class activists, many with jobs in the public sector, have begun to assume the leadership of Labour constituency parties and to challenge Labour's working class activists in their former preserve of local government.

Middle class dominance of the major institutions is a feature of all liberal democracies. But in Scotland the middle-class grip is all the tighter for the absence of the countervailing class power which in other industrial societies is supplied by a politically assertive trade union movement. The British trade union movement may be an imperfect vehicle for working class interests and ambitions but for most of the period since the beginning of the Second World War it has successfully asserted, through the TUC, labour's right to a share in economic policy making. The centralisation of power within the British trade unions has, however, left the Scottish TUC and Scottish regional councils of most unions without any industrial muscle or any significant role in the political process, a lack for which the STUC consoles itself by a good deal of political breast-beating and make-believe.

The social distance between the majority of the Scottish population and Scotland's public institutions is increased further by the growing number of English personnel in senior positions. Part of this distancing effect arises from a residual nationalist resentment of the English. But the more important part is a consequence of the middle and upper-middle class stereotype which most Scots pin on Englishmen.

To sum up: Scotland in 1981 remains a socially divided community with relatively low levels of social mobility, a more unequal distribution of wealth, income and power than in England let alone countries like Norway, Denmark and the Netherlands, and with an exceptionally high proportion of its population living in relative poverty.

How Many Nations?

Against this background of social division Scottish Nationalists should not be surprised if their talk of 'the Scottish nation' is often dismissed as sentimental rubbish. The Edinburgh advocate in his New Town Flat and the Glasgow bus driver in a Red Road high rise may share a sentimental attachment to Scotland on the football field or athletics track and feel a similar irritation when 'England' is used for 'Britain' by TV newsreaders. But in their everyday concerns – their jobs, their incomes, their hopes for their children, their anxieties about retirement, the quality of their housing, their health – they might as well live in different countries. When Nationalists talk of Scotland the nation they must expect the questions: whose nation? What kind of Scotland?

Three – Voting Behaviour

Class Voting

Neither the electoral nor the policy case for left wing nationalism follows automatically from the persistence of the class system in Scotland. Indeed in the United Kingdom there has been a significant weakening of the link between class identity and party loyalty. Professor Richard Rose of the University of Strathclyde found that only 49 per cent of voters in the 1979 election supported their traditional 'class' Party, compared to 54 per cent in 1970 and 57 per cent in 1964. Of all the social groups the working class was the most 'deviant'. Whereas 62 per cent of the upper-middle class (professional, administrative and business) voted Conservative, only 45 per cent of the working class (skilled, semi-skilled, unskilled manual and welfare recipients) voted Labour. While the Conservative lead over Labour among the upper-middle class has declined from 53 per cent in 1964 to 44 per cent in 1979, Labour's lead over the Conservatives among working class voters declined from 28 per cent to only 7 per cent.

However, the United Kingdom figures conceal important differences between England, Wales and Scotland. Whereas in England in 1979, 41 per cent of the working class voted Conservative, in Wales only 29 per cent did so, and in Scotland only 24 per cent. Labour gained the support of 50 per cent of the Scottish working class vote, SNP 19 per cent and Liberals 6 per cent.

If the Scottish working class remains predominantly anti-Tory, the Scottish middle class is deeply split in its political loyalties. While 66 per cent of the English upper-middle class voted Conservative, only 53 per cent of the proportionately slightly smaller Scottish middle class did so, and in Wales only 34 per cent. The Scottish lower-middle class, also slightly smaller than its English counterpart, gave only 43 per cent to the Conservatives against 56 per cent in England.

Why is Scotland Anti-Tory?

The effective introduction of the adult male franchise in 1885 confounded those who had predicted that it would destroy the Conservative Party. Instead the Conservative Party has flourished. In few elections this century has it failed to win at least 30 per cent of the English working class vote. One source of Conservative support among the English working class has been the survival into industrial England of the rural 'deference' vote. But a more important factor in the post-war period has been the impact of direct taxation on rising working-class incomes. The impact has been felt most keenly in the economically most confident regions of England, like the Midlands and South East, where sections of the working class have come to regard home and car ownership, foreign holidays, and the other pleasures of middle-class affluence, as the norm. Under financial pressure from such new commitments, these newly affluent sections of the working class began to sympathise with the middle-class preference for tax cuts over improved public services. So they moved from Labour, the party traditionally associated with the welfare state and high public expenditure, to the Tories, the party of tax cuts.

Although the Scottish working class has not been immune to these influences, it has been subject to a wider range of countervailing influences. Scotland's post-war boom was too short to repair the damage to Scottish confidence done by the interwar depression. The effects of Britain's post-war decline were beginning to be felt in Scotland by the late 1950s, while the Midlands and South East of England continued to be relatively buoyant into the 1970s. So the balance sheet of costs and benefits between cuts in personal taxation and increases in the social wage was judged differently in Scotland, to the benefit of the Labour Party.

But Scotland's anti-Tory bias has deeper historical roots. As Presbyterians, Scots had a natural suspicion of the Tories as the party of the Episcopalian establishment. After all what is the Church of England but the Tory Party at prayer? Some at least of that religious antipathy survived into the 19th century to join with a residual anti-English sentiment to prejudice the Scottish industrial working class against the Tories as the party of the English establishment. That same image offended both the religious faith and the sense of nationality of the Irish sections of Scotland's working class. Meanwhile the third element, the disposed highlanders, identified the Tories as the party of the landowners.

Industrialisation brought a new element of class awareness to reinforce Scotland's anti-establishment sentiment. Even by 19th-century standards Scotland's experience was harsh. Scottish housing was of a lower standard than south of the border, Scottish wages were lower until the end of the century, the Poor Law was harsher and the disciplinarian attitudes of Scottish employers were less likely to be softened by the sort of paternalism which inspired the reforms of Shaftesbury and his colleagues in England. Until its split in 1886 over Irish Home Rule, the Liberal Party with its strong radical traditions succeeded in absorbing the emerging class consciousness. But the formation of the first Scottish Labour Party in 1888 was an early sign that working class political institutions were preparing to challenge the Liberals' failing grip. Meanwhile, those Orange sections of the Scottish working class, who began to look to the Tories as an alternative to the unreliable Liberals, did so for religious-cum-ideological reasons quite different from the social and economic interests of the working class in England.

The effect of the inter-war depression on Scotland's economic confidence has already been mentioned. But the experience of those years had a wider impact on working class attitudes. The strong export bias of its capital goods industries made the Scottish economy exceptionally vulnerable to the Depression. As unemployment rose, Scottish employers were among the most enthusiastic advocates of wage cuts as the way to restore competitiveness. The bitterness which the employers' attitudes created in the working class was compounded by the political defeats which the working class suffered in the General Strike of 1926 and in the 1931 election. The immediate effect was a swing towards conservatism, in the shape of the National Government, at the expense of the emerging Labour Party. The longer term effect was to impress even more deeply on the Scottish working class a psychology of defensiveness which came to identify the Labour Party as its natural vehicle. That mood yielded temporarily to Scotland's post-war reconstruction boom, helping to give the Tories just over 50 per cent of the Scottish vote in 1955, as it yielded in the early 1970s to the oil boom to swing support to the SNP. But as the UK's economic

THE CASE FOR LEFT WING NATIONALISM

decline gathered momentum from the late 1950s, the defensiveness established itself as the most persistent theme in working-class political attitudes.

The Middle Class

The ambivalence of the Scottish middle class towards the Conservative Party also has a historical role. More than the working class, the middle class was sensitive to the religious dimension of politics. Westminster's handling of Scottish church issues continued to generate political controversy for most of the 19th century. Although the Liberals and Tories shared responsibility for the mishandling of the Veto Act which led to the Disruption of 1843, that traumatic event confirmed important sections of the Scottish middle class in 'dissenting' attitudes which predisposed them against the Tories. As chief legatees of the Union settlement the Scottish middle class also resented the retreat of the remaining Scottish institutions before the superior political power and social prestige of English institutions. In the 20th century, an awareness of Scotland's economic and social vulnerability among sections of the Scottish middle class predisposed them in favour of the public sector, which by the 1970s supplied 34 per cent of total Scots' employment compared to 30 per cent of English employment.

Socialism

To be anti-Tory is not necessarily to be in favour of socialism. The survey evidence suggests that many of the individual socialist policies of the British Labour left are only slightly less unpopular among Scottish than among English working class voters. While the SNP has the opportunity to develop a left wing programme for Scotland, free of the anti-democratic and centralist tendencies of the British left, it certainly could not expect all of its policies to be popular.

The electors, however, do not decide their votes by their response to individual policies but by how far they are able to identify with the party as a whole. The overall tendency of the party's policies and the position it takes up on controversial issues are the important factors. Given the strength of class feeling in Scotland a socialist reputation may be attractive even to voters who reject individual socialist policies. And for a party like the SNP which has a reputation for being opportunistic on social and economic issues and which cannot claim a long track-record of identification with working class interests at the grassroots, a clear ideological commitment to the left would signal to working class voters a new readiness to stand with them on the socially divisive issues of the day.

The survey evidence gives no support to those Nationalists who believe that the SNP's future lies in competing with the Social Democrats for the moderate/centre vote. A large proportion of the potential Social Democratic vote consists of former Labour voters who swung to the Tories at the last election and who are now, in their disillusionment, looking for a moderate alternative. Such disappointed Labour converts to Thatcherism are rarer in Scotland than in England. In Scotland the SNP, not the Tories, has been the natural working-class alternative to Labour.

The Labour defector to the SNP, however, appears to have a different range of political values from the English Labour defector to the Tories. The Strathclyde Election Survey reveals that SNP voters in 1979 were much closer on social and economic issues to Labour voters than to Conservatives. Furthermore, almost twice as many Conservative as Labour voters (64 per cent to 34 per cent) thought there was a big difference between their own party and the SNP. Also only 17 per cent of Conservative voters in the General Election had voted 'Yes' in the Assembly Referendum compared to 42 per cent of Labour voters. So the evidence suggests that the SNP should challenge for the Labour vote by presenting itself, *inter alia*, as a party better equipped than Labour to achieve the goals of full employment and social welfare.

Opinion surveys are not a substitute for a political strategy. Parties of radical change like the SNP are in business to challenge public opinion not to echo it. Their strategy should follow not from nice electoral calculations but from an analysis of society's needs and problems.

The class structure of Scotland has already been summarised. This is not the place to detail the reforms necessary to achieve the egalitarian goals which the Labour Party has so conspicuously failed to achieve in Scotland. Suffice it here to say that Scotland's class system will not yield to anything less than a coordinated and mutually reinforcing redistribution of income, power and wealth.

The Scottish Economy

Scotland's economic problems point no less emphatically than her social problems to left wing solutions.

The two dominant trends in the Scottish economy in the 20th century have been the decline of its manufacturing industry and the progressive takeover of its economic assets by external capital. Since 1951, Scottish manufacturing industry has suffered a net loss of over 150,000 jobs. Service employment has meanwhile grown more slowly in Scotland than in other industrialised countries. Between the mid-1960s and the mid-1970s it grew by only 13 per cent to reach 56 per cent of total employment, compared to 18 per cent in the UK, 43 per cent in the United States, 40 per cent in the Netherlands and Sweden, and 16 per cent in West Germany. Since 1959, Scottish unemployment has grown from 88,000 to 286,000.

The external takeover of Scottish assets which began in the 19th century accelerated in the 1960s and 1970s. Today 60 per cent of Scotland's manufacturing labour force is employed in non-Scottish firms and the remaining Scottish controlled jobs are concentrated in the older and technologically less sophisticated sectors of Scottish industry. In the last decade external capital has also invested heavily in Scotland's natural resources – land, timber and above all energy.

If Scotland today has many of the features of a 'neo-colony' it was not always so. In the nineteenth century Scotland was the centre of an international trading and transport network covering much of Asia and Africa. She also developed a range of financial institutions geared to overseas portfolio investment. Since the founding of the first investment trust in Dundee in 1873, a significant share of the profits of Scottish industry has been exported, chiefly to the Dominions and North America. One estimate is that by the 1900s Scottish institutions had overseas investments worth £500m. In the post-war period, Scotland's financial sector has grown while her manufacturing base has shrunk. Today, Scottish investment trusts alone have overseas investments worth about £1bn.

Scotland's financial institutions have certainly brought new jobs to the service sector. But as they have become progressively more integrated with the international financial system they have encouraged the Scottish investor to disengage further from the Scottish economy and to look for investment opportunities overseas.

The decline in Scottish manufacturing, the slow growth of Scottish services, the progressive takeover of Scotland's firms and natural resources by foreign capital, the integration of Scotland's financial institutions into an international system in which Scotland features chiefly as a location for high-yielding energy investments – all these are among the symptoms of a chronic sickness in the locally controlled private sector of the Scottish economy. The Scottish private sector is simply no longer large enough or independent enough to serve as the basis of a revived Scottish 'mixed' economy. Scottish controlled manufacturing firms now supply only 12 per cent of total Scottish employment. Small firms will certainly have an important role in Scotland's economic revival but they cannot carry the burden of economic reconstruction. In any case without a determined policy of state support, the most successful of the small firms would succumb to takeover bids by multinational companies determined to defend their market dominance.

Scotland's economic revival, therefore, depends on a major extension of the public sector in the form of improved public services, increased public finance for industry conditional on the adoption of co-operative ownership and other forms of industrial democracy, and public control of Scotland's financial institutions (as I write, the Bank of Scotland is negotiating a merger with the South African Standard Chartered Bank).

Bourgeois Nationalism

The long decline of the Scottish private sector has destroyed the social and economic base in Scotland for 'bourgeois nationalism'. When such a base existed in the 19th century, the strong orientation of Scottish industry towards imperial markets tied the industrial bourgeoisie to the Union and the world-wide trading system which the Union supported.

The Scottish industrial bourgeoisie retained an identifiable social base, albeit if gravely weakened, into the 20th century. But even in the exceptional circumstances of the Depression, the Scottish bourgeoisie's continued interest in overseas markets and in armaments' manufacture dependent on Britain's world role prevented it from conceiving a nationalist political strategy to support the corporatist programme of economic reconstruction which it evolved through such bodies as the Scottish Development Council and the Scottish Economic Committee.

The accelerated takeover of Scottish assets by foreign capital since the War has virtually eliminated the Scottish industrial middle class as an independent sector in Scottish political life, except occasionally in a defensive role. Its impotence is confirmed by its failure to exploit the bargaining power of Scottish oil in the way the Albertan business community has used the province's energy wealth to extend its economic and political clout in Canada, or in the way the Norwegian business community has secured the use of Norway's oil revenues to subsidise Norwegian industry at the time of the world recession.

The Scottish professional middle class meanwhile is ill-equipped to provide an alternative base for middle class nationalism. The Church is dying in Scotland as elsewhere. The Scottish legal community appears largely content with its captive market and with the shabby provincial privileges conferred by the Union. And such key groups as academics, journalists and broadcasters are dependent on the British state or some other external agency and anyway are increasingly dominated by English personnel.

There remains the wider public sector middle class in the civil service, local government, the health social and educational services. These groups have a clearer economic interest than any other middle class group in supporting the creation of a political system which would insulate the public sector from the periodic assaults of British governments struggling with a shrinking economic base and confronting an English electorate with a pronounced list to the right. But strong integrating forces are at work too. One is the power of centralised public service unions. Another is the extent to which senior posts are held by non-Scots. But perhaps the most important is the fact that the great post-war expansion of the public sector was sponsored by central government. In Quebec, where the extension of the public sector in the Quiet Revolution of the 1960s was largely the result of provincial initiative, the new public sector middle class has supplied the Parti Quebecois with many of its most determined cadres.

These factors do not completely explain the passivity of the Scottish middle class in the face of the enormous opportunity which oil-financed self-government presents. The scale of the social change which the Scottish working class has suffered under the Union should not be allowed to conceal the more discreet injury which the Union has inflicted on the Scottish middle class. In the course of its long battle against economic odds, the Scottish working class has developed a keen sense of its own identity. But in rejecting a role of national political leadership even during its period of social and economic dominance, the Scottish middle class mutilated itself psychologically, perhaps beyond recovery. One consequence is seen in the contrast between the relative wealth of fiction and drama about the Scottish working-class experience and the dearth of imaginative literature about middle-class experience. Scotland must be the only Western society where the working class is more fertile of literature than the middle class. No doubt the Scottish middle class will continue to supply activists and intellectual champions to the Nationalist movement but as a collective interest it will be hostile or apathetic.

The Working Class

If the Scottish working class has developed a sense of its own identity it is an identity which bears little resemblance to the heroic proletarianism encapsulated in the myth of Red Clydeside. Politically it is dourer, more defensive, while culturally it is so pickled in tartan sentimentality that it exists today only as a caricature. In this form, an appeal to a working-class sense of nationality may elicit a political response in the short term. But the schizophrenia of the Scottish imagination presents a barrier to any more lasting effect. That familiar working-class, figure the fiery or maudlin Nationalist of the night before, is invariably the tame Unionist of the morning after.

Yet, in an old industrial society with a weak middle class, the working class offers the only possible base for popular nationalism. The Upper Clyde campaign of 1971, the swing of working-class support to the SNP in the mid-1970s and the working-class support for the 'Yes' vote in the referendum of 1979 suggests that the Scottish working class has retained at least some potential for radical action despite the haemorrhage of working class jobs which has occurred over the last 30 years.

Certainly no other class has such an overwhelming interest in breaking out of the decaying political and economic system of post-imperial Britain. The cycle of Britain's industrialisation and deindustrialisation has exacted a higher price, socially, economically and culturally, from the Scottish working class than any other section of the native British working class. And in the last ten years the transformation of Scotland's economic potential has thrown the continued wasting of the Scottish working class into a harsh, even grotesque, profile.

The challenge for Scottish Nationalists is to articulate this working-class interest into a new sense of political nationality capable of challenging the defensive and self-deluding nationality which helps to attach the working class to the Labour Party.

This argument does not mean that a Nationalist party should look for support only from the urban working class. A clear commitment to the public sector should prove attractive to elements of the public sector middle class. And, building on the existing strengths of the Nationalist case, the SNP's platform should embrace land and agricultural policies attractive to the rural working class, policies on the EEC and on fishing attractive to fishing communities, policies on energy attractive to conservationists of the anti-nuclear movement, policies on social issues attractive to the women's movement and to a range of welfare recipients such as old age pensioners and single parents.

But what it does mean is that the SNP must look to the urban working class to supply the indispensable core of its vote. Without that support, the other votes which the SNP can hope to attract will always fall short of the popular and stable mandate required to break Westminster's grip on Scotland's future.

There is no prospect of Scotland's decline being reversed from a British base. Even leaving aside the implications of the emergence of the Social Democratic Party for the Labour vote, English voting patterns, in particular the large minority of the English working class which habitually votes Tory, make it improbable that any British Labour government will survive into a second five year term. In any case, while the social democratic policies of recent Labour governments have failed in Scotland, the policies of the new Labour left, based on a massive increase in centralised decision making with 'democratic' control channelled through the Labour Party itself rather than new public institutions, offer little hope to Scotland. Indeed their only certain result would be to intensify British exploitation of Scotland's energy resources as the left wing government, lacking a stable popular base in either the English electorate or the labour movement, faced the retaliation of the international financial agencies and the multinationals.

Scottish Labour

The Scottish Council of the Labour Party will provide a poor defence against the new wave of British centralisation and exploitation. It has failed hopelessly to exploit the new bargaining power which North Sea oil has given Scotland. Although it has a wide base in Scottish local government, the trade unions, media, higher education and voluntary organisations, it has made no contribution of any significance to the recent strategic debates about the future of the Labour Party. Indeed, in almost ninety years since the foundation of the independent Labour Party by Keir Hardie, only two other Scottish personalities have made any contribution of note to the Party's major debates: John Wheatley in the 1920s and John Mackintosh in the 1970s.

Perhaps Scottish Labour's lack of political and intellectual vitality reflects its own self-definition as a provincial and subordinate component of the British Labour Party. It was only this year that the Scottish Conference of the Party founded by the noted internationalist Kier Hardie even allowed international issues on its agenda.

The Labour Party in Scotland was born of a desire to challenge the class structure of power. Today it reflects and sustains both the class structure of Scottish society and Scotland's subordinate role within the United Kingdom power structure. Two-thirds of Scotland's Labour MPs come from middle class backgrounds or occupations and at constituency and local government level working class activists are being steadily replaced by recruits from the public sector middle class, many of whom are English incomers.

In spite of Scotland's constancy to the Labour cause, Scottish Labour MPs feature as the NCOs of Labour parliamentary politics, seldom officers. The recent Labour leadership contest was fought between four Oxbridge educated Englishmen with another public school and Oxford educated Englishman waiting in the wings. Apart from the Scottish Secretary only three Scottish MPs have been members of Labour cabinets since the War – and one of those was an Englishman sitting for a Scottish seat. More and more the Labour Party in Scotland operates as a device by which a provincial and provincialised middle class mobilises the Scottish working class vote in support of a dissenting section of the English middle class which cannot count on the loyalty of its own working class. In return the

Scottish middle class is given a properly subordinate place in the British power structure and the Scottish working class, the poor bloody infantry of the civil war within the English middle class which passes for politics in Britain, is repaid with chronic unemployment, some of the worst housing in Western Europe, record rates of ill health and forced migration. What matter if they fall, the council estates and industrial wastelands of Scotland will furnish abundant replacements.

Conclusion

To summarise the argument, the historic sense of Scottish political and cultural nationality is too weak to serve as the basis for modern political nationalism.

With the decline of the Scottish middle class the Scottish working class offers the only possible social base for a Nationalist movement in Scotland.

Given the persistence of class divisions in Scotland, a nationalist case which concentrates on the promise of economic growth while ignoring the divisive issue of how the fruits of growth are to be distributed will never win the trust of the largest block of Scottish voters, the urban working class.

The SNP's credibility – with working class and middle class voters alike – depends on the Party pursuing a consistent line on the key issues of the day based on an analysis of Scotland's economic and social needs.

Given the collapse of the Scottish private sector and the major social and economic inequalities which persist in Scottish society, that analysis will lead to a socialist response.

The growing gap between the reality and the potential of the Scottish economy, and the growing divergence between English and Scottish voting patterns, offers Nationalists an opportunity to create a new, aggressive sense of political nationality to challenge the traditional defensiveness which ties the working class to Labour.

The SNP's target should be to establish itself as the radical Scottish alternative to the Labour Party.

To succeed left wing nationalism must look to Scotland's future, not her past. It could do worse than adopt as its slogan Hugh MacDiarmid's prescription for a Scottish renaissance: 'Not Traditions – Precedents!'

Scotland's Cruel Paradox

Radical Scotland, February / March 1983

SOCIALISTS LIVE TODAY in the shadow of a cruel paradox. They are surrounded by the evidence of capitalism in crisis. Thirty million people in the capitalist economies of Europe and North America are out of work. Tens of thousands of companies go bankrupt each year. The international monetary and trading system sponsored by the capitalist democracies after the Second World War totters under the impact of rising protectionism and financing problems.

Yet, in the midst of this crisis of capitalism, it is socialists who feel lost and confused, while the apologists of capitalism confidently trumpet their faith even as they dodge the falling masonry of their own system.

The reasons for this loss of socialist confidence have been well documented. The millenialist hopes of earlier generations of socialists have been confounded by capitalism's ability to adapt to new challenges. Where capitalism has been overthrown, efforts to build socialism in its place have too often spawned one-party states which have recreated privilege and inequality – in the classic case in a welter of blood and persecution. The achievements of later generations of socialist reformers have failed to destroy the class system and are now in retreat before the revival of free market ideologies. And new issues cutting across the traditional lines of socialist politics – the environment, equality of the sexes, the approach of the post-industrial society – have emerged to increase the socialist's sense of intellectual disorientation.

The Left's Paralysis

In Britain, the Left appears paralysed in the face of a steady erosion of working class support for the traditional objectives of the labour movement. Lacking a vision of an alternative socialist society capable of generating the popular enthusiasm which supported the reforms of the post-war Labour Government, a new generation of Labour militants has concentrated on winning control of the party machine only to find that its reserves of electoral fuel are running dangerously low.

Of course, the ideals of socialism survive this accumulation of defeats and disappointments. The presumption of equal rights based on a common humanity; the belief that the welfare of each member of society is the responsibility of all members of society; that social need not private gain should determine the use society makes of its material and human resources; that without economic and social democracy political democracy remains a stunted growth; that without a generous sharing of experience and responsibility the human personality cannot achieve its fullest expression. These values and insights endure.

But to what purpose, in the absence both of a theory of social change to identify the possibilities of reform capable of reconciling socialism's egalitarian ambitions with the demand for a democratic, even libertarian, society?

Labour's Failure in Scotland

No section of the socialist movement is so exposed to the charge of intellectual failure as Scottish socialists. The Labour movement enjoys a more stable base of electoral support in Scotland than in any other country in the United Kingdom. Yet, after decades of Labour dominance, the Labour movement has not only failed to produce a socialist culture in Scotland – or even provide a hint of what a socialist culture might be – but has failed to make any noticeable contribution to those attempts which have been made to rethink socialism. Overwhelmingly the ideas behind the Alternative Economic Strategy, the campaign for labour democracy, the debate about the relationship between feminism and socialism, the elaboration of new strategies for European nuclear disarmament, have come from the established sources of intellectual dissent in Britain. This is a southern radical middle class which, as it loses any substantial base of electoral support among the English working class, has to look increasingly to the Labour loyalties of Scotland and Wales to salvage its hopes of political power.

The next election promises to throw a harsh spotlight both on the political dilemma of English socialists and the intellectual failure of Scottish socialists. The odds are heavily in favour of a Tory majority in England and a Labour majority in Scotland. But even if Labour were to defeat the odds and win an overall majority in Parliament, the socialist crisis would have been delayed not avoided. A parliamentary majority based on a minority share of the vote, perhaps no more than 35 or 36 per cent, will provide an inadequate base for the implementation of a radical socialist manifesto. In 1945 the incoming Labour majority rode a wave of popular support. It had won the battle for the hearts and minds of the British people, the battle of ideas. There was a cross-party consensus, born of the pre-war and wartime experience in favour of many of the reforms Labour proposed.

Vested Interests

The contrast with the political mood today could not be more obvious. Instead of consensus there is polarisation. Labour has not even engaged in an educational campaign on behalf of its radical manifesto. Without any substantial popular base from which to launch a programme of socialist reform, a radical Labour government would fall easy victim to a counter-attack by vested interests backed by much of the press and the opposition parties. Radical socialism has little future in the United Kingdom.

Whether Labour fails to win the next election or finds its radical ambitions frustrated in government, the challenge for Scotland's Labour majority will be clear – to continue as an impotent rump at Westminster or to claim the power to apply in Scotland the radical socialist remedies rejected by the English body politic. If it chooses the first course it will deserve nothing but contempt. If it is to choose the second, it will need to arm itself with courage and vision.

The problems are daunting. Scottish manufacturing industry has suffered a net loss of over 200,000 jobs since the mid-1950s, contributing to a current official unemployment rate of 14.5 per cent and an unofficial rate probably close to 16 per cent. External control of the economy – now well advanced in both the manufacturing and service sectors – has eroded the institutional base from which any programme of economic recovery must be launched.

At a conservative estimate, one in five of the Scottish population lives on an income at or below the supplementary benefit rate. The scale of Scotland's problems of physical and mental ill-health, many of them products of a culture of poverty, is notorious.

Inequality and Restoring Incentives

Nor has Scotland been immune from the effects of the social 'counter-revolution' launched south of the border. Even before Thatcher came to power the distribution of income and wealth in Scotland was more unequal than in England. The economic policies of the Thatcher Government have been aimed quite deliberately at increasing economic differentials in order to restore incentives. The economic changes, however, are only the first instalment of the counter-revolution. Market forces helped along by privatisation now threaten to institutionalise the growing economic inequalities. Scotland is being invaded by private hospitals backed by financial interests in London and the United States. The Government is encouraging the growth of fee-paying schools by the restoration of grants removed by the last Labour Government. The ground is being prepared for an assault on the principle of free health and education services by a campaign to introduce vouchers, to be topped up as the holder decides – or can afford.

The MP for Hamilton, George Robertson, may complain that the sale of Hamilton College of Education to an English company that intends to turn it into a private school offends against Scotland's educational traditions. But he and his fellow Scots Labour MPs are responsible for their own impotence.

Unemployment and the Working Class

Unemployment and the social counter-revolution carry dangers for the left in Scotland. Present experience confirms the lesson of the 1930s – that high unemployment does not radicalise the working class: rather it makes them timid and conservative, deflecting them from radical solutions towards whatever is familiar and established. In England the Tories, aided by repeated and heavy doses of Falklands chauvinism, have maintained their appeal to working class voters even in areas like the West Midlands where the rate of growth of unemployment has been higher than anywhere else in the country. It is true that in Scotland the Labour Party has won back support from the SNP. But it has done so as the party of the local status quo, as the representative of the provincial establishment, not as a Bennite crusade. And the SNP, after all, offered its distinctive brand of radicalism. If high unemployment does help to consolidate Labour's dominance in Scotland, it may be at the price of further weakening the will for radical change among the Scottish working class. In the absence of a countervailing socialist culture, high unemployment tends to create a culture of despair quite as hostile to the prospects of socialist advance in Scotland as Tory populism is to the hope of a Labour revival in England.

The social counter-revolution will also weaken Scotland's socialist potential. While Labour's dominance in Scotland is built on the exceptional loyalty of the Scottish working class to Labour, it is reinforced by the higher levels of middle-class support Labour enjoys north of the Border. (According to one estimate only 53 per cent of the Scottish upper-middle class and 43 per cent lower-middle class voted Tory, Labour sharing the defectors with the Liberals and Nationalists.) But will the Scottish middle class be able to resist the appeal of counter-revolution? Scottish consultants recorded a 55 per cent majority against pay beds four years ago, but the schemes for private hospitals in Glasgow and Edinburgh are not short of eager backers among Scottish consultants.

If Scottish socialists face formidable problems, they also enjoy some distinct advantages. The most obvious is Labour's electoral strength. Of course, the mass of Labour voters are not socialist in any positive sense. To make them so is the central educational and inspirational challenge which Scottish socialists face. But the task is slightly eased by two factors. Scottish opinion seems to be far less susceptible to the appeal of populist British nationalism than English opinion. Fewer than 60 per cent of Scots thought the recapture of the Falklands was worth the cost in human lives and resources compared to 80 per cent of English people. And the absence of a large ethnic minority population means that the 'race issue' is less likely to divide, or divert, Scottish energies.

The second advantage is the electoral weakness of the Tory Party. Since 1959, the Tory vote has declined with few interruptions. It is probably now too weak to support an indigenous right wing revival. Increasingly the counter-revolution in Scotland will be imported from south of the border.

The Spirit of Scottish Capitalism

The potential for a right wing revival in Scotland is further undermined by the collapse of Scottish capitalism. If economic revival through a resurgence of native capitalism is increasingly problematic in England, in Scotland it is almost inconceivable. The eagerness of the directors of the Royal Bank – the largest private employer in Scotland – to sell out to Standard Charter is more representative of the spirit of Scottish capitalism than the resistance Anderson Strathclyde is putting up to the Consolidated Charter bid or the aggressive talk about Scottish overseas expansion by Angus Grossart. As a social and political interest, Scottish capitalism is capable at most of mounting a rear-guard action. Multinational capital in Scotland is another matter.

The fourth advantage is Scottish oil. True, the faith that North Sea oil can transform Scotland's economy has gone, destroyed not by the slump in oil prices or the gloomy prognostications of stockbrokers, but by the demonstration under Labour and Conservative governments that the oil was no panacea for Britain's economic ills and the consequent decline in Scottish expectations. But the facts – that Scotland is the world's seventh largest oil producer, that it yields £6 billion a year in government revenue, that it has enabled Scotland's North Sea neighbour Norway to keep its unemployment down to 2 per cent in a world recession – could be potent forces for Scottish socialism if used as part of a strategy to challenge defeatism and fuel a revolution of rising expectations. It depends like so much else in Scotland on Labour's willingness to lift its veto on change by mobilising its Scottish majority in pursuit of Scottish ends.

The most that can be claimed for these advantages are that they indicate a *possibility* of socialist advance in Scotland. But that is one possibility more than the English enjoy, and surely enough to inspire Scots to start reconstructing Scottish socialism.

Scottish Universities

Radical Scotland, February / March 1984

The Scottish universities lie close to the heart of the Scottish paradox. Scottish identity has survived, according to the conventional wisdom, because of the national institutions of law, church and education preserved from pre-Union days. Yet these carriers of Scottish identity have steadily refused a role of national leadership. They have enjoyed the privileges of their established status while disowning the responsibility for the political, economic or social health of the national community in which they live. They seem prepared to accept even the most extreme consequences of their own inactivity – the erosion of the national community. They flaunt the plumage of national identity but ignore the dying bird.

For many liberals the failure of the Scottish universities to exercise any national leadership has been harder to forgive than the failure of the Church and the Law. The Church is a dying institution with a shrinking social base. A revitalised Scotland would be likely to push it further to the sidelines of national life. A Scottish parliament would finally explode the tattered claim of the General Assembly to be 'Scotland's Parliament'. The Law is by its nature the natural ally of state power. Scots Law exists by sufferance of an English majority at Westminster, and it is steadily dying at its hands. No matter, Scots lawyers have a protected market and social changes – the expansion of home ownership, the increased rates of divorce, the spread of personal and family insurance – more than compensate for the failure of Scots Law to develop in other directions.

But the universities should have been different. As centres of free thought, they should have been the focus and the source springs of new thinking. The interaction in the privileged precincts of the university between the guardians of the nation's intellectual traditions and the young and hopeful makes the university the centre of radical thought and action. Was that not the role of the universities of Germany in the liberal nationalist movements of the 19th century or the role of the Norwegian and Swedish universities in the pan-Scandinavian movement or even in the championing of *avant garde* theatre with Ibsen? Surely the universities of the Third World have been frontrunners in demanding radical change?

Even in the West – in the United States, France and West Germany, even in stale old Britain – as recently as the 1960s did the universities not take the lead in challenging the status quo? Surely then the Scottish universities would be the first to reflect the changing prospects and expectations of the people of Scotland?

Much of the nationalist criticism of the role of the Scottish universities in the early 1970s was based on this naïve liberal concept of the university. During the years of British imperial success, the Scottish universities had been assimilated to the dominant English model and had themselves become agents of Scotland's assimilation. But in changing political circumstances, an injection of Scottish teaching and research staff, and a broadening of the curriculum to include new Scottish studies, would rehabilitate the universities to equip them to play a positive and enlightening role in Scottish society.

It was a delusion. If the liberal ideal of the university has ever been realised in Britain, it has been for brief periods only. In England and Scotland alike, the free spirits imagined by the liberals have operated always at the margin, parasitic on the vocational roles of the university. In Scotland, certainly the general degree with its philosophical foundation and the relative ease of access to the university, gave the university a wider social role than it had in the United Kingdom. But then the Scottish universities had a particularly weak tradition of cultural leadership. Indeed, in the 20th century, none of the foremost critics of Scottish culture – figures such as Neill, MacDiarmid, the nationalist critics of the '30s such as Power, contemporaries such as Tom Nairn or Chris Harvie – have been employed at Scottish universities. Far from acting as a catalyst in the nationalist upsurge of the late 1960s and early 1970s, the Scottish universities responded reluctantly and inadequately. The expansion of Scottish studies that has taken place was the result of the efforts of committed individuals willing to exploit the prospect of political change to put pressure on the university establishment to accommodate them and make resources available. Even today the provision of Scottish studies at undergraduate, postgraduate and post-doctorate levels remains woefully inadequate.

In the eyes of many critics, the modest advances which have been achieved in Scottish studies have been more than cancelled out by the successful campaign waged by the Scottish universities to be omitted from the proposed assembly's range of functions in the referendum campaign of 1979. The case presented by the universities reads like a unionist litany. Under the control of the assembly the universities would be subject to the decisions of the parochial assembly men and women. Nationalists would insist on more Scottish studies: Labourites would seek to divert funds from the universities to less selective education. Without the link to other British universities afforded by the membership of the Universities Grants Committee (UGC), the Scottish universities would quickly retreat into the academic kailyard. They would no longer be able to attract the most able and ambitious of British academics. In short, under Scottish control the lights would go out all over Scotland.

Of course, the Scottish universities did not oppose the assembly as such. They had to maintain an official political impartiality. But they knew what they were doing. They knew that, in a nation chronically unsure of itself, if the most prestigious of national institutions were seen to disassociate themselves from the assembly, devolution would be damned in the minds of many Scots. When the referendum vote showed a pro-assembly majority below the 40 per cent level – and too narrow to force Westminster's hand – the universities had cause to congratulate themselves on their contribution to the debacle.

Or so they thought. With the return of a Conservative Government, elected by the majority nation of the political system they had helped defend, the Scottish universities quickly learned that a Parliament of ideologically purblind English suburbanites might be as great an evil as an assembly of spiteful and parochial Scots. Under pressure from the Government, the favoured UGC itself became an instrument of state direction. The level of admissions, the balance of courses, capital projects, staffing levels, even in some cases survival itself, all became matters of desperate negotiation between universities and their former benefactors.

For the Scottish universities the ironies proliferated. By their opposition to the assembly they fashioned the instruments of their own humiliation, hastened a general election which returned a Tory Government committed to cutting public expenditure. Distinctive features of the Scottish tradition made the Scottish universities particularly vulnerable to a cuts-obsessed government – the higher proportion of university students in the population, the four year honours degree and the survival of the ordinary degree. The universities' neglect of their corporate Scottish identity made it all the more difficult to weld a common front against the government, so leaving the weak like Stirling and Heriot Watt to fight their own battles. In any case, their opposition to the assembly had alienated important sections of Scottish political opinion, including some of the younger Labour MPs or aspiring MPs who might have been expected fight their political battles. Even those Scottish universities who were relatively favoured by the UGC – such as Edinburgh and Glasgow – were left at an added disadvantage to their historic rivals, Oxford and Cambridge. Even the oldest Scottish universities are poorly endowed. Although the facts about the wealth of Oxbridge colleges are hard to come by, the richest among them (Trinity at Cambridge, for example) certainly has an endowment income greater than any singly Scottish university – and perhaps even greater than the Scottish universities combined. Using their traditional wealth, those Oxbridge colleges with canny investment advisers are probably drawing substantial incomes from investments in Scottish oil developments, even as Aberdeen University is being forced to consider amalgamation with Robert Gordon's to extend its own resource base. The fact that the two political authors of this consolidation of the Oxbridge supremacy – Keith Joseph and William Waldergrave – are the products of Eton and Fellows of All Souls – the antithesis of the Scottish democratic tradition – adds piquancy to the humiliation of the Scottish universities.

Given the erosion of Scottish control over the Scottish economy, the potential for financial support from private commercial interests is smaller in Scotland than south of the border. The efforts of Edinburgh and other Scottish universities to build up 'science parks' have been completely overshadowed by the success of Cambridge and some other English universities.

In these circumstances what is surprising is not that a Scottish academic leader like Graham Hills, Principal of Glasgow University, has begun to question the assumption that membership of the all-British UGC is the best possible arrangement for the funding of the Scottish universities, but that so few Scottish academics have joined him in seeking a public debate. There is nothing to suggest that Graham Hills is more representative of Scottish university opinion than say the organisers of last year's 400th anniversary celebrations at Edinburgh University. The academic showpiece of those celebrations - a conference on *The University in Society* – was opened by a talk on the *English* universities and the sections on the universities in contemporary society had no keynote contribution from any Scottish academic or public figure nor any consideration of any topical issue, just three years after the referendum, of the role of *Scottish* universities in *Scottish* society. There was indeed a series of 'popular' lectures covering the Scottish themes, rather in the style of Extra Mural Department afternoon lectures, but the contrast spoke volumes for the university's sense of distinction between the academic and the vulgar. It was a great pity that the conference did not include a critical discussion of the myth of the Democratic Intellect.

If, against the odds, the Scottish universities were to reassess their relationship with Scotland, how should the left react? Certainly to welcome the change of mind not to scorn it. Like the conversion of certain Labour MPs to the principle of devolution, it will, of course, be an expedient move. But a weakening of the unionists bonds throttling Scotland is a necessary, but by no means sufficient, condition of radical change in Scotland. In welcoming the change, radicals should be clear about the terms on which the Scottish universities might be reintegrated into the Scottish educational system. Certainly they will have lost any liberal illusions about the role of the modern university. They will be armed, too, by the knowledge that the expansion of the universities in the 1960s and 1970s has not achieved a widening of the social base of university entry. Above all, they will be aware that the greatest educational challenge which now faces Scotland, as it faces most developed countries, in its time a challenge as great as that of providing primary education in the nineteenth century or secondary or higher education in the twentieth century, is the extension of post-school education to the majority of the Scottish people who are presently denied it. The structure within which the Scottish universities, with their traditional concern to educate a tiny proportion of the population to a relatively high level, can contribute to that educational challenge will have little room for a Scottish UGC. If the Scottish universities are being persuaded by bitter experience of the need to change they will have to accept their own privileged role may have to change too.

The Fall and Fall of Toryism in Scotland

Radical Scotland, June / July 1985

ACCORDING TO THE pundits, a new mood was evident at the Scottish Conservative Party conference in Perth. For the first time motions explicitly critical of the leadership were allowed to appear on the agenda. A speaker was heard to declare that he did not like to be used as walk-on support for the platform. Behind the chorus of *Land of Hope and Glory*, some claimed to detect a discordant note of rebellion.

The sceptics will say that they have heard the story before. The trouble is that from one year's conference to the next the grumble does not develop into organised dissent from official strategy. At this year's conference the greater vigour in the criticisms was entirely due to outrage at the effects of rates revaluation. Not – it is noted – outrage over the fact that 360,000 Scots are on the dole, and over 1.6 million are living in poverty, nor even over the Government's failure to fulfil its pledge to cut income tax significantly. No, the 'make or break' issue is rates.

That could be taken as confirmation of the modesty of Conservative expectations in Scotland. For the rates issue, like the issue of student grants, is an issue which strikes at Conservative 'core' support. Conservatives fear the rates issue could lose them the support of many of those voters who have remained loyal during the party's 20-year electoral decline in Scotland. Indeed, poll figures published during conference week suggested the Conservatives might be left with only four seats in Scotland in an immediate general election.

Conservatives' obsession with the rates issue helps to explain the party's lack of moral authority in Scotland. Of the established parties, the Tories are the most vulnerable to the accusation that they have no soul. Each of the other parties expresses, however fitfully or hypocritically, an identifiable tradition or aspiration in Scotland's complex identity. One source of Labour's moral authority in Scotland is its role as spokesman for an ideal of social justice. Its rhetoric carries echoes of historic personalities who are part of a common Scottish inheritance – Burns, Hardie, Maxton and the ILP-ers. The Scottish Liberals can plausibly claim to be the legatees of the political radicalism of Scottish Church politics and of Gladstone. Behind the pronouncements of David Steel and other Scottish Liberals it is still possible to detect the influence of nonconformist nationalism. The SNP is inspired by a vision of a revived – or perhaps newly created – political and cultural community.

But the voice of the Scottish Conservatives today, like the voice of the Social Democrats in Scotland, seems to contain no reference to any distinctive tradition or ideal which might support its claim to national Scottish rule. In the case of the SDP the absence is understandable. The party is four years old and neither its origins nor its leadership owe anything to Scotland. But the Scottish Conservative Party has roots deep in the history of Scotland. How can its voice have so little contemporary resonance here?

It was not always so. Scottish Conservatism has distinctive intellectual roots. Walter Scott's fusion of political unionism and a defensive cultural nationalism provided an ideology for the Scottish aristocrats, often Episcopalian rather than Presbyterian, who upheld the Tory interest against the Whig interest in the 19th century.

In spite of its origins and its social base, the Tory tradition in Scotland was as capable as English Toryism of recognising the social problems of industrialism. The main debate on social provision for the poor in mid-19th-century Scotland was between two Scots Tories – leading Free Churchman Thomas Chalmers, who struggled to extend the parochial system to the problems of Glasgow's urban poor, and High Tory and Episcopalian Archibald Alison, who argued the case for a publicly financed system of poor relief which would be extended to the able-bodied unemployed.

In the 20th century, the formation of the Scottish Unionist Party in reaction to the Liberal Party's Irish policy extended the social base of Scottish conservatism into the industrial areas.

The working class support which this development made available to the Tories was as important in the longer term as the professional and industrial middle class support which it brought to the Conservatives. The Unionists injected a meritocracy into the Scottish Tories' intellectual bloodstream. It also gave Scottish Conservatism the opportunity to secure a base among the Protestant industrial working class which was to support the plausibility of the party's claim to be the party of 'all the nation' until the 1970s.

The 1920s and '30s were an era in which the Scottish industrial middle class still had sufficient self-confidence and energy to intervene positively in Scottish and British politics. Scottish industrial leaders – Weir, Duncan, Maclay, Lithgow – were prominent in advancing 'statist' solutions to the problems of the British economy. They helped to set up the Scottish National Development Council in 1930 to lobby for the diversification of the Scottish economy away from traditional heavy industries. Under Sir Godfrey Collins as Scottish Secretary - himself a member of the Glasgow publishing family – another Scottish businessman, Sir Hugh Rose, pioneered the Special Areas Act of 1934 and became Scottish Commissioner.

The epitome of this period of innovative conservatism which drew on the confidence and cohesion of a Scottish industrial and commercial bourgeoisie was Walter Elliot. Elliot straddled at least three sections of Scottish middle-class life: the professions, the universities and commerce. As Minister for Agriculture (1932–33) he supported Boyd Orr's researches on malnutrition and unemployment. As Scottish Secretary (1936-38) he promoted the work of the Scottish Economic Committee, set up Films of Scotland with John Grierson and helped create the Scottish Special Housing Association. Despite the economic problems Scotland faced, it was possible in Elliot's time for social radicals such as Boyd Orr and literary figures as different as Neil Gunn and Eric Linklater to identify themselves as Tories, if not necessarily supporters of the National Government.

The 1930s were a grim period for many Scots, but the industrial structure, although weakened by both recession and structural change, supported a Scottish bourgeoisie which was still sufficiently integrated and cohesive to provide Scottish conservatism with a firm base in Scottish society.

The level of popular support which the Conservatives, in the guise of Unionists and National Liberals, enjoyed in the 1930s was matched in the post-war period only between 1950 and 1955. The rise of the Conservative vote to just over 50 per cent in the 1955 election was the product of a conjunction of new political factors. One was the exploitation of a mood of nationalist resentment against the effects of the Labour Government's policy of centralisation, illustrated by Churchill's announcement in the 1950 election campaign: 'I should never adopt the view that

Scotland should be forced into serfdom of socialism as a result of a vote in the House of Commons'. Another was the record of Conservative Scottish Secretary, J. Stuart (1951–56), in beating Labour's house-building record and securing government support for the Forth Road Bridge and the electrification of Glasgow's railways. More significant perhaps was the fact that the Scottish economy had fared relatively well under the stimulus of reconstruction and that the Scots were as grateful as any others at being liberated from the ration book.

But the social base of conservatism in urban and industrial Scotland was already being undermined. When Scotland began to suffer the effects of Britain's economic decline in the late 1950s, Scotland's own industrial leadership had been so weakened and penetrated by non-Scottish capital that it could no longer provide the base for a positive response. Scottish conservatism had to look to other sections of Scottish society for leadership.

The changes were symbolised by two events in the early 1960s. In 1960 the Scottish Council (Development and Industry), with Government backing, set up an inquiry into the future of the Scottish economy. It was chaired by an Englishman, John Toothill, who had come to Scotland to work for the Manchester-based company Ferranti. And in 1961 the Scottish Secretaryship was given not to a Scottish industrial grandee or active businessman but to the estate-owning, Eton educated MP for Argyll, Michael Noble. Although Noble's period as Scottish Secretary saw major government initiatives in bringing new industry to Scotland – notably the formation of the Scottish Development Department and the winning of the Ravenscraig strip mill and the British Leyland factory – Conservative politics came to be seen as increasingly dominated by landowners with English public school educations.

With great fanfare Sir Alec Douglas-Home was manoeuvred into a safe seat. The next Conservative Scottish Secretary, Gordon Campbell, was from the same stable as Noble. Although from a family background in brewing, George Younger became known to the Scottish public as a former Regular Army officer and landowner. Only now, with aristocrat Michael Ancram's presence in the Scottish Office team balanced by a school teacher, a university lecturer and a manager, as well as a new generation of young professionals rising through the hierarchy, is the party ridding itself of the damaging 'grouse-moor' caricature.

Other factors were working to undermine the Conservatives' social base. During the 1960s Scotland's unemployment rate was between one and a half times and twice the UK average, even after a net emigration rate which rose in its peak year to 40,000. The sight of lengthening dole queues reactivated the defensive instincts of the Scottish working class – dormant during 15 post-war years of economic revival – and strengthened working class identification with Labour as their traditional protector during hard times. The result was that the Conservatives in Scotland never enjoyed the electoral benefit of that process of working class 'embourgeoisement' which took place in some areas of England where the economy remained more or less buoyant into the 1970s.

Working-class Protestant identification with the Conservatives was also on the wane. In spite of the revival of civil strife in Northern Ireland, the secularisation of Scottish life had undermined the force of religious loyalties, freeing former Tory voters among the Protestant working class to consider the SNP and Labour.

The Conservatives' conversion under Heath's leadership to the cause of Scottish devolution in 1968 did nothing to reverse the retreat of the Tory vote towards the rural areas and the east. As in the Labour Party, devolution was initially imposed on a resentful Scottish party by the London leadership. Endorsement by Alec Douglas-Home's constitutional committee sweetened the pill but still left convinced devolutionists in the minority and exposed to the charge that they were planning to hand Scotland over to the Labour 'mafia'.

The bitterness of Heath's ten year old feud with Thatcher obscures the fact that, as 'Selsdon Man', Heath was among the first Tories to argue that if Britain's decline was to be halted the social democratic consensus had to be broken. It was in Scotland, at Upper Clyde Shipbuilders, that he was forced to make a U-turn from that radicalism by an extraordinary alliance of Scottish industrialists, trade unionists, churches and every Scottish political party including the Conservatives. It was the last occasion under a Tory government that a Scottish interest was successfully defended against the government by a Scottish political consensus. In future, the Scottish economy was to be exposed to the free working of the market.

Symbolic of the Tory attitude to Scotland was Margaret Thatcher's quick dismissal, on taking over the leadership of the Conservatives, of the SNP as a 'Snap, Crackle and Pop' party. Days later the SNP won a crucial local by-election which obliged the Labour government to act on its election pledge. When the devolution referendum was held, the Conservative Party had officially transferred to the 'No' camp where it was joined on spurious grounds by one of the architects of devolution, Alec Douglas-Home. The rump of the Scottish business middle class based in the west of Scotland showed that if it had lost the energy and confidence for positive initiatives it could still aspire to a blocking role in Scottish affairs by sponsoring the 'Scotland is British' campaign. Significantly, the younger business class associated with the financial sector in the east of Scotland supported devolution.

The hollowness of contemporary Scottish conservatism is marked by its lack of intellectual vitality. Although a majority of Scottish Conservative MPs backed Heath against Thatcher in the leadership elections, none has emerged as a major critic of Thatcher's policies, despite their cruel impact in Scotland. If the Scottish Office role is to moderate government policies, it appears to be moved more by the imperatives of political survival in Scotland than by social conscience or intellectual conviction.

Leaving aside the maverick expatriates from St Andrews University, Scotland hasn't contributed much to the evolution of Thatcherism either. At this year's conference, a conspicuously defective case for a poll tax represented the peak of political argument. Which leaves the freelance ideologues associated with the former Dundas Institute – now the Hume Institute – as the guardians of Scottish Toryism's intellectual identity. And, in its indifference to the cultural as well as the social and economic effects of Scotland's industrialisation and de-industrialisation, their vision of Scotland as a Singapore of the North-West Atlantic suggests that utopianism may serve as evidence of infantile disorder on the right as well as on the left.

The '79 Group: A Critical Retrospect

Cencrastus, 1985

The Scottish National Party '79 Group was officially launched in the summer of 1979. Some of its members saw its purpose as the more effective representation of a left wing point of view within the SNP. Others saw it as nothing less than the conversion of the SNP into a socialist party. Either way, the dissolution of the Group three years later in response to a decision of the SNP's Annual Conference to proscribe all organised groups within the Party marked the end of the most determined attempt in the fifty-year life of the SNP to strengthen its left wing identity.

THE ORIGINS OF THE '79 Group lay in the disappointments of 1979 – the failure to win a decisive majority for the Scottish assembly in the referendum of 1979 and the reverses which the SNP suffered in the general election which followed. In informal meetings following the general election a number of SNP activists found themselves in agreement on the reasons for the SNP's failure. The radical momentum and working class support which the SNP had built up from Margo MacDonald's victory in the Govan by-election of winter 1973, through the general election of 1974 and a series of local government by-election victories in 1975 and 1976, had been thrown away by the strategic blunders of a Party unwilling to pursue a consistent policy on the increasingly divisive issues thrown up by an economy plunging into recession. The Party's strategic confusion was evident at the parliamentary level in a series of voting alliances with the Conservative opposition – on shipbuilding nationalisation and budgetary issues, for example – against a Labour government which the SNP could not afford to destroy before it had made clear its intentions on devolution, and at local government level in the failure of SNP councillors to agree on their response to the cutbacks imposed by the Labour government after 1976. If the SNP was to succeed in creating a popular mandate for independence, or for any major change in Scotland's constitutional status, it would have to abandon the search for a 'consensual' road to independence and equip itself with a strategy for building an anti-Tory coalition of Scottish interests around a working class core.

The early, informal meetings of dissidents attracted three types of SNP members. One group was composed of Nationalists who had joined the Party in the 1960s and by the 1970s held elected posts at national and constituency levels. Margo MacDonald, Rob Gibson, Andrew Currie and myself were prominent in this group. A second, smaller group was composed of academics who had joined the Party in the 1970s, usually from the Labour Party. Edinburgh University historian and cultural man o' pairts Owen Dudley Edwards, Strathclyde economist and defence specialist Gavin Kennedy and Jack Brand, Strathclyde political scientist and former chairman of Glasgow City Labour Party, were its best known members.

But the meetings were dominated by another generation of National- ists, mainly in their twenties, who had joined the Party in the 1970s and by the end of the decade held elected positions at branch constituency level, mostly in urban areas. Their perception of the SNP was of a Party which during the 1970s had begun the process of weaning itself from a traditional nationalism based on an appeal to an assumed sentiment of nationality, in favour of a nationalism which spoke directly to the economic and social needs of the Scottish people. The group included most of the Party's Headquarters staff – Research Officer Robert Crawford, Assistant Research Officer Roseanna Cunningham, Press Officer Duncan Maclaren, Trace Union Officer Steve Butler. It was this generation which created the '79 Group and largely determined its tactics.

Through their informal meetings the dissidents quickly agreed on the basic form and ideology of the Group. In June 1979 the '79 Group was officially launched as an organised SNP faction, with a membership restricted to SNP members but with meetings open to all Party members, and committed to campaigning both within and outwith the SNP in support of three aims: Scottish independence, a republican Scottish consti- tution and a socialist distribution of income, power and wealth.

The Intellectual Formation of the Group

The Group was fired by the ambition to develop a radical critique of Scottish politics. In the event, the Group's intellectual contribution, while radical and original in terms of the SNP's internal debate, was derivative from the wider debate on the Scottish Left, whose intellectual conservatism it faithfully reflected.

Perhaps the Group's most important contribution was a more thorough critique of fundamentalist nationalism than had previously been attempted, at least from within the ranks of the SNP. But it also presented analyses of the shortcomings of social democracy as a response to Scotland's economic and social ills, explored the consequences of Scotland's economic dependence with particular reference to the weakness of the Scottish private sector, and adapted and publicised a Scottish critique of Labourism. It also produced an early analysis of the political implications of the divergence of English and Scottish voting patterns and, in the form of the 'Scottish Resistance' proposals, described the outlines of what remains the only coherent strategy available to the Scottish left in response to the emergence of a right wing Government lacking a Scottish mandate.

This list of topics helps to identify the Group's intellectual limitations. The problematic issues of contemporary socialism – the decline of the working-class vote; the barriers to socialism created by the individualistic ethos of a consumer society; the relations between socialism, feminism and environmentalism; the tension between equality and individual liberties; the popular resentment of growing dependence on a state bureaucracy, however welfare oriented; the role of the market in a socialist society – received brief reference in Group publications and debate but were not in any serious sense on the Group's agenda. If Group members realised that in raising the socialist banner they were declaring for an ideology in crisis, they interpreted that crisis in parochial terms – the failure of the British Labour Party to hold the working-class vote south of the Border and the anti-democratic character of state-socialism as expounded by the Labour Party. The solutions were obvious, in principle at least: community socialism on a Scottish political base.

The reasons for the confined intellectual horizons of the '79 Group are to be found in the particular circumstances and ambition of the Group and in the general conditions of Scottish political culture.

The main impulse behind the formation of the '79 Group was the desire to find a solution to the electoral problems of the SNP. Opponents of the Group within the Party described the Group's ideology as 'expedient socialism born out of frustrated nationalism'. Certainly most members of the Group were more interested in the impact on the balance of power within the SNP and on the SNP's electoral prospects than they were in confronting the dilemmas of modern socialism, or in constructing a credible socialist programme for Scotland. It was a precept of the Group that it was the SNP's political strategy, not its official policy programme, which was defective. Significantly, in three year's existence, the Group was to offer no elaboration of the brief outline of republican and socialist principles adopted at its launch.

The effect of this severely practical orientation on the Group's intellectual formation was demonstrated at the launch meeting itself when the suggestion that the Group might summarise its decentralist and egalitarian vision of Scotland's future in a word less compromised by association with the British Labour Party than 'socialism' – 'radical democracy' was one suggestion – was scornfully rejected not on theoretical grounds, but because it would confuse traditional Labour voters, whom the '79 Group wished the SNP to direct its appeal.

Perhaps it is not surprising against this background that among the chief intellectual influences on the '79 Group must be counted the Labour Party or, more precisely, the Labour Party's success in retaining its working class support in Scotland when it was being steadily eroded in England. To many Group members this success constituted clear evidence that class identity was still the decisive political factor in Scottish politics and that Scotland's centre of political gravity was several points to the left of England's. The Group's complaint was that the Labour Party had at best wasted Scotland's radical potential and at worst cynically exploited it in the interest of sustaining the Party's challenge at Westminster for the empty title of Her Majesty's Government. For all that, the Labour Party's electoral success demonstrated the durability of a class-based politics articulated through the trade union movement.

Another source of the Group's intellectual conservatism lay in the SNP's own intellectual, or at least rhetorical, traditions. While in its political ambitions and its organisational form the Group represented a major departure from SNP practice, it was able to claim some ideological legitimacy within the SNP from one of the most persistent strands of SNP rhetoric – the appeal to the socialist home rule tradition of Keir Hardie and the Scottish ILPers. In recent years this tradition had been nurtured out of sentiment by personalities like George Reid and Billy Wolfe, and exploited by some to their right simply to score debating points off

Labour. Its influence in the '79 Group was reinforced by the entry to the Group of Jim Sillars whose powerful rhetoric was reinforced by the authority of his South Ayrshire antecedents and of his own record of initiatives on the Scottish left. Whatever the political advantages within the SNP of invoking that tradition, its impact on the Group's intellectual ambitions could only be pernicious. Scottish socialists have been more distinguished for the passion of their moral indignation at the injustices of capitalism than for the brilliance of their socialist analysis.

Another, potentially more creative, influence was the reappraisal of Scottish politics carried out by Marxist (or *Marxisant*) writers during the 1970s in response to the SNP's emergence as a vehicle for progressive nationalism. Foremost among these writers was Tom Nairn through his long essay 'The Anatomy of the Labour Party', his book *The Break-Up of Britain* and his contribution to the first Group seminar on *Scotland and the British Crisis* in February 1980. Other writers who contributed to a pool of left wing historical or structural analysis of Scottish developments into which members of the Group dipped haphazardly were Scott and Hughes (*The Anatomy of Scottish Capital*), Dickinson (*Scottish Capitalism*) and James D. Young (*The Rousing of the Scottish Working Class*). The journalistic contributions of Neal Ascherson and Christopher Harvie were also closely followed by Group members.

However, the potential of the left wing influence was never realised. The Group's response was on the whole uncritical. If a select minority knew Nairn's writings at first hand, fewer had read the responses of such left critics of Nairn's views as E.P. Thompson and Eric Hobsbawm. Nairn and Ascherson were valued more as prestigious names with which to accuse the unionist left than as a source of working ideas. The Marxist influence certainly introduced Group members to the idea that there might be structural explanations for the SNP's emergence and for its uneven progress. But the Group had neither the ideological skill nor, as an embattled cadre, either the inclination or the time to explore the structural factors. The net effect was to reinforce a schematic view of Scottish society dominated by a few actors or factors – a dependent bourgeoisie, a depoliticised proletariat, uneven development, the world capitalist economy – which the Group simply superimposed on its traditional view of Scottish society.

What the Scottish left was unable to supply was access to a wider range of non-Marxist or 'post-Marxist' writing about the dynamics of social change. The concept of post-industrial politics as expounded in the United States by Daniel Bell or Ronald Inglehart or in France by Alain Touraine was no more familiar to the Scottish left as a whole than it was to the '79 Group. And a knowledge of more recent revisionist writing – André Gorz's assault on the myth of the revolutionary potential of the working class, Alain Touraine's exploration of new social movements, Rudolf Babro's critique of bureaucratic socialism or his advocacy of environmentalism, even the British debate on the relationship between socialism and feminism – would have forced the Group to recognise that its cherished socialism was in a state of transition and perhaps encouraged it to look for sources of radical energy outside the official cast-list of Scottish politics.

A further influence internal to the Group also deserves a mention. The most influential constituency representation within the Group was from West Lothian. Not only did the West Lothian members enjoy the prestige of West Lothian SNP's long and vigorous challenge to the Labour Party in an industrial constituency but they were well organised and led by two of the 'discoveries' of the Group: Alex Salmond, a recent economics graduate of St Andrews and a founder of the successful Free Student Press of the later 1970s, and Ken MacAskill, a radical young lawyer attracted to the SNP after the 1979 election and the formation of the '79 Group. In the 1980s, West Lothian was in the front-line of Scotland's struggle against industrial decline. Salmond and MacAskill, along with other Group members, were actively involved in the major campaigns in the area against factory closures and redundancies at Plessey and British Leyland. Their influence within the Group helped to confirm a model of Scottish society in which the industrial working class figured as the only potential challenger to the British state. As a guide to the immediately available campaign opportunities in a Scotland experiencing 'deindustrialisation' the model was of obvious value. But it may be doubted whether it offered an adequate account of the political possibilities in a society in which barely one third of the labour force remained in manufacturing; and it may have contributed to the Group's neglect of the potential of other sectors of the labour force – and of other sections of the electorate.

Electoral Strategy

To win in Scotland the SNP needed to break the Labour vote – not the Conservative vote – therefore it should challenge Labour on its own territory: socialism.

Henry Drucker, *The Curious Incident: Scottish Party Competition Since 1979, The Scottish Government Year Book 1983*

Such was one account of the '79 Group's electoral strategy. In fact the Group's reasoning was more complicated than this bare summary suggests. The Group had a two-stage strategy. The first stage was the politicisation of the SNP itself, to be accomplished by provoking a debate about the SNP's political future which would identify the strategic choices facing the Party, and then by polarising opinion for or against the left wing option by mounting challenges for elected offices in the Party from candidates standing explicitly on a left wing platform. At best, the left would win the contest: at worst, the process of debate and division might educate the Party in the need for a consistent strategy on the divisive issues of the day with all that such a strategy entailed in terms of political education and leadership.

The Group never suffered from the delusion that the raising of the banner of socialism – let alone the banner of republicanism – by the SNP would bring the Scottish working class flocking to the Party's side. While it argued that the campaigns and interventions which composed the SNP's electoral appeal should grow from socialist commitment rather than from short-term and often local judgements of electoral advantage in the SNP tradition, it acknowledged that socialist principle had to be interpreted in the light of political practicalities. The Group also admitted that the evidence to support its case for a consistent left strategy was inconclusive. The greater support from Labour than Tory voters for the assembly, the closer agreement on social and economic issues between Labour and SNP voters than between SNP and Tory voters, Scotland's record of support for Labour, SNP's own success in the mid-'70s in attracting the younger, skilled working class vote, the evidence that Scottish opinion was slightly less hostile than English opinion to some of the traditional socialist goals such as greater state intervention in the economy or income redistribution, the wider constituency of support for the health service in Scotland

– it was conceded that all this circumstantial evidence failed to establish that the Scottish voter would respond positively to a left wing appeal. The Group's claim was rather that in conditions of economic recession a left wing appeal, if supported by actions to match the rhetoric, would enhance SNP credibility in the eyes of key sections of the trade union and Labour movement. When the trade union movement finally accepted that the Labour Party would never be in a position to form a British government with anything remotely resembling a popular mandate for radical change, its response to the SNP would then be free of the class-based suspicions of nationalism which had inhibited it in the past.

It was a further premise of the Group's electoral thinking that in a society such as Scotland, culturally deracinated and experiencing industrial decline, the case for independence had to be argued in economic and social terms. As democratic socialism was the only philosophy capable of yielding a programme of reform which had any hope of overcoming Scotland's multiple problems, the case for independence had to be presented as the case for socialism, whatever the difficulties of winning public support for socialism.

The argument within the SNP about the electoral consequences of the '79 Group's strategy was crystallised by the emergence of the SDP. While the '79 Group favoured assaulting the Labour vote from the left, the SDP represented the alternative of attacking it from the centre.

During the autumn of 1981, when the SDP had all the attractions of novelty, SNP Chairman Gordon Wilson cited the 25 per cent opinion poll support for the SDP/Liberal Alliance in Scotland against the '79 Group's left wing strategy. The Group's initial response was to argue that the gap between the peak 25 per cent support for the Alliance in Scotland and the 48 per cent in England reflected the limited base for the SDP among disaffected Tory voters in Scotland, a judgement which in the light of the 1983 election result seriously underestimated the SDP's potential appeal to disaffected Labour voters in Scotland, not to say SNP voters.

But increasingly the Group pointed to other considerations. One was the implausibility of building a convincing programme to solve Scotland's problems in the 1980s and 1990s out of the débris of the social democratic policies of the 1950s and 1960s. Another was the probability that even if, by operating from the political centre, the SNP succeeded in attracting Labour voters it would be at the expense of the hostility of the Labour institutions – the unions, the STUC and the Trades' Councils – whose support would be vital in any prolonged campaign to extract constitutional reform from Westminster. Further, if the SNP presented itself as Scotland's very own social democratic party, it would be obliged to underplay the growing divergence between English and Scottish politics. In the medium term that divergence threatened to expose the Labour Party as the weakest link in the British political system, isolating Scotland's Labour majority in parliament from the prospect of power and thereby undermining the credibility of Scottish Labour's claim to be Scotland's defence against hard times. In the longer term the divergence opened up the possibility that the political cultures of Scotland and England were polarising – a pro-nuclear English Tory government against an anti-nuclear Scotland, a Tory England determined to cut the health service against a broad Scottish constituency of support for the principle of a public health service, a Tory England bullish about the potential of private enterprise in the new service industries of the south-east against a Scotland nervous of the weakness of the Scottish private sector. Against this background, the role of the SNP should be to exert the greatest possible electoral pressure on the Labour Party in the short and medium terms while promoting the case for an independent socialist response to Scotland's problems in the longer term.

Internal Strategy

The members of the '79 Group were well aware of the perils of setting up an organised political group within the SNP. They knew that the SNP had a history of reacting strongly against organised dissent to the point of expelling the dissidents.

At the earliest meetings warnings were exchanged that even if members escaped disciplinary action they would face a period of unpopularity until developments in British politics persuaded the SNP of the validity of the left wing strategy. Yet, there was no serious challenge to the view that, with all its risks, an organised group was essential to the project of 'politicising' the SNP as a first step towards committing it to a left wing strategy for independence.

The Party membership would no doubt have given a polite hearing to those urging a left wing strategy in their individual capacities as members of Party branches or constituencies or as delegates to the National Council. But the Group considered that the SNP had grown during the 1970s to such a size that a debate could not be sustained by the uncoordinated efforts of individuals. Nothing less than a collaborative effort in working out a shared analysis of the SNP's role in Scottish politics, publicising it through a programme of publications and conferences and then offering a slate of candidates to assume collective leadership of the Party, had any chance of breaking down the SNP's instinctive aversion to ideological debate.

The Group members fortified themselves for their task with two considerations. One was the belief that during the growth years of the 1970s under Billy Wolfe's leadership the Party had developed a social democratic identity in defence of which moderates in the Party would be prepared to ally with socialists against a right wing or 'fundamentalist' backlash. The second was that quite apart from the internal political balance, a majority of Party members would be prepared to defend the right of political combination within the Party on democratic grounds, whatever their views of the Group's case.

The Group's expectations of the Party's responses were fulfilled in the early period of the Group's existence. Billy Wolfe, Isobel Lindsay, Tom McAlpine, Jim Fairlie and other representatives of the reformism of the mid-'70s defended the Group's right to exist while dissociating themselves from the Group's strategy. But the tolerance of the moderates ebbed as the Group demonstrated its capacity to win victories against the Party leadership. When it became clear that the momentum of the Group's advance had been broken, Lindsay, McAlpine and Fairlie – though not Wolfe – joined the traditionalists in clamouring for the banning of the Group.

From the outset, most members of the Group recognised that the timing of the challenge to the leadership for the strategic direction of the Party would be crucial. At the early meetings there was general agreement that the Group was embarking on a 'long march' through the SNP institutions which would take not less than five years. At a time when rising unemployment was depressing Scottish expectations from the oil-fired peaks they had attained in the mid-1970s, an SNP revival would be elusive. It was part of the Group's case that the SNP had to replace its oil-inspired 'hyping' of Scotland's economic prospects with a closer identification with a and trade union movement now engaged in a grim rear-guard action to defend jobs and living standards. The strategy would yield no quick electoral benefits, but it would start to rebuild working class trust in the SNP against the day when Labour's continued decline in England finally discredited Scottish Labour's claims to be the defender of Scottish working people. But the Group's members were aware that if the Group peaked within the SNP before a new left wing strategy had had time to strengthen the SNP's appeal to key cadres of the labour movement, the Group would be held responsible for the Party's failure to make progress.

In this perspective the Group's strategy was to seek every opportunity to explain the left wing strategy through publications, seminars and the sponsorship of keynote resolutions for National Council and Annual Conference, to promote slates of avowedly Left-wing candidates for Party office, and, not least, to set the Party an example by giving practical and political support to the campaigns waged by the people of Scotland to defend jobs and living standards against the attacks of the English Tory government.

This long-term strategy might have proved too great a strain on the stamina of the Group's members. In the event it was the Group's patience rather than its stamina that was tested and found wanting.

In the spring of 1980, a few days before the SNP's 1980 Annual Conference in Rothesay, Jim Sillars joined the SNP and immediately became a member of the '79 Group. Sillars provided the Group with a more effective spokesman than it had previously possessed, attested by the 300-strong audience he attracted as guest speaker at the '79 Group fringe meeting and the wide media publicity his move attracted. Sillars brought with him a more optimistic assessment of the SNP's short-term prospects than many of the senior members of the Group. Supported by the West Lothian members, whose experience of local campaigns gave them a bullish outlook, Sillars insisted that the SNP could achieve a significant revival of support by the mid-term of Parliament.

Sillars had a crucial influence on the content of the Group's strategy as well as its timing. It was he who extended the Group's critique of parliamentalism into a call for a programme of 'Scottish resistance', including civil disobedience.

The critics of the civil disobedience proposal within the Group warned of the potentially divisive effects it might have within the Party, if not the Group itself, and of the danger of the Group becoming identified with civil disobedience to the detriment of its wider ideological and educational role. But again by the strength of his advocacy and enthusiasm Sillars overcame the doubters in Group meetings during the winter of 1980.

These meetings were part of the Group's preparations for the 1981 conference of the Party in Aberdeen. The Group identified three keynote resolutions to suggest to branches and constituency associations for submission for the conference agenda – a resolution calling on the SNP to lead a 'Scottish resistance' to the destruction of Scottish industry, not excluding civil disobedience; a resolution calling for an independent Scotland to withdraw from NATO and adopt a policy of armed neutrality; and a resolution calling on the Party to recognise the collapse of the Scottish-controlled private sector of the economy and to plan for an enlarged, democratically controlled public sector.

The telescoping of the Group's original timetable entailed a revision of the Group's strategy on contesting elections. If it was important to establish the Group as one element in the Party leadership in anticipation of an upturn in the Party's fortunes in the short term, then it was impolitic to alienate moderate opinion within the Party by putting up a Group candidate to challenge Gordon Wilson as Chairman. In any case, Wilson was believed by some members of the Group, including Sillars, to be open to being influenced by them. So the Group agreed to leave Wilson unopposed while contesting other executive offices.

The revised '79 Group strategy was successful in rallying support at the Aberdeen conference. The resistance and neutrality resolutions were carried, though Gordon Wilson, who had declined to contribute to the debates, immediately dissociated himself from the conference decisions, distinguishing himself among Nationalist leaders by declaring that as a professional lawyer he could not be expected to condone any action in breach of the law! More important, without consulting any of his colleagues, he publicly announced that he would be inviting Jim Sillars – who along with two other Group members had been elected to a position as a Party Vice-Chairman – to take responsibility for the resistance campaign.

Shortly after the Aberdeen conference, widely advertised in the media as a major advance for the left within the SNP, the SNP's poll rating rose briefly above the 20 per cent level. But the internal divisions made it impossible to test whether this poll finding was a freak or an early response to Aberdeen's promise of a more militant and purposeful SNP. Sillars' brave attempt to implement the resistance strategy was undermined by the public attacks on the whole strategy and on Sillars himself by other office bearers, as well as by his own fear that any act of mass civil disobedience might lead to violent clashes between the police and members of the Siol nan Gaidheal, a fringe group of young SNP activists upholding a romantic and vaguely militaristic style of nationalism. Following Sillars' arrest with five other '79 Group members for breaking into the proposed Scottish assembly building, Sillars almost certainly enjoyed sufficient moral authority to control the more excitable of the 2,000-strong crowd which rallied on Calton Hill overlooking the building. But Sillars' mind was made up, and perhaps the only opportunity to vindicate the resistance strategy by an act of organised non-violent mass civil disobedience was missed. The less spectacular acts of symbolic resistance to industrial closure carried out under the resistance strategy were not enough to salvage the strategy at the 1982 Annual Conference at Ayr.

The Group's position was further weakened by the SNP's poor performance in the 1982 regional elections. Consistent with the Group's telescoped timetable the author, after contesting the Party Chairmanship in 1979 and the Senior Vice-Chairmanship in 1980 in line with the original longer-term strategy of the Group, had contested and won the Local Government Vice-Chairmanship in 1981 and subsequently gained the endorsement of the Party's National Council for the 1982 regional elections to be fought on the resistance theme. But not all Party associations and candidates supported the strategy. The voters, unimpressed either by the resistance theme or by the Party's performance as a whole, gave SNP a meagre 13.5 per cent of the vote, down 7 per cent from the 1978 regional elections.

When, on the first full day of the 1982 Ayr Annual Conference, a public exchange of insults between '79 Group members and supporters of a new Party group called the 'Campaign for Nationalism' provoked Gordon Wilson to put the continuation of his Chairmanship behind a call for the proscription of all organised groups, the influence of the '79 Group within the Party was already on the wane.

Conclusion

The Group failed to achieve its most ambitious aim: to convert the SNP into a socialist party. It is doubtful whether it achieved its more realistic ambition of strengthening the left wing voice within the SNP. While it helped to bring on a number of outstanding younger left wing activists, other left wingers dropped out of active membership of the Party in disgust at the proscription of the '79 Group and a few left the SNP altogether. If a younger generation of left wingers is spreading through the grass roots it has yet to demonstrate a capacity for decisive leadership even at branch level. Left wingers still find it easier to win resolutions of support for radical causes like the miners' strike at National Council than to mobilise campaigns of support. The SNP's 1983 and 1984 Annual Conferences suggest that the Party has reverted to its traditional preoccupations – adjusting its policy on the EEC, reaffirming is stance on neutrality, straddling the lines of devolution or independence, advertising the 'cure-all' of independence. The issue which the '79 Group had forced to the top of the agenda of the three previous conferences – the SNP's role in concerting a Scottish response to British crisis – was conspicuous by its absence. The events of May 1982 had forced the left to diffuse its challenge to the traditionalists with the consequence that the SNP is today ill-equipped to put either intellectual or electoral pressure on the Labour Party in Scotland as it surveys the darkening prospects for British socialism.

There is no simple explanation of the Group's failure. The odds against success were long. To shift the centre of gravity of any political party is difficult. The difficulty is compounded when the attempt is made in the aftermath of a series of defeats when the instinct to return to the 'old-time religion' is always strong. Furthermore, the '79 Group was attempting it within a Nationalist party, in the name of an ideology of social division which offended against the nationalist axiom that the nation is 'one and indivisible'.

The Group's own dispositions and decisions lengthened the odds even further. The Group's theoretical base was narrow. It offered a stereotyped model of Scottish society which focused on traditional class divisions to the neglect of new sources of social change and radical dissent. The Group failed to develop its ideological position from that narrow base, as finally confirmed for the author by the Group's failure at the Ayr conference in 1982 to challenge the collusion of the SNP's parliamentary leadership in Mrs Thatcher's Falklands adventure.

There were also serious mistakes of political judgement. The Group overestimated the stability of the social democratic identity of the SNP established in the 1970s. It failed to appreciate the contradictions between relying on that base to defend it against a traditionalist backlash while seeking to polarise opinion for or against its left wing strategy. It abandoned its original five-year-plus timetable for a shortened one based on a hopelessly unrealistic assessment of the short-term potential for an SNP revival. As a consequence, the challenge to the Party Chairman was suspended, allowing him to establish a reputation as being above the battle – a reputation neither his own ideological position nor his electoral interests as an MP dependent on an 'anti-Labour' Tory vote in his constituency warranted.

Perhaps in the end the most significant contribution the '79 Group has made to Scottish politics lies outwith the SNP. By fighting the left wing battle against long odds within the SNP, the Group promoted among the wider Scottish left the credibility of left wing nationalism. By so doing it has helped to erode one of the few alibis for inaction remaining to the Labour Party in Scotland.

Review: The Crisis of the Democratic Intellect

Radical Scotland, October / November 1986

THE OPENING YEARS of the 1960s witnessed the publication of two books whose impact has reverberated down the last 25 years in Scotland. 1961 was the year of publication of George Davie's study of the Scottish universities in the 19th century, *The Democratic Intellect*. It was followed the next year by the first edition, by Oliver and Boyd, of *The Collected Poems of Hugh MacDiarmid*.

To an expatriate Scot at the time studying philosophy at Cambridge the two books had the force of revelation. They shattered the delusion fostered by a secondary schooling at a Yorkshire direct grant grammar indecently proud of its membership of that cabal of English public schools, the Headmasters' Conference, that Bloomsbury – along with Auden and Spender – represented the high point of British cultural achievement in the 20th century.

My response to the impact of Davie and MacDiarmid may have been the sharper because of the complete novelty of the themes they treated, and because by circumstance of place my appreciation was solitary. In spite of reviews in the *New Statesman* of both books – the reviewer of *The Democratic Intellect* was C. P. Snow – I cannot remember a single allusion to either book by fellow students or tutors and lecturers in Moral Sciences Tripos at Cambridge. No doubt Davie and MacDiarmid could have predicted such indifference in a rival citadel to the Scottish culture they were so ardent to revive.

Happily, in Scotland the books were widely, though by no means universally, welcomed as seminal contributions to the reconstitution of a vigorous and self-critical 'high culture' in Scotland. While in the subsequent years Davie's contribution was somewhat over-shadowed by the acclaim – and the literary polemics – generated by MacDiarmid, he continued to develop and broaden the theme of the Democratic Intellect: the struggle of the Scottish universities to redefine the role of the Scottish intellectual tradition, generalist and metaphysical, in response to the pressures for greater specialisation from south of the border and for a new vocational emphasis from the rising new educational interests with Scotland. Far less prolific than MacDiarmid, Davie's very occasional publications after 1961 were the merest tips of a mountain of research which has been fully exposed only with the publication this September of a major sequel to *The Democratic Intellect*, *The Crisis of the Democratic Intellect*.

Not the least impressive feature of Davie's work has been the continuity not only of the theme but of intellectual ambition and imaginative range. His dense and allusive style – each reading of Davie brings to mind Wittgenstein's metaphor of language and meaning as a 'seamless web' – makes summary hazardous, but the briefest account of his few publications confirms these strengths. *The Democratic Intellect* described how the vacuum in national leadership in Scotland created by the fragmentation of the Churches in the Disruption of 1843 stimulated the Scottish universities, with the grudging support of Parliament in the Universities (Scotland) Act 1858, to restate the democratic vocation of the Scottish universities in the shape of a generalist degree course centred on philosophy and deliberately designed to neutralise the inequalities of scholastic and family backgrounds among aspiring students. Without the sympathy of Parliament the project had succumbed within two decades to English pressure for a more specialised, less philosophical, curriculum, supported by powerful social interests within Scotland concerned to ensure that talented Scots were educationally equipped to compete on something like even terms with the products of the English universities for posts in the burgeoning bureaucracies of imperial Britain.

In his next publication, the 1973 Dow Lecture on *The Social Significance of the Scottish Philosophy of Common Sense*, Davie offers a defence of the Scottish Enlightenment thinkers against the judgement of such social historians as Christopher Smout in his *History of the Scottish People 1560–1830* that the Scottish philosophers failed to adapt their conservative class-bound perspectives on the scope for social advance to the promise of unbounded material abundance opened up by the Industrial Revolution, in this falling sadly behind such English (and Anglo-Scottish) radicals as Priestley, Bentham and the Mills. On the contrary, argues Davie, the Scots thinkers' insistence that a society which postponed confronting the spiritual and cultural problems created by the increasing specialisation of economic and social roles imposed by industrialisation in contemplation of its promised material fruits, risks the loss of civic virtue and intellectual integrity as social separation grows between the technically expert and the uncultured masses. The best defence against these dangers was precisely the Scottish generalist tradition of education based on a reflective common sense philosophy and accessible to what was for the time an unusually wide spectrum of classes.

Davie's third publication in this epic project to revive the Scots' intellectual self-confidence was the Historical Association pamphlet *The Scottish Enlightenment*. The defeat of the Platonic scheme for the forced development of Scotland advanced by the anti-Union patriot Andrew Fletcher served to trigger the spread of scepticism in Scotland which reached its climax in Hume's destructive analysis of causality. The native tradition reasserted itself variously through Adam Smith and Thomas Reid in the form of a common sense philosophy which re-established the credibility of scientific procedure within a philosophy which accepted the general and the specialised in the sphere of philosophy, and the vulgar and the learned in the social field, as complementary in the way that relations between the ministers and the laity were complementary in Presbyterian democracy.

The Crisis of the Democratic Intellect describes a secular, twentieth century version of the 19th century schism between Church and State. The antagonists this time were the Scottish universities on the one hand and the Scottish Education Department (SED) on the other. The outcome of the struggle between the universities' attachment to the generalist tradition and the SED's demand for a more selective and specialised system of education better suited to the aptitudes and the vocational needs of pupils led to a split between the universities and the SED. While in the 1920s the universities successfully upheld the 'democratic intellectualism' of the Ordinary Arts degree and the privileged position of philosophy within it, in the 1930s the philosophy departments surrendered their subject's claim for pre-eminence in the university curriculum by succumbing to the fashion for technical and specialist philosophy. The longer-term result of these developments, conspicuous even to the lay public by the 1970s, was that the Scottish universities ceased to make any claim for cultural leadership within Scotland.

Davie takes some ironic satisfaction from the fact that, having been abandoned by the philosophy departments, Scottish metaphysics found new and somewhat unexpected homes elsewhere in the modern Scottish universities, in Edinburgh's exploration of the limits of the biological sciences, in the computer-based inquiries into the nature of artificial intelligence, and above all in the reawakened interest in the Scottish Enlightenment among social scientists. Scotch metaphysics is dead. Long live Scotch metaphysics!

The ambition and force of Davie's arguments will attract criticisms from academic specialists in educational and social history and philosophy as inevitably as the honey pot attracts bees. The book may raise a different range of issues for lay readers, left and right.

Hopefully left wing readers will not dismiss Davie as a historian of the philosophical eccentricities of the fading Scottish bourgeoisie. A bourgeois society – such as Scotland – whose bourgeoisie has lost its vigour and sense of identity is a society labouring under an intellectual handicap which cannot be compensated for by the most vigorous working class culture. The reconstruction of Scotland's bourgeois history is an essential step towards rekindling a collective will in Scotland to command its own future.

Davie's case for the peculiar value of a generalist education in a time of growing specialisation and vocationalism will be widely accepted. Less widely accepted, but still – in the opinion of this reviewer – highly persuasive, is his case that metaphysics should have a central place in that generalist education. More problematic is Davie's assumption of the social importance of the metaphysical tradition in the universities. Davie argues that the Scottish tradition was justified as training for a national elite recruited from a wider social spectrum than the elite of Oxford and Cambridge. But if we are to assess the effectiveness of that elite within the universities by the ebb and flow of the academic status of metaphysics, where are we to look for evidence of its contribution outwith the university? In one of the most exciting chapters of the book Davie explores the influence of Scotch metaphysics on the poetry of MacDiarmid. Where is the evidence of its impact in the political and social spheres? The record on social and democratic reform of the Scottish bourgeoisie in the latter half of the 19th century is unimpressive. In the 20th is evidence of influence to be sought in the petit bourgeois leadership of the ILP? Or more hopefully perhaps in the 'conservative radicalism' of middle class Scots prominent in educational, cultural and even social innovations in the inter-war years – John Grierson documentaries; A. D. Lindsay of Balliol, the WEA and the new 'generalist' University of Keele; John Reith of the BBC; Walter Elliot and John Boyd Orr in health and social policy initiatives?

How far in any case can Elliot's notion of 'democratic intellectualism' be extended beyond the bourgeois perspectives of Scottish Enlightenment thinkers, 19th-century metaphysicians and inter-war innovators to encompass an alternative vision of a secularised democracy – founded on a moral idealism free of utopian illusions about human perfectibility, individualist in its respect for individual conscience, collectivist in its insistence on the right of the majority to organise public institutions in accord with strenu-ously debated values, scornful of the pretensions of the worldly powerful *sub specie aeternitas*?

Characteristically George Davie will have his own agenda of the issues outstanding from his work to date. The vigour of his latest publication gives reason to hope that they will be addressed in further contributions with the same scope and intellectual quality of *The Crisis of the Democratic Intellect*.

Scotland International

Cencrastus, Winter 1989

UNLIKE THE MYTHS of Scottish democracy, of Scotland as a crucible of socialism, or of Scotland's educational superiority, the myth of Scottish internationalism has no classic texts. It has led an elusive half-life sustained in the popular imagination by a sentimental belief that 'A man's a man the warld o'er', by the multi-national social links of the Scottish diaspora and by the national prejudice that if the Englishman is a chauvinist, then the Scot must be an internationalist. It has been a sleeping myth. It has no role in Scotland's civil life to compare with the roles of the democratic, socialist and educational myths in supporting particular cultural, political or professional interests. Because of Scotland's lack of a constitutional identity in international affairs and her slight political influence on the official foreign policy positions of UK governments, it has seldom been invoked in political controversy. The fact that it has survived at all in this discouraging environment is surprising: that it appears in recent years to have become more potent suggests that something may be shifting in Scotland's firmament.

As England extended her cultural and political dominance of Scotland from the 16th century on, Scotland had to work increasingly hard to resist complex pressures to forsake her self-image as a nation among nations and reconcile herself to the status of a province of Britain with suitably provincial expectations. The sources of resistance have been various. The institutional legacy of the Union – particularly the distinctive system of education and law – has provided contacts and comparisons with national systems beyond England. The Church of Scotland, partly through its membership of the Presbyterian international, partly through its activities in Africa and elsewhere, has sometimes offered an alternative perspective on international affairs to that fashionable in the south. Through its Edinburgh and Glasgow colleges, Scots medicine has continued to press a claim for international recognition. At a more popular level, Scotland's separate representation in a number of international sporting events, notably football, has helped the Scots sustain a perception of themselves as Scottish members of an international community rather than British ones.

But the resistance has been more than an institutional reflex. Among Scottish intellectuals it has often been a self-conscious appeal to a European vocation in defiance of the presumption that Scotland is England's cultural colony. Conspicuously, Hugh MacDiarmid scoured the literature of Europe, east and west, to reconstruct a Scottish identity which would be as offensive to English values in its cultural cosmopolitanism as in its revolutionary politics.

But as MacDiarmid was forced to acknowledge, the historical faults running through Scotland's culture in the end undermine any attempt to reconstruct Scotland's national identity from a cultural base.

In the last two decades, Scottish politics has offered a firmer base than Scottish culture from which to promote a Scottish identity adapted to an interdependent world at the end of the 20th century.

The political developments which have sharpened the Scots' sense of their international identity have not occurred in a historic vacuum. The vein of internationalist sentiment which has survived the provincialisation of Scotland has fed a popular idealism which at different times has celebrated Mazzini, Kossuth and Garibaldi as heroes of democratic nationalism, acclaimed Gladstone's denunciation of Bulgarian atrocities, encouraged the pacifist internationalism of Keir Hardie and Ramsay Macdonald and warmed Scottish support for the cause of Republican Spain. That this internationalist impulse has acquired a fresh impetus in recent years is shown in the activities of bodies such as the Scottish Medical Aid Campaign for Nicaragua, the international contacts promoted by the Scottish Trades Union Congress, the demonstration of solidarity with the African National Congress by Scottish local authorities and political parties, and the determination of the Scottish Campaign for Nuclear Disarmament and of environmentalist groups in Scotland to maintain a separate and vigorous Scottish presence in their respective international movements.

Although public campaigning for Third World development aid was introduced into Scotland by English-based agencies, by the early 1980s it too had taken on a distinct Scottish identity through the activities of bodies such as Scottish Education and Action for Development (SEAD), the Scottish Catholic International Aid Fund (SCIAF), Campaign Coffee Scotland and Oxfam in Scotland. A recent SEAD survey claimed that the Scots are notably more generous towards the Third World than the English, both in direct giving and in their political attitudes.

This latest assertion of Scottish identity in international affairs is more strongly associated with the labour movement than with the nationalist movement. But the labour movement has contained it within what remains a fundamentally provincial perspective on Scotland's political role. With few exceptions, Labour's 'Third World' activists have acquiesced in the Labour Party's rejection of a separate voice for Scotland in world affairs.

The reasons for challenging that acquiescence have an extra urgency in Thatcher's Britain. Scots can take little satisfaction in their generosity as donors to Third World appeals when as citizens of the United Kingdom they give less than one-third as much of their national wealth in development aid as the Norwegians, Dutch or Swedes. What satisfaction can anti-nuclear Scots take in the proliferation of local authority 'nuclear-free' zones in Scotland when their country is the site of one of the densest concentrations of foreign military facilities in the world? What are we to make of prominent Labour members of Scottish delegations to Nicaragua who express solidarity with the Nicaraguans' struggle for freedom while resolutely opposing a political status for Scotland which would enable them to give more effective help to popular struggles in Nicaragua and elsewhere than they could ever give as private citizens?

The gap between the values of Scottish voters and the foreign policy positions of the London government is not the only ground for urging a separate voice for Scotland in international politics. More potent in political terms is the growing awareness of the impact on Scotland of the growth of international interdependence.

As a small open economy Scotland has always been vulnerable to the effects of changes in international competitiveness as illustrated most recently by the loss of more than one-third of the Scottish manufacturing labour force between 1974 and 1985 (Buxton, 1986). Scotland has one of the highest levels of foreign investment of any developed country, with 19 per cent of her manufacturing labour force, including 40 per cent of the labour force in the electrical and instrument engineering industries, employed by non-UK companies, and another 40 per cent provided by non-Scottish UK companies. The development of Scotland's oil reserves has been dominated by foreign companies. Scotland's geographical location has ensured Scotland would be colonised by the new globe-straddling military technologies. Scotland's geology has combined with its location to make it a favoured site for nuclear dumping. New transport technologies have made Scotland's countryside more accessible to distant centres of power and population, adding further layers of foreign ownership to the existing spread of external ownership of Scottish land and exposing more Scottish communities to colonisation by incomers.

The impact of these transnational forces has been reinforced by changes in Scotland's political environment. The growth of international interdependence has coincided with a dramatic decline in the economic and political power of the UK and hence in the UK's capacity to shelter Scotland from adverse international forces. The reckless, and from a Scottish point of view counter-productive, haste with which London governments have exploited Scottish oil reserves in order to relieve pressure on the UK's balance of payments is a case in point. The UK's entry to the European Community – both symbol of and response to British decline – further increased Scotland's exposure to external forces. Even more important, the divergence of the pattern of voting in England and Scotland, culminating in the return in 1987 of a Conservative government which gained the support of only 24 per cent of Scottish voters, has made British institutions less responsive than ever to Scotland's needs. Thus regional development aid is cut as the Scottish economy faces the challenge of the European Community's single internal market; the government finally dispenses with the 'ring fence' around Scottish companies as the pace of international takeovers and rationalisation quickens; and the nuclear waste disposal company, Nirex, is deflected from England by Conservative party pressure towards Tory-free Scotland.

In spite of the dramatic nature of these changes in Scotland's political environment, Scottish opinion has been slow to draw political conclusions. None of the unionist political parties has allowed the changes to overturn its established view of Scotland's political future. The Scottish media have failed to make any systematic connection between the external forces assailing Scotland and the country's political options. If only by elimination, the main stimulus to public debate has been the Scottish National Party, whose emergence as a significant political force in the late 1960s and the early 1970s probably owed as much to the impact of transnational forces as it did to relative deprivation, the 'overload' of central government or other factors internal to the UK which have been favoured as explanations by academic commentators.

Within the SNP the main focus of debate in the 1970s was Scotland's relationship with a Western Europe in the throes of integration, though Scotland's role in the nuclear balance of power and her responsibility as an oil-rich country towards the developing countries were important secondary foci.

Opinion within the SNP was split. The predominant view was that whatever the short-term disadvantages for Scotland of UK membership of the European Economic Community, its future lay as an independent member of the Community with representation in the Community's policy-making and decision-taking institutions on the same basis as other small member states. Although this pro-Community view used an internationalist rhetoric, it was primarily interested in the Community as a framework for Scotland's passage to independence, not in its merits as a model for the management of international interdependence or its impact on the development prospects of the Third World.

But a substantial minority of Nationalists combined scepticism about the benefits which an independent Scotland might derive from membership with a critique of the Community's international role. Influenced partly by their fear of a future united Western Europe arming itself with nuclear weapons and partly by a strong commitment to political and economic decentralisation, they argued that the European Community was a centralising and protectionist force hostile alike to Scotland's economic interest and to a more equitable distribution of economic and political power in the international system. In place of the integrationist model of Europe's future represented by the European Community they championed the decentralist model of the European Free Trade Association composed of those Western European states which had declined to join the Community.

The international community has developed two main organisational models for managing international interdependence. The most widely used model – represented in Western Europe by agencies as diverse as the European Broadcasting Union (EBU), the European Free Trade Association (EFTA), the European Centre for Nuclear Research (CERN) and the Council of Europe, and in the wider international community by such agencies as the General Agreement on Tariffs and Trade (GATT), the International Monetary Fund (IMF), the International Telecommunications Union (ITU) and the International Seabed Authority – has been the development of specialised intergovernmental organisations. These organisations have usually been con-federal in structure requiring their members to surrender only as much of the objective of the organisation. Between them the global and regional networks of these agencies provide a flexible and politically decentralised system for the management of international interdependence.

Western Europe has been the site of the second, more radical response to the growth of international interdependence. The European Community is distinct in three vital ways from the decentralised intergovernmental model. Its ultimate objective is the political union of its members. Its declared path to that objective lies through the creation of an internal common market providing uniform conditions for the movement of capital, labour and goods throughout the member states. And it has equipped itself with supranational institutions in the Commission, Parliament and Court to supervise its passage along the road. Its central decision-taking body, the Council of Ministers composed of representatives of the member governments, was committed from the beginning of the Community to progress from decision by unanimity to decision by majority voting with votes weighted according to the size of the member state's population. Although the 1966 Luxembourg compromise imposed by de Gaulle halted that progress, the Single European Act of 1987 providing for an extension of majority voting and created a new momentum for the transfer of decision-taking powers from national governments to the central institutions of the Community.

While the GATT/EFTA model and the European Community model of international organisation remain distinct in their political structure, the economic scenarios they offer are converging. GATT and EFTA were inspired by the belief that the creation and maintenance of a liberal trading system was the key to the successful management of international interdependence. But as international trade has diversified and grown in economic importance, the term 'free trade' has been extended to cover new areas. Freedom from quota or tariff restrictions has been extended to embrace freedom from distortion by industrial subsidy and a multitude of other discretionary instruments available to governments. Free trade in services, including financial services, is now high on GATT's agenda while other intergovernmental agencies such as the International Monetary Fund and the World Bank insist on the liberalisation of capital movements. The dynamic of growth in the post-war world has gone far to break down the distinction between an interdependent world economy and an integrated world economy, with implications for economic management and by extension for political democracy which are not fully understood.

Scotland has a choice of four main options for her future in Europe – the continuation of her present status as a region of a unitary UK, a Scottish legislative Assembly within the UK either with powers devolved from Westminster or with powers assigned by a federal constitution, an independent Scotland within the European Community, and an independent Scotland outwith the Community.

The continuation of her current status would leave Scotland without any institutional defence against the impact of external forces. The Single European Act of 1987 serves both as a sign that these external forces are continuing to strengthen and a warning that British institutions will be even less capable of protecting Scotland. This is not to say that as a region of the UK Scotland need be a passive victim of these forces: Scotland's civil institutions in industry, education, the arts, the labour movement and the media will continue to develop their international links in response to the growth of Scotland's interdependence with other members of the international community. But they will lack the vital support which official Scottish institutions with powers to represent Scottish interests in international forums could provide. With Scotland's direct voice in the European Community limited to eight members of a European Parliament of 518, the representation of Scotland's interests in the main policy-making and decision-taking bodies of the Community would continue to be subject to an English veto.

The devolutionary and federal options would provide a political base from which to promote Scottish interests abroad and to support the international projects of Scotland's civil institutions. Even a devolved Assembly could emulate the German Länder, which maintain a representative in Brussels to promote their interests to the makers of Community policy. It could promote inward investment and give support to Scottish exporters. Like some Canadian provinces, a state legislature within a federation could enter a claim to represent its interests abroad in the areas reserved to it by the constitution. The weakest form of a devolved Assembly would be able to deploy cultural and educational policy in support of its international aims. From devolved Assembly through to state legislature within a federal constitution, the spectrum of powers embraces fiscal powers, budgetary powers within federal limits, scope for industrial, research and labour market policies, ownership of natural resources and environmental controls, as well as housing, transport, arts, broadcasting, education and at least some aspects of health and social policy.

Yet even within a federal United Kingdom the powers withheld from a Scottish legislature would be at least as important to Scotland's future as those possessed by it. Monetary policy, including control of the currency, would be the responsibility of the federal authority with its in-built English majority. Fiscal and budgetary powers would be shared. Trade policy, including agricultural trade, would be a federal responsibility as would be the international aspects of the environmental policy. Control over the exploitation of natural resources, including offshore resources, would be shared. And control over foreign and defence policies with their requirement for access to land would be the exclusive function of the federal authority.

The role assigned to Scotland in the UK's nuclear defence policy might be thought sufficient in itself to discredit the federal option for Scotland. In fact in an age of interdependence, decisions in almost all the areas reserved to the federal authority can have a profound impact at state level. The UK's decision in 1973 to enter the European Economic Community exposed Scottish jobs to intensified competition while at the same time imposing higher costs on Scottish industry and Scottish household budgets through the increased prices of the Common Agricultural Policy. The policy of maintaining a high value for sterling in the early years of the Thatcher government contributed to the loss of tens of thousands of Scottish manufacturing jobs. The government's refusal in 1986 to co-operate with OPEC and other oil producers in restricting oil output to support the world price of oil contributed to the loss of between 12,000 and 20,000 more. For a country as exposed as Scotland is to the transnational forces, the federal option, with its bar on official Scottish participation in the international management of interdependence, has few attractions.

In a country which has had many reasons to be suspicious of the European Community, some Scottish Nationalists have nevertheless looked to the European Community to clear a path to Scottish independence by undermining the power of Westminster. If the slow progress of integration during the 1970s and the first half of the 1980s disappointed that expectation, the Community has recently come back into favour as a support for independence. Under the influence of Jim Sillars, who had committed his short-lived breakaway Scottish Labour Party in the mid-1970s to a policy of Scottish independence within the European Community, the SNP has moved in the 1980s from a position of suspicion of the European Community to one of firm support for Scotland's membership, subject to a referendum of the Scottish people. But where the Nationalists had previously seen the European Community as undermining the powers of Westminster, the Community's chief role in the 1980s is to dispose finally of the charge of separatism levelled against independence in the 1970s.

There is nothing specifically internationalist about the SNP's position. It assesses the European Community almost entirely in terms of its useful-ness to the cause of Scotland's independence. The Community's role in the wider international system, and its impact on the Third World, barely feature in the debates. More remarkable still, even the internal develop-ment of the European Community, and its implications for Scotland's economic and political prospects have been side-lined.

While the call for 'Scotland in Europe' has undoubted advantages as a tactic to lay the separatist bogey, as a long-term strategy for Scotland it faces some major problems. The first problem is an economic one. The European Commission's Cecchini Report on the single internal market identifies major gains in output and jobs for the Community as a whole, conditional on the member governments committing themselves to growth policies. But it says nothing about the regional distribution of the benefits. There is a clear danger that these will be concentrated in the more dynamic central regions of the Community, to the disadvantage of Scotland as a region of industrial decline on Europe's northern periphery. Some Scottish economists, including Scottish Office advisers, fear that sectors of Scottish industry, including electronics, with a relatively poor technological performance and a high level of external ownership, may be vulnerable to import competition, takeover and rationalisation with a further loss of headquarters function from Scotland.

An independent Scotland within the Community would certainly be better able to defend herself against these hostile tendencies than Scotland as a region of the United Kingdom. But even an independent Scotland might find it difficult to secure stable prosperity within a European Community progressing through the single international market to yet closer integration. The founding rules of the European Community on equal competition and non-discrimination against nationals of member states have a wide-ranging application. If, until recently, they were honoured as much in the breach as in the observance, the restoration of the momentum towards integration following the Single European Act has given the Commission a new zeal as guardian of the Community rules. The implications for a Scottish government committed to the radical restructuring of Scottish industry with public as well as private capital are profound.

Among the policy instruments which Community rules could deny to a Scottish government are industrial subsidies and capital aid above stipulated levels, preferential treatment for national suppliers in public procurement, the requirement to purchase from local suppliers as a condition of licences for oil and gas developments, preference for nationally owned or based companies or labour, requiring investors from Community member states to commit themselves to setting up research facilities in Scotland, limitation of right of ownership of land in Scotland to Scottish citizens and control of takeovers of the largest Scottish companies by companies in other member states.

The single internal market is also creating pressure for fiscal harmonisation, including VAT, excise and company taxation, and in the longer term for monetary union and the convergence of economic and social policies. No doubt Commission President, Jacques Delors, was exaggerating when he claimed recently that within ten years 80 per cent of economic decision-taking within the member states would be done at Community level. But he is surely closer to the reality of an integrating Community than those Nationalists who embrace European integration as a campaigning slogan while denying that it need entail any significant limitations on the freedom of action of a future Scottish government.

An independent Scotland would have no difficulty in finding allies among other Community members for increased regional spending to counteract the centralising tendencies of the internal market, but to find allies on how those funds should be distributed might be more difficult. The bulk of the enhanced £9bn structural budget following the Single European Act has been allocated to Spain, Greece and Portugal, consistent with a shift in Community priority from regions of 'industrial decline' to the 'less developed' regions. In any case the record of regional spending within the single United Kingdom market suggests that even relatively large transfers of resources may have a limited effect on regional disparities. While the social package promoted by Jacques Delors as a complement to the single internal market – industrial democracy, strengthening women's rights in the labour market, extending rights to retaining environmental protection – are urgently required they would be neither compensation nor substitute for the national policies required to counteract the disadvantages of greater economic centralisation.

An independent Scottish government within the community would retain wide powers over education, housing social policy, the arts, industrial promotion, the attraction of investment, agriculture and fisheries. It could also, as Alex Salmond, has pointed out, pursue its own macro-economic policy. But the more open the economy the more difficult it is to secure the benefits of expansion for the domestic economy. In any case, the capacity of macro-economic measures alone to tackle the structural supply-side problem of the Scottish economy is doubtful.

The continuation of the national veto, possessed by small states as well as large, will provide some defence against hostile Community initiatives. But the veto is a double-edged weapon, particularly for a small country. In the complex interstate bargaining through which the European Community takes most of its decision, the use of the veto by one member has always been liable to prompt retaliatory use by another. Furthermore the extended social and regional policies required to counteract the regionally divisive effects of the single market will be difficult to sustain without extension of majority voting beyond the provisions in the Single European Act. The three votes which Scotland would have in the Council of Ministers and the 16 Scottish members in the European Parliament out of a total of 526 would be a very narrow political base from which to defend the interests of a small country with major social and economic problems on the northern most periphery of the Community.

Scotland's membership of a Community rediscovering its zest for integration also threatens to constrain Scotland's options in other important areas. It could, for example, foreclose Scotland's options in the development of her own political structure. The supranational feature of decision-taking in the Community and the wide reach of Community rules combine to limit the scope for decentralisation of power to regional and local levels. The Swiss government recently gave as one of its reasons for deciding not to apply for Community membership its fear that the

Community's rules and structures would prove incompatible with the Swiss system of decentralised and direct democracy, particularly the autonomy of the canton and the provision for referenda by 'citizens' initiative'. Even on the most optimistic assumptions about the evolution of the Community's political institutions, its commitment to the removal of all local distortions to free and equal competition dictates a centralised structure.

In a community of 323 million, the national and even the civic roots of democracy may begin to be threatened at what the zealots for European unification may consider an early stage of integration. The fact that Scotland's population of five million would be represented by just 16 people in the Community's legislature is a reminder of how far the civic substance of democracy may be diluted even when the form is present.

Scotland's Claim of Right

The Claim of Right for Scotland, 1989

THE PUBLICATION OF *A Claim of Right for Scotland* in July 1988 shot a beam of republican optimism through the mirk of Scottish politics. It held out the promise of an escape from the long tunnel of depression in which Scotland had been trapped since the referendum of 1979. It suggested, even before the decade had been concluded, that the view of the 1980s as a cruel mould misshaping Scotland's future might one day be replaced by the memory of a dishonourable interregnum between two complementary periods of national revival.

The 1970s had been years of hope borne up by rising expectations. By and large, political debate had been infused with the spirit of reason. *Pace* Neil Kinnock, for all the excitement of those turning times, more thinking was done with the head than with the blood. Books like *The Red Paper on Scotland* (ed. G. Brown, 1975), *Scotland and Nationalism* (C. Harvie, 1977), *The Radical Approach* (ed. G. Kennedy, 1976) and *The Break-Up of Britain* ('T. Nairn, 1977), and journals such as *Scottish International Review* and *Question*, applied some progressive thinking of the 1960s to a critical analysis of Scotland's political paralysis, its cultural dilemmas and its psychological preoccupations. As befits a nation of economists, the political options were exhaustively assessed against their economic effects. As an active member of the Scottish National Party, the optimistic rationalism of those years is symbolised for me by the SNP's extended series of policy documents remaking Scotland in the image of Scandinavian social democracy.

In retrospect, the defects in the intellectual foundations of this optimism appear obvious. The contradiction between the rhetoric of decentralisation and community control and the urge for a more powerful interventionist state – 'POWERHOUSE SCOTLAND' was the headline slogan of Labour's Scottish manifesto for the election of October 1984 – was identified but never resolved. The powerful impetus to individualism built into the consumer revolution was barely acknowledged, its political ramifications not even guessed at. English politics was assumed to be irredeemably pragmatic and conservative. Feminism had to scramble for

a place at the bottom of the agenda. The dilemmas posed for a Nationalist movement by the growth of international interdependence and integration were left as vague question marks. But if the intellect was often weak
the will for rational public debate was manifest.

By the mid-1980s, the optimism had soured into despair. Here was a
nation which appeared to have lost its faith in the public role of reason,
turned its back on a dazzling opportunity for economic revival and resigned
itself to chronic unemployment, spreading poverty and political impotence.
From the vantage point of the previous decade it must have seemed that
only the grim and graphic irony of Jonathan Swift's *A Modest Proposal for
Preventing the Children of Ireland from being a Burden to their Parents or
Country* was adequate to express the depth of Scotland's humiliation.

If *A Claim of Right for Scotland* has a more modest claim to literary
fame than *A Modest Proposal* it is surely a more hopeful augury for
Scotland's future than Swift's satire was for Ireland's. In their Prologue the
authors of the *Claim* place themselves in a line of descent from the Scottish
Claims of Right of 1689 and 1842. Far more important is the *Claim*'s role
in the modern revival of republican thinking in Scotland. The first evidence
of this revival was the Scottish National Party's 'Constitution for an
independent Scotland' published in the mid-1970s. It asserted the sovereign
right of the Scottish people to self-determination, laid down the principles
of a written constitution guaranteeing fundamental rights and liberties
and provided, *inter alia*, for proportional representation, initiative and
referendum.

Notable developments of this modern tradition include Neal Ascherson's *Ancient Britons and the Republican Dream* (1986) and Tom Nairn's
The Enchanted Glass (1988), each exposing the myths and cultural stratag-
ems by which the British, and more particularly the English, conceal from
themselves the gravity of their political and cultural crisis.

A Claim of Right for Scotland makes a distinctive and very practical
contribution to this modern revival of Scottish republicanism. The first is
the demolition of the presumption of Westminster's democratic legitimacy
in Scotland. It exposes the flaw in a constitution which permits – indeed
through its electoral system positively encourages – the assumption, in the
name of parliamentary sovereignty, of absolute power by a party representing a minority of the voters in a general election.

In Scotland this perversion of democracy is measured by the powerlessness of parties which between them won 57 per cent of the United Kingdom vote and 76 per cent of the Scottish vote to redeem in parliament their election pledges to set up a Scottish Assembly.

The *Claim*'s second distinctive contribution to the development of republican thinking is the proposals it makes for a Constitutional Convention as a mechanism to allow the Scottish people to pursue their right of self-determination. If the *Claim* is revolutionary in its logic, it is notably cautious and evolutionary in its conclusions. This caution is no doubt a by-product of the practical purpose which inspired its instigators. It was conceived by the Campaign for a Scottish Assembly not as an academic treatise on the defects of the British Constitution or the relative democratic merits of popular and parliamentary sovereignty but as the intellectual underpinning of a campaign for a Scottish Assembly which would be representative of majority Scottish opinion. The fact that the Constitutional Convention has been launched – even though the composition of its crew and its course are as yet uncertain – may be considered sufficient vindication of the original project.

But the practical political purpose behind the *Claim* does appear to have blunted the subversive edge of its argument. The *Claim* is firm in its conclusion that the British Constitution offers the Scots no consistent opportunity for self-determination and that they are therefore entitled to act outwith the constitution. It is less confident in identifying the implications of the unrepresentative character of Westminster government for the individual citizen's obligation to obey the law of the land.

The moral legitimacy of democratic government derives from its observance of two principles – the inviolability of a core of individual rights and the right of the majority to determine issues of public interest consistent with those individual rights. Where either of these principles is consistently breached democracy falls. A political system in which more often than not a minority of voters assumes the power to govern fails to satisfy the most basic requirement of democracy. When the elected representatives of that minority, having assumed power, deliberately use it to attack and undermine the values of the majority the very idea of democracy is mocked. Minority rule of this sort sacrifices the moral credit which democratic theory assigns to majority decisions.

Of course, the fact that a law represents the preference of a minority does not of itself free the citizen from his obligation to obey the law.

A law passed by representatives of a minority of voters may still be a good law deserving of obedience. But it does mean that where a law passed by a minority administration offends the deeply held beliefs of individuals or groups it cannot deploy in its support the moral credit which is due in a democracy to the majority preference.

The dilemma of the individual citizen under the unrepresentative British system of government has a practical bearing on the political purpose which inspired the *Claim*. Many Scots find the policies imposed upon them by the present minority government offensive to basic moral beliefs. The more individual citizens are emboldened publicly to defy the unjust laws of an unrepresentative – and in crucial ways an anti-democratic government – the more likely it is the Constitutional Convention will command public sympathy when it is forced to act outwith the constitution in execution of Scotland's right of self-determination.

Perhaps the caution which the *Claim* demonstrates in extending its republican logic to the right of individual resistance is a tribute to the bourgeois character of the Committee which drafted the *Claim*. That is not intended in a dismissive sense. In the 1970s the middle classes in Scotland remained largely indifferent, if not actively hostile, to the cause of constitutional change. The Nationalist movement suffered from the paradox that it was a bourgeois nationalism which lacked the support of any significant section of the bourgeoisie. Today the capital owning and capital managing elements of the Scottish bourgeoisie remain hostile: indeed as a result of the polarisation of opinion secured by Mrs Thatcher and Michael Forsyth they are more purposefully hostile today than they were a decade ago. But under the pressure of the Thatcherite attack on Scottish institutions, particularly public sector institutions, other sections of the middle classes have been forced to reassess their political attitudes. Even so, middle class support for a significant measure of constitutional change is a tender plant whose growth and flowering cannot be taken for granted. If sustained for long enough the Government's efforts to create by force of state a social and economic base for Thatcherism in Scotland may succeed.

One can imagine the passionate ambivalence with which Hugh MacDiarmid would have contemplated a radical Claim of Scottish Right drafted *inter alia* by a former Chief Planner at the Scottish Office, a former Permanent Under-Secretary at the Scottish Office, an Methodist clergyman, an Edinburgh Professor of Public Law, a former Foreign Office diplomat and a former chairman of the Scottish Postal Board. But such authorship reinforces the hope that the Convention can help to crystallise the sense of dislocation felt by many middle class groups in Scotland into a firm will for political change. It is this prospect which among other reasons makes an SNP withdrawal from the Convention a grave strategic error.

The launch in London of Charter 88 with its call for constitutional reform within the United Kingdom prompted claims from some right wing commentators that the left had turned to constitutional tinkering, despairing of success on the ideological battle front. As we have seen the purpose of the *Claim* was to provide intellectual underpinning for a broadly based Scottish initiative for constitutional reform, not to provide a new image of democracy to challenge the ideology of 'freedom through the market'. But the political context in which the *Claim* was conceived, particularly the ideological dominance of market theories, makes it pertinent to inquire whether the *Claim* contains elements of a republican ideology capable of carrying the battle to champions of the market.

The immediate targets of the *Claim*'s criticisms of Britain's system of government are the constitutional arrangements which make the Crown-in-Parliament the sole source of political legitimacy. Although alternative bases of legitimacy are not explored, the *Claim* identifies the rights of the citizen as the chief victims of this monopoly: 'Every feature of the English constitution, every right the citizen has, can be changed by a simple majority of this subordinated Parliament' (*A Claim of Right for Scotland*, 4.3).

The belief that every citizen is a member of a political community of shared rights embracing individual liberties and the right to an equal share in the determination of issues in the public domain lies at the heart of the republican idea. The concept of political community as the basis of democratic rights may help to combat some of the New Right's cruder essays in market individualism. For example, it helps to expose the undemocratic character of the Government's proposals to give a single generation of parents, by virtue of their role as proxy consumers, the power to remove a school from democratic control of their fellow citizens whose interest in education as a public good is no less than theirs, who have contributed through generations to build up assets of the school and who will continue to provide the funds for the school.

The right's deployment of the individual's presumed right to choose through the market against the democratic presumption in favour of a collective determination of public issues can be countered only if the attractions of the market definition of freedom are first properly appreciated. The brief references to issues of individual freedom contained in the *Claim* suggest that its authors may underestimate the appeal of market freedoms. The *Claim* asserts that there are two kinds of choice – 'choice from what is offered and choice of what is to be offered' (*Claim*, 7.2) and asserts that stripping away the power of politicians restores power 'not to the people but to the powerful'.

It is doubtful whether in Britain, or in Scotland, in 1989 that is how the majority of people actually experience the effect of Mrs Thatcher's reforms. At least some of those reforms – the privatisation of publicly owned industries (public utilities are a distinct case), the sale of council houses, the Parents' Charter, School Boards and opting-out – are as likely to be experienced as a liberation from the bureaucratic power of public authorities than as a subjection to powerful private interests. And if, in some areas at least, freedom is felt to lie in choosing between the 'given' options of the market rather than edited options of public authorities, the issue of where the options are edited, in London or Edinburgh or Brussels, and by whom, becomes superfluous.

The republican idea need not be helpless before this public perception. It can give a greater presence to the concept of political community by reforming the electoral system to secure majority government; by entrenching core liberties in a Bill of Rights; by correcting some of the shortcomings of representative government; by providing opportunities for direct democracy in the form of initiative referenda or directly elected boards to supervise local services, including School Boards elected not by the spurious community of consumers but by the political community of citizens; and by consolidating such changes in a written constitution asserting the will of the people as the source of political legitimacy.

Secondly, republicanism's insistence that the only safeguard of individual liberties is the community's will to defend them puts it in a strong position to contest Mrs Thatcher's assertion that there is no such thing as society only individuals and families. In almost every aspect of life in a modern society the opportunities for the enjoyment even of those goods which are indisputably private depend critically on public policy, as the householders of Kent struggling to defend the peace of their homes – in some cases the very existence of their homes – from the British generation of TGV's will attest.

Thirdly, the republican idea is well equipped to contest the colonisation of public good by private rights. The principle of the community of citizens identifies the deliberative process of democratic government as a public good in itself. In the same perspective education, general culture including the arts and the media appear as much as public goods as they are private goods, while other goods such health and material prosperity contain at the least significant elements of public good.

The republican concept can be extended to issues of distributive justice. Gross inequalities of income and wealth conflict with the requirement that all members of the political community should have at least a rough equality of opportunity to participate in the determination of public issues. And the essential interdependence of the individual and the community is held by some to endow the citizen with social rights to accompany his or her political and civic rights.

However, this extension of republican claims is not only theoretically problematic. From an egalitarian point of view it has the disadvantage of being open to 'minimalist' interpretations which would leave the materially less fortunate members of the community with no more than 'threshold' provision in an increasingly unequal society.

Egalitarianism needs to be supported within the republican frame work by a more robust principle of distributive justice capable of responding to the dynamic of change in modern society. That 'principle' may be found to be nothing more, and nothing less, than an ethic of human solidarity creating duties to complement the citizen's political rights. In this 'social' republic each citizen will be assumed to have a core of common needs which it will be the prime purpose of the political community to meet, consistent with the principle that no citizen can accept for his fellows a level of provision lower than he judges necessary for his own welfare.

These republican speculations take us some way from the practical political concerns of the *Claim*. But Scottish self-government will be a poor thing if it is not informed by a vision of radical democracy beyond the ken of the market.

The Scottish Middle Class and the National Debate

Nationalism in the Nineties
(ed. Tom Gallagher), 1991

THERE IS A mystery about the Scottish middle class. In most liberal democracies the middle class has been not only the dominant social group but also the main source of national leadership. From its bases of power in the national institutions of government, law, education and the church, and in commerce, industry, finance and the media, the middle class has provided the most sensitive register of the changing prospects of its national community and the directing force of the community's response.

Chief among its objectives have been the perpetuation of its own privilege and power at home and the extension of its prestige and power abroad. But in most countries the middle class has acted on the assumption that its own security and power depend on the strength and cohesion of the national community as a whole.

The Scottish middle class is an exception. In recent decades, as Scotland's circumstances have undergone rapid and dramatic change, the Scottish middle class has managed only a stuttering, hesitant and ineffectual response. In the last 20 years Scotland has emerged as the world's fifth largest producer of oil. She has suffered a massive takeover of her industrial assets. She has experienced a near doubling of the proportion of her people living in relative poverty. She has been subjected to a decade of radical government by a party which her voters have rejected with increasing insistence at three successive elections. More and more areas of her national life have been exposed to the impact of an accelerating pace of international integration. Yet, in this period of tumultuous change, the Scottish imagination has seemed unable to comprehend, let alone bridge, the growing gulf between Scotland's reality and Scotland's potential. Responsibility for that failure lies primarily on the shoulders of those groups in society which, by privilege of education and advantage of position in the institutions which shape opinion, determine society's potential for collective action – that is to say, the middle classes.

The strength of the Labourist tradition and its attendant mythology in Scotland makes it necessary to insist – in a way which would be superfluous in any other Western country – on the fact of middle class dominance. There are, it is true, statistical differences in the occupational structures of Scotland and of England and Wales, for example in the proportionate size of the professional, managerial and administrative groups and manual workers. But small differences of two or three per cent in the proportionate shares of different occupational groups do not make a difference between middle class dominance and non-dominance. The long years of Labour's political dominance in Scotland has eroded the social dominance of the middle class only at the margins. People of middle-class education and family background dominate virtually every institution which possesses significant power: Scottish industry and finance, education, media, the law, central and local government, the political parties including the Labour Party, the churches – all are conspicuously 'bourgeois' in character. If it is a little less unusual in Scotland than in England to find someone of working class background in a commanding position in, say, the media or education, the difference is of very modest degree and certainly far too little to explain the difference between the national roles of the middle class in Scotland and the middle classes in other Western countries.

If the Scottish middle class is peculiarly defective in its capacity for national leadership the implications for Scotland's future are grave. In 'post-industrial' society the dominance of the middle class looks set to increase. The decline of the manufacturing labour force has been even more rapid in Scotland than in most other industrialised societies. The non-manufacturing sections of the labour force are dispersed and difficult to organise. It is improbable that any distinctively working class formation will be able to act as a determining force in the affairs of a Western democracy for the foreseeable future. The live issues in the politics of the 21st century are likely to reflect middle-class not working-class concerns. Of course, the issues themselves – the environment, the centralisation of power, cultural autonomy in an age of mass communications, relations between developed and developing countries – affect working class people as much as middle class people. But the ideological formulations of these problems, the terms in which they are debated, the organisational forms they inspire, are likely to reflect middle-class values and skills. If Scotland is to define and negotiate her own interest in the 'post-industrial' world, the Scottish middle class will have to find a new will for public leadership.

The Scottish middle class is not being treated here in some sub-Marxist way as a cohesive economic interest with a predetermined role in Scotland's history. The term middle class is used only to describe those members of society who make their living through utilising significant accumulated assets, whether in the form of education or training or financial capital. The only assumptions made – and then as elements of a working hypothesis – are that members of these middle class groups, such as doctors, teachers, businessmen, administrators and managers, have an interest in maximising the career opportunities available to themselves and to their children within their own community and that they recognise that their prospects depend crucially on the fortunes of the national community as a whole. No further assumption is made about a common middle-class interest. Indeed, we shall see that in the 1980s London governments have attempted, with some success, to polarise the interests of middle class groups in Scotland.

The failure of the Scottish middle class in recent decades can be illuminated, with appropriate caveats about the hazards of comparisons through time and across cultures, by comparisons both with Scotland's past and with the contemporary experience of other developed societies.

In the 18th and 19th centuries the Scottish middle class played a role of national leadership with considerable, if diminishing, energy. The Scottish Enlightenment represented an effort by Scottish intellectuals with their roots in Scotland's commercial, legal and church middle classes to liberate Scotland from religious obscurantism and establish her claim to membership of rational, enlightened Europe.

In the early 19th century Walter Scott, of impeccably bourgeois background, reacted to the English encroachment on Scottish institutions by promoting an image of historical Scotland even as the succeeding generation of Edinburgh lawyers represented by Cockburn was preparing a campaign to reform Scotland's political system after an English model, and sections of the West of Scotland middle classes were laying the foundations of Scotland's industrial pre-eminence.

In the mid-19th century, when traditional Scottish institutions were clearly on the defensive, the Disruption of 1843 demonstrated the vigour with which one section of the Scottish middle class could defend Scottish tradition against the attacks of a meddling Westminster Parliament. By the mid-century the Scottish industrial middle class had established itself as one of the driving forces of Britain's imperial economy.

The erosion of the economic base of bourgeois Scotland which took place in the first half of the 20th century did not drain Scotland's middle classes of all their vitality. The Independent Labour Party drew notably on middle class leadership. Scots industrialists took a leading role in the rationalisation of British industry in the inter-war period, as well as leading campaigns to restructure the Scottish economy. Boyd Orr and Walter Elliot confronted some of Scotland's social problems while contemporaries such as A. D. Lindsay, John Grierson and John Reith explored, in their very different styles, the implications of the new technologies of communication for the future of democracy in a mass society.

After the Second World War, however, the springs of vitality began to dry up. As wartime Scottish Secretary, Tom Johnston created an all-party Council of State through which to pursue nation-building initiatives such as the creation of the North of Scotland Hydro Electric Board. But the momentum of Scottish reform did not survive into the 1950s. The limited but significant autonomy which Johnston enjoyed was lost in the programmes of British reform initiated by the post-war Labour government. While these reforms brought major benefits to the working class people of Scotland, they limited the opportunities for the exercise of public leadership from a Scottish base. Where the effort was made, as with the Scottish Covenant for Home Rule, it was on too narrow an ideological base and was quickly smothered by the exigencies of British politics. If Johnston left a legacy to the Scottish middle class, it lay in the reinforcement of the belief that Scottish problems could be tackled most effectively through a state-sponsored consensus and in the founding of the corporate or sub-corporatist system of Scottish government.

The 1960s witnessed the publication of a variety of diagnoses and prognoses of Scotland's social and economic problems: the Toothill report on economic development, the Oceanspan strategy, the Cullingworth report on Scotland's housing. But if there was anything approaching a coherent and sustained response it was found in the elaboration of regional development policies within a corporatist framework, supported by the vigorous promotional activities of the Scottish Council (Development and Industry). With hindsight the parameters of this response were too confined and parochial to allow an adequate response to the changes in Scotland's environment signalled by the United Kingdom's loss of international political and economic power.

It was in the 1970s, however, that the weakness of the Scottish middle class was most cruelly exposed. In spite of a conjunction of circumstances more favourable to Scotland's prospects for economic development and social progress than had obtained for many decades, the Scottish middle class produced only a mouse of a response.

For most of the 20th century, the weakness of the Scottish economy has provided the Scottish middle class with an alibi for inaction. The discovery at the very end of the 1960s of major reserves of oil off Scotland's coasts and the multiple rise in the world price of oil in 1973 blew that alibi away. The discoveries gave Scotland a potential for economic development greater than at any time since her economic 'take-off' in the 18th century on the basis of her coal and iron ore reserves. What is more, the economic constraint on Scottish initiative was lifted at a time when the penalties for inaction were growing steadily more severe.

In 1960 the United Kingdom stood fourth in the world league of income per head. By the end of the 1970s she was struggling to hold a place in the top 20. Scotland's unemployment was pointing sharply upwards for most of the seventies: the 100,000 mark was passed – for the first time since the war – in 1973 under the Conservative government of Edward Heath. The 200,000 mark was touched in 1978 under the succeeding Labour government. From 1973 onwards a series of reports drew public attention to the revival of large-scale poverty in Scotland with claims that nearly one in five Scots was living in poverty or on its margins. Scotland's housing problems were exhaustively publicised. The role of foreign multinational companies in developing the oil reserves heightened Scots' awareness of the high level of external ownership of their industrial assets as of the land itself. In the 1970s the opportunity for positive action and the need for radical change were in dramatic coincidence.

Elsewhere in the world, societies whose economic potential had been similarly transformed by the revaluation of natural resources were in a ferment of change. Developing countries such as Libya, Nigeria and Kuwait rushed to seize the development opportunities offered by the oil boom. So too did developed societies such as the Canadian provinces of Alberta and Quebec and Scotland's North Sea neighbour Norway.

In 1971 the 30 year reign of the Social Credit Party in Alberta was brought to an end by the election of the Progressive Conservative Party. The Progressives were fired with an ambition to carry through an industrial revolution based on the local processing of Alberta's natural resources. Their vigorously interventionist policies produced a series of notable initiatives including the creation of the Alberta Energy Company, the purchase of Pacific Western Airlines, the creation of the Alberta Heritage Fund to secure a long-term income to the people of Alberta from the oil developments, the creation of an Albertan Energy Resources Conservation Board control industrial development and the development by the Alberta Gas Trunk Company of plans for Albertan-controlled petrochemical projects. These institutional innovations were supported by no less radical interventions on oil prices and taxes. For a government of provincial businessmen ideologically hostile to state intervention this record was eloquent testimony to the energising impact of the world revolution in oil prices.

The impact was no less profound in Norway. The Norwegian government seized the opportunity to launch a major policy initiative to adapt the Norwegian economy to the challenge of world recession. Most notable was a counter-cyclical policy which held unemployment below two per cent in a period which saw Scotland's unemployment rise to eight per cent. Institutional innovations included the creation of Statoil, a state-owned oil company, as the vehicle for the state's 'carried interest' in oil developments. Of equal significance was the close collaboration between the Norwegian government and Norwegian business in maximising Norway's industrial benefit from its natural wealth.

The prospect of oil wealth also extended the horizons of Norwegian policy-makers beyond economics. The first in the series of Norway's long-term economic programmes gave priority to making Norway a 'qualitatively better society' through a narrowing of income differentials, the decentralisation of power, sexual equality and a commitment to generous levels of aid to developing countries.

The wave of reforms which began in Quebec with the 'Quiet Revolution' of the 1960s perhaps owed less to economic causes than developments in Norway or Alberta. But the strengthening of Quebec's role as an exporter of hydroelectric energy underpinned the rise of the nationalist Parti Quebecois in the 1970s. While the new party had some success in attracting the support of working class Quebecers, its cadres came from the rapidly expanding public sector salariat recruited from an educational system which had been modernised and freed from the control of Catholic clerics in the 1960s. Quebec provides a clear example of the transformation of a traditionalist defensive nationalism into an aggressive reforming nationalism.

The Scottish response to the discovery and revaluation of its oil assets was altogether more modest. The creation of the Scottish Development Agency in 1975 represented the only institutional development of note to put against Alberta's Energy Board and Heritage Trust, against Statoil or Hydro-Quebec. But by the end of the decade the amount of money made available for industrial investment by the Scottish Development Agency was far closer to the subsequent cuts in the annual value of other forms of regional assistance – approximately £70m – than to the £5bn which the oil revenues contributed to the London Exchequer in those years.

There remained the proposals for a Scottish assembly as a token of Scotland's will to be innovative. But whatever the historic and symbolic value of an assembly, its powers would have been dwarfed by the scale of the opportunities opening up for Scotland. It would have had fewer powers than the Generalitat restored to Catalonia by the 1978 referendum, fewer than the German Lander, fewer even than the Greenland Parliament endorsed by the 23,000 voters of Greenland in January 1979. As a test of the will to innovate across the social spectrum, the assembly referendum showed the middle class as the least enthusiastic section of Scottish society, with only 35 per cent of AB voters intending to vote 'Yes' in February 1979 compared with 65 per cent of DE voters.

Of course, the response to the assembly proposals provides only the crudest of measures. After all, the proposals provoked opposition even from committed Nationalists whose will for change can be taken as read. What continues to astonish fifteen years or so later is not so much the hostility or indifference of the majority of the Scottish middle class to the assembly legislation but the weakness of their gut response to the dramatic change in Scotland's potential in the 1970s.

Why did Scotland's business community not seize the opportunity of Scotland's new wealth to secure a major adjustment of the economic balance in favour of Scotland, as the business class did in Alberta? Why did Scotland's public administrators not demand the opportunity to prove their capacity for 'nation-building' in the way the state bureaucracy of

Quebec had been doing since the 1960s? Why were Scotland's 'caring' professions so loath to demand that Scotland's new wealth be applied to reducing the poverty and deprivation that blighted the lives of so many Scots, in the spirit of the Norwegian programme for welfare reform? Why did Scotland's health professionals not insist that they be given the means to launch new programmes of community health and health education among a population whose health record was abysmal by the standards of Western European countries? Why were Scottish architects and designers not clamouring for the public commissions which would challenge them to shape a new public face for Scotland in the way that Alvar Alto and his colleagues gave architectural expression to Finland's post-war revival? Why did Scotland's university teachers and administrators not seize the moment to demand major new provision for research to challenge the dominance of Oxford, Cambridge and London, and lay the basis for a bid to make Scotland once again an international centre of learning and inquiry? Why, in short, did the Scottish middle class in this moment of blossoming opportunity evince so little ambition for the public welfare of Scotland, or even for their own and their children's career prospects in Scotland?

Social and historical factors can be offered in speculative explanation. As noted earlier, the core middle-class groups of employers, managers and professional workers formed a smaller proportion of the population in Scotland in 1971 than of the populations of England and Wales, 11.6 per cent compared to 13.5 per cent. And the gap had widened slightly by 1981 with 13.4 per cent of the Scottish population in these groups compared to 16.3 per cent in England and Wales. But this difference is too small to be taken seriously as an explanation.

Other structural factors concealed by an analysis based on occupational groups may have been at work. One such is the displacement of Scots by non-Scots in decision-taking posts in Scotland. The takeover of Scottish businesses by non-Scottish companies has been a matter of public debate in Scotland for decades. By the mid-'70s 40 per cent of Scotland's manufacturing labour force worked in companies controlled from outwith Scotland along with a significant but un-quantified proportion of Scotland's service industries. The record shows that takeover often led to a loss of top decision-taking jobs within the company and the loss of business for Scottish professional and other service companies as contracts were moved south. Where the top jobs remained in Scotland it became more likely that they would be filled by non-Scots.

Even where there has been no transfer of ownership or control a process of displacement of Scots by non-Scots in top jobs seems to have been taking place. Public sector employers have increasingly recruited managerial and professional staff from a UK if not international labour market. The high proportion of non-Scots among the teaching staff of Scottish universities was actively debated in the early 1970s. During the '70s non-Scots were becoming steadily more numerous in top jobs in other sectors: local government administration and services, the arts, the voluntary organisations. It is conceivable that this displacement hindered the growth of a 'critical mass' of Scottish concern and ambition.

Another factor which may have operated to obstruct the growth of a clear Scottish focus was the absence of independent trade union structures across a wide range of public sector employment, in particular the fast-growing local government services. This has not always prevented public sector employees in Scotland pursuing their distinct strategies in industrial disputes but it has certainly restricted the role of the trade unions as a base for independent Scottish initiative. The political initiatives of the Scottish Trades Union Congress (STUC) provided partial compensation but in the 1970s the STUC was not active across such a wide range of Scottish issues of Scottish concern as it has been under the leadership of Campbell Christie in the 1980s.

These factors of displacement and assimilation were, of course, not operating in the traditional middle classes of the church, law and school teaching which recruited from a protected Scottish labour market. Surely these traditional professions with their key roles as carriers of Scottish identity would be eager to seize the moment for '*unde grade revanche*' for the centuries of subordination to English middle class models and traditions rooted in London, Cambridge and Oxford?

But though they were still nationally distinct these groups were exposed to other factors which may have confined their political horizons. The Church of Scotland was clearly an institution in decline, both numerically and in social status. Although historically Scotland's national church, the Catholic Church was beginning to overtake it in terms of members. Its General Assembly might still claim the title of 'Scotland's Parliament' but its deliberations were received by the public more and more as one voice among many, religious and secular, advertising their views on Scotland's future.

While the teaching profession had a firmer social base – its numbers had grown by 60 per cent since the early 1950s – its members felt that their social and economic status was declining. The prolonged 'work-to-rule' actions of 1973–76 were symptoms of a deep unease about the profession's prospects and social role.

By comparison, the Scottish legal profession seemed secure in its social status and economic prospects. But even here there were uncertainties. Scots law was constantly exposed to the danger of erosion and injury by ignorant legislators. And in some of the fastest-growing and most lucrative areas of legal practice – tax law, administrative law, company law – the law was more British than Scottish and the opportunities were concentrated in London.

A further factor inhibiting the growth of radicalism among these traditional middle class groups is their status as beneficiaries of the 'historic compromise' between English and Scottish interests built on the Act of Union of 1707. That settlement secured a position of provincial privilege within the emerging imperial state of Great Britain for the Church of Scotland, Scots law and Scottish education. The privileges of Church and law followed directly from the Act itself. The entrenchment of the privileges of the teaching profession was a longer process marked by the formation of the Scotch Education Department in 1874 and of the General Teaching Council for Scotland in 1966.

The benefits have been significant. The lawyers have enjoyed a protected market, the prestige of serving an imperial state and the prospect of promotion to senior legal office, not excluding the Lord Chancellorship of England. The Church of Scotland gained recognition as the National Church, and enjoyed the social privileges which went with that role. The teachers eventually gained a protected labour market, professional autonomy, membership of Scotland's educational 'policy community', and even – they could argue – preferential financial provision for Scottish education.

The 'historic compromise' thesis can be applied beyond these three historic middle class interests. Scottish business benefited by trading its protected market for access to expanding markets in England and her colonies. In the 20th century the growth of the Scottish Office provided a 'semi-protected' market in well-paid administrative jobs. The devolved structure of broadcasting in Scotland, with its 'semi-protected' market, can be seen as a late product of the compromise.

However, as an explanation of the conservatism of the Scottish middle classes the thesis is of limited value. The compromise provided the Church of Scotland with no protection against the Veto Act which led to the Disruption of 1843, nor Scots law with protection against the growth of law into new areas on an English foundation. It could never have provided protection against long-term secular trends such as the decline in Church membership, the loss of prestige by British state institutions and the impact of social and cultural changes on the attraction of teaching as a career. And of course it cannot apply to the wide range of middle class professions which have never enjoyed any Scottish 'privilege'.

Scotland's main political parties have reinforced rather than challenged the conservatism of the Scottish middle class. They have at once reflected and institutionalised middle class inhibitions.

In the 1970s the historic unionism of the Scottish Conservatives was reinforced by the hostility of Scotland's business community to any change in Scotland's political status. The base of this opposition lay in the West of Scotland industrial leadership represented by such figures as Lord Weir. It judged that even the modest change proposed in the Labour government's devolution proposals would impose unacceptable costs on the business community, producing a left wing socialist administration committed to class war and to punitive taxation on business and leading to an independent Scotland cut off by tariff walls from its traditional markets in England and overseas.

This was a notable case of thinking with the blood rather than with the head. Such fears were a direct legacy of the Scottish engineering industry's history of bitter labour disputes and its traditional dependence on government war contracts and imperial markets. That they were still so salient in the 1970s owes much to the fact that the confidence in the Scottish manufacturing industry in general – and the West of Scotland engineering industry in particular – had been undermined by a crisis of closures and takeovers.

There were dissenting voices within the business community. Some of the 'Young Turks' of Edinburgh's financial community such as Ian Noble and Angus Grossart argued on cultural as well as economic grounds for a Scottish assembly. It was significant that they were innovators in an economic sector which was expanding, had no history of labour militancy, had never been dependent on government contracts and was used to operating across national frontiers. But even in the financial sector theirs were minority voices. The big Scottish insurance companies and the clearing banks remained hostile or at best determinedly sceptical.

Indeed, it was in the financial sector that the defensiveness and lack of confidence of the Scottish business community was most dramatically revealed when in 1981 the Scottish public learned that the Board of the Royal Bank of Scotland was seeking a takeover bid from the Standard Chartered Bank. Despite much expert opinion to the contrary, the directors of the Royal Bank maintained that the bank – which provided approximately one half of all Scotland's banking services – was too small to expand internationally by itself. Ironically, the independence of the bank was finally secured by the London-based Monopolies and Mergers Commission. Denied its preferred option, the Royal Bank demonstrated that contrary to the wisdom of its own board it did after all have the resources to diversify successfully within the UK and abroad.

Under such defeatist influence the Scottish Conservative Party showed no inclination to respond directly to the change in Scotland's external circumstances. It did respond to the internal challenge of the emergence of the Scottish National Party. From Edward Heath's Declaration of Perth in 1968 in support of the principle of a Scottish assembly, it had moved by 1974 to endorsing the call for a Scottish oil fund. But that marked the limit of official Conservatism's tolerance of nationalist aspirations. On assuming leadership of the party in 1975, Mrs Thatcher began hauling in the line. By the time of the 1979 referendum the Conservative Party was sharing the leadership of the 'No' campaign with its allies in the business community.

But, by 1979, the Conservative Party shared its role as political representative of the middle class in Scotland. It retained a bare majority (53 per cent) of the electoral support of the upper-middle class in the 1979 election but only 43 per cent of the lower-middle class vote. The Labour, Liberal and Scottish National Parties attracted respectively 18, 15 and 14 per cent of the upper-middle class vote and 30, 9 and 17 per cent of the lower-middle class vote.

By classic nationalist precedent the Scottish National Party should, at least, have been a keen rival to the Conservatives for the Scottish middle-class vote. But the SNP was a classic bourgeois party only in the sense that its leadership was drawn from the professional middle class of solicitors, teachers, doctors, journalists and accountants along with small business-men. It never won majority support from any cohesive middle-class interest. Traditionally, it drew it support more evenly from across the social spectrum than the other parties. When it was at its peak in the mid-70s its additional support came not primarily from the middle-class groups but from the skilled manual workers in the 18 to 35 age group.

The group which always seemed the least likely to support the Nationalists was precisely the core bourgeoisie of the business class, fearful of losing traditional markets and state support. The only major business figure to come out in support of the SNP was the maverick Sir Hugh Fraser. For the rest the SNP had to content itself with the support of smaller businessmen whose markets were predominantly local, and a sprinkling of management consultants and financial specialists. If the Scottish owners of the companies servicing the oil developments sometimes looked enviously at the advantages conferred on their Norwegian-owned counterparts by the Norwegian government's protection policies, their dependence in the short term on Whitehall and in the longer term on the multinational oil companies deterred them from drawing any radical political conclusions.

Following the restraints on public expenditure imposed by the Labour government in 1976 the Nationalists might have been expected to attract more support from Scotland's public sector salariat. That it did not do so may be attributed partly to the presumed increase in the number of non-Scots in influential positions, partly to the lack of clarity in the SNP's own ideological position, and partly to the influence of British trade unions and the Labour Party itself.

The Labour Party was indeed the SNP's chief rival for the support of Scotland's 'deviant' middle-class voters. In 1979 it attracted more than twice the number of middle-class votes that the SNP attracted. Significantly its lead was greatest among the lower-middle-class voters where the bulk of the public sector salariat was located. While the Liberal Party was a close rival of Labour and the SNP among upper-middle-class voters, it fell badly behind in its appeal to lower-middle-class voters. Not surprisingly the Liberal Party led both Labour and the SNP in middle-class support as a proportion of total support for the party. Indeed, the class profile of support for Labour and the SNP was very similar, with the upper-middle class contributing three per cent more of the SNP's support than of Labour support and the lower-middle class contributing one per cent more of Labour support than of SNP support. The Liberal profile was much closer to the Conservative profile with both attracting levels of support from working-class voters 29 to 30 per cent lower than the SNP and Labour.

The Conservative Party's failure to attract a higher proportion of Scotland's middle class votes no doubt owes something to traditional tensions between English and Scottish 'establishments' which persisted after the 'historic compromise' of the Union. But Labour's relative success in attracting Scottish middle-class support probably owes more to a perception of Labour as the champion of state intervention to correct regional inequalities, particularly economic inequalities. Beginning with Tom Johnston, the Labour Party had established itself as the party of a 'managed economy' with strong regional development policies. The climax of this approach was reached with the creation of the Scottish Development Agency to provide planning, leadership and finance for the Scottish economy. In the October 1974 election the Labour Party had advertised its plans for the Agency under the immodest slogan POWERHOUSE SCOTLAND. From its position of weakness the Scottish business community was able to join other sections of Scottish opinion in welcoming the Agency as a powerful support for Scotland's economic development.

During the 1970s the Labour Party itself became noticeably more middle class. A new generation of activists, many of them with 'public sector' middle-class jobs, emerged to claim leadership of Labour's local government in Eastern Scotland, although in the West and in Central Region the working-class trade union leadership proved more resilient. At both the national level and the parliamentary level Scottish Labour presented an increasingly middle-class face to the world. By the mid-'70s, two-thirds of Scots Labour MPs had a middle class background or education. By 1988 only 13 out of 49 Scottish Labour MPs had a working class occupational background.

As a vehicle for ambitious, politically minded middle-class Scots, the Labour Party served to divert energy and concern away from Scottish priorities to British political exigencies. It provided a system of political rewards based in London in which Scotland featured as a proving ground and rear base. This regionalist perspective obscured the scale of the changes in Scotland's external circumstances during the 1970s.

Even when the Labour Party's role is added to the wider inhibitions to which Labour's middle-class career politicians were heir, the sum of explanation remains obstinately less than its parts. Each of the factors specific to the Labour Party – its vested interest in a British system of power, its ideological hostility to any threat to working class unity, its institutional conservatism – were exposed to and failed the judgement of time. Scotland's record under Westminster governments of both parties in the 1960s and 1970s declared its own verdict on the effectiveness of London rule while the oil discoveries gave dramatic credibility to the alternatives. The reality and potential of Scotland were opposed to each other more directly than at any previous moment in Scotland's modern history. Yet few Scots Labour MPs demonstrated any zeal for their own Government's constitutional proposals, modest as they were. Of those who did – John Mackintosh, Jim Sillars, Harry Ewing, Alex Eadie, John Robertson, Dennis Canavan – it may be significant that only one, John Mackintosh, was from an established middle-class background.

How was it that personalities such as John Smith, Donald Dewar, Robin Cook and Gordon Brown were so little excited by the opportunities which the 1970s opened up for Scotland? By class and culture they should have been highly sensitive to the changing status and opportunities of their national community and institutions. All four were from the marrow of the Scottish middle class. Their fathers' professions were respectively a primary head teacher, a doctor, a high school rector and a Church of Scotland minister. All were educated at Scottish schools and universities. They were well informed about Scotland's circumstances: Cook and Brown had a special knowledge of Scotland's social problems. As professional politicians they had no excuse for underestimating the problems of obtaining remedies from Westminster. Here, surely, were the elements to fire a passion to redress Scotland's wrongs? Who, indeed, was better equipped than they to lead an alliance of Scotland's frustrated middle class and its hard-pressed working class in a campaign to secure the benefits of Scotland's new-found wealth for the Scottish people? Instead these exemplars of middle-class Scotland responded, grudgingly, only when their electoral base came under direct threat from nationalism. Only one, Gordon Brown, showed any notable enthusiasm for constitutional change and then rather less enthusiasm than another, Robin Cook, put into opposing his own Labour government's proposals for a Scottish assembly. The two lawyers meanwhile conveyed the impression that the whole issue was an unfortunate diversion from the real world of politics in the corridors of Westminster. It seemed that there was little room in these well-educated heads for the notion that Scotland might be facing an historic opportunity to escape at last from the cruelly lingering legacy of the industrial revolution or to vindicate the ideals of Scottish democracy. In these middle-class deadlands of the imagination, history happened in other places.

Perhaps it is the lack of vitality of the middle-class Scottish imagination which brings us closest to the heart of the mystery about the Scottish middle class. There is a striking dearth in the recent imaginative literature in Scotland of middle-class characters and experience. Scottish fiction and drama have been dominated for the last three decades by images of working-class Scotland. William McIlvanney, Gordon Williams, Alan Sharp, James Kelman, John Byrne, Bill Bryden, Hector MacMillan, Archie Hind, Peter MacDougall, Agnes Owens: the roll-call of working-class Scots writers is extensive and impressive. Middle-class writers, or at least writers who use middle-class characters in their Scottish context, are rare birds by comparison. Only two writers – Robin Jenkins and Elspeth Davie – have persisted with middle-class themes. Other names can be cited – James Allan Ford, Stuart Hood, James Kennaway, Allan Massie. But Ford's best-known novel, *The Brave White Flag* (1961), is set in the Second World War, and Hood's novels are set in pre-war or early post-war periods. James Kennaway certainly knew how to conjure up the demons of the Scottish soul but his particular constituency was the Anglo-Scottish upper-middle class from which he himself came. Massie's closest engagement with the contemporary Scottish middle classes, *One Night in Winter* (1984), is one of his less successful novels, particularly in its treatment of characters who are not of Massie's own Anglo-Scottish background. Significantly the most widely read modern novel of the Scottish middle class, *The Prime of Miss Jean Brodie*, was a glorious one-off for its author Muriel Spark. Scottish drama post-James Bridie is even less well-endowed with characters from the Scottish middle class.

Recent Scottish autobiography has also been dominated by working-class experience. Jimmy Reid, Jimmy Boyle, Ralph Glasser, Ian Jack, Jim Sillars, Molly Weir are among those who have written of their working-class background and upbringing. Again middle class examples can be cited – Billy Wolfe's political autobiography *Scotland Lives* (1973) stands out – but the working-class bias of the output is overwhelming. Assuming that the bias reflects the tastes of Scottish readers many middle-class Scots must identify more strongly with images of working-class Scotland than with images of middle-class Scotland.

The working-class dominance of Scottish imaginative and interpretative literature, poetry apart, is the mirror image of the situation in England where middle-class character and context dominate and working-class experience is marginalised. There are signs of a revival of middle-class confidence and vitality in other areas of Scottish culture (among them historical and political writing and journalism) but if the urge, and capacity, to articulate one's experience through reconstructing it imaginatively in fiction and drama is taken as the test then the 'inarticulate Scot' is revealed as typically middle class not working class. It seems that the Scottish working class has developed a keener sense of identity from its long record of struggle against harsh odds than the Scottish middle class has learned from its complacent enjoyment of provincial privilege.

The 1980s presented a sharp challenge to the complacency and inertia of the Scottish middle class. The domestic reforms of Mrs Thatcher's administrations proved a stronger stimulus to the Scottish middle class to reassess its role than the changes in Scotland's external environment had proved in the previous decade. By the end of the '80s there was hardly a section of the Scottish middle class which remained untouched by the Thatcherite revolution.

The middle class was only affected at the margins by the dramatic rise in unemployment which took place in the first five years of Mrs Thatcher's rule. It felt the impact of the Thatcherite economic whirlwind rather more through the accelerated destruction by closure or takeover, or both, of a very large part of what remained of a Scottish-controlled economic base. The list of victims included Distillers, Coats, Anderson Strathclyde, Stenhouse, Arthur Bell, Scottish Agricultural Industries and United Wire. By 1986 half of the 140 biggest Scottish registered companies in 1979 were under external control. While some Scots businessmen and commentators had armed themselves ideologically to accept the process as a necessary and invigorating part of the working of the market many others voiced their fears that the takeovers were part of a vicious circle of relative economic decline.

The public sector middle class in Scotland was certainly not less exposed to the effects of Thatcherism. The Conservative cuts in public expenditure were targeted in particular at public services. With a smaller proportion of middle-class Scots than of middle-class English people opting out of the public health and education systems the Scottish middle class was more sensitive to the effect of government policy on the standard of the services. And with a higher proportion of the Scottish labour force dependent on the public sector for jobs – 34 per cent compared to 30 per cent in England – the Scottish middle class had greater reason to feel concerned about job security and career prospects.

Other government measures reinforced concerns about jobs and careers. The privatisation of state industries and public utilities reduced the government's political stake in the maintenance of jobs and opened the way to market-led rationalisation. The push for privatisation of services provided by local authorities and health boards forced many middle-class employees to consider the options of returning to the private sector perhaps through management buy-outs. While primary and secondary education escaped significant job losses, higher and further education and state-financed research institutes lost jobs and security of tenure.

The Thatcherite campaign to recreate an enterprise society had a particular urgency in Scotland. Thatcherism diagnosed Scotland as an extreme example of the 'dependency culture' which had sapped the vitality of British society as a whole. In Scotland the 'disease' of dependency had spread further through the social body than in England, disabling sections of both the working class and the middle class which should have been natural supporters of Mrs Thatcher's mission. Symptoms of the Scottish disease were found not only in Scotland's inability to generate the economic dynamism of the south of England but also in the electoral unpopularity of the Conservative Party under Mrs Thatcher's leadership. By the 1987 election the Conservative share of the two-party vote in the average Scottish constituency was nearly 20 per cent below what it would have been if Scotland had voted in line with Britain as a whole, and the proportion of the professional, administrative and managerial class voting for the Conservative Party fell below 30 per cent in Scotland.

Even before the debacle of 1987 the Conservative Party had been persuaded of the need for exceptional measures to stem the loss of middle-class support in Scotland. It responded to the dismay spread among the middle class in Scotland by domestic property revaluation of 1984 by pledging to replace the rates by a flat-rate community charge designed to relieve the middle class of its 'disproportionate' contribution to local government expenditure.

But the 1985 commitment to the poll tax was a defensive measure. If the Conservative Party was to be revived in Scotland the Scottish middle class had to be persuaded to become active in Scottish public life in support of the ideal of a free market enterprise society.

The Thatcherite strategy for a middle-class revival in Scotland had two elements. It sought first to create new opportunities and incentives for the Scottish middle class to assume a leadership role in Scottish society. And it contrived, secondly, to polarise Scottish opinion between a public sector corporatist interest on the one hand and a private sector free-market interest on the other.

Public authorities had already been put under severe expenditure constraints by the government. Local authorities were now to be subjected to the further political constraint created by the replacement of the roughly progressive property tax by a regressive poll tax. Having bound the public sector victim the government then invited the middle class led by the business sector to despoil his assets.

Councils were legally required to put designated services out to competitive tender while the government actively promoted the 'contracting out' of a wider range of local authority and health services. Health Boards were shamelessly packed with Conservative supporters or Thatcherite fellow-travellers. The power of the health professions was curbed by new styles of business management and new forms of funding and by government encouragement to hospital management to initiate 'opting-out'. College Councils were placed under business leadership and given new management powers. Universities were forced to move closer to the market by cuts in public funding. The creation of School Boards presented middle class parents with the opportunity through the 'opting-out' option to transfer even more of their social privileges to their offspring, largely at public expense.

The climax of these government efforts to recreate a private sector middle-class leadership came with the proposal to merge the training functions of the Training Agency in Scotland with the economic development role of the Scottish Development Agency in a new body called

Scottish Enterprise. Both the Central Board and the Boards of the 22 Local Enterprise Companies which Scottish Enterprise will fund to deliver training and economic development services locally are to have a statutory two-thirds majority of businessmen.

The advance claims made for the economic effectiveness of Scottish Enterprise rest on highly contentious ideological assumptions about the sources of wealth creation. What is clear is that with an annual budget of £500m Scottish Enterprise represents – in intention – a massive transfer of power from the public to the private sector. For a government ideologically opposed to state intervention it is an audacious piece of social engineering.

In response to the impact of Thatcherism, the 1980s have seen a wider range of middle-class interventions in Scottish politics than in any other post-war decade.

Provoked by the introduction of School Boards, the Educational Institute of Scotland abandoned its preference for 'insider' lobbying to appeal directly to Scottish opinion in a campaign against the Anglicisation of Scotland's educational system. Scottish doctors and consultants canvassed public support for their opposition to government plans to extend the role of market forces in the health services. The Association of University Teachers reversed its former opposition to the universities' inclusion in the responsibilities of the Scottish assembly to campaign for their inclusion in future schemes for a Scottish parliament, a position now endorsed by the Principals of the Scottish universities. The Church of Scotland and the Catholic Church have been forthright in their condemnation not just of specific Thatcherite policies but of the whole Thatcherite ethos. The Standing Commission on the Scottish Economy under the chairmanship of a former Principal of a Scottish university detailed a 'democratic corporatist' alternative to Thatcherism for the Scottish economy. Scotland's two 'quality' daily newspapers, *The Scotsman* and *The Glasgow Herald*, along with *Scotland on Sunday* and *Observer Sunday*, have been unremittingly critical of the application of Thatcherism in Scotland. Both the Faculty of Advocates and the Law Society of Scotland have publicised their case against the government's proposed legal reforms. While the focus of the campaign for the non-payment of the poll tax has been on the Anti-Poll Tax Unions with their militant leadership and largely working class constituency, the ranks of non-payers embrace many tens of thousands of principled middle-class non-payers.

The most significant evidence of a radicalisation of Scottish middle-class attitudes is found in the publication of *A Claim of Right for Scotland* by the Scottish Constitutional Convention asserting the sovereign right of the Scottish people to determine its own constitutional future. Although the Convention was set up by a broad coalition of Scotland's oppositional groups – the churches, trade unions, local authorities, political parties – the committee which drafted the *Claim* was conspicuously 'bourgeois', embracing a former chief planner at the Scottish office, a former member of the British Diplomatic Service, a *regius* professor of Public Law, a former convener of the Church and Nation Committee of the Church of Scotland, the chairman of the Scottish Postal Board and a former under-secretary at the Scottish Office. As well as being an expression of a more radical mood, the Convention exerted its own radicalising influence on the debate about Scotland's constitutional options. It stimulated new thinking about the voting system and about the need for regional balance in a Scottish parliament. It also provided moral support and a source of leverage for Scottish Labour Action, a grouping of Labour MPs and activists who wanted to push the Labour Party towards a more radical form of devolution embracing proportional representation and backed by a doctrine of a 'dual' Scottish and British mandate.

The most noteworthy evidence of a mobilisation of middle-class opinion on the political right was the formation in May 1989 of the Scottish Business Group (SBG) to promote more active support by business-men at the local level for the Conservative Party. The group included some big names such as James Gulliver, Sir Hector Laing and Sir Ian MacGregor whose business interests were not primarily Scottish, along with a wide cross-section of the leaders of Scottish business. According to reports, it was at meetings of the core group of the SBG that the proposals for Scottish Enterprise were developed. The Group also played a key part in persuading the Scottish Office to back down on its opposition to unifying business rates on both sides of the border. A key figure in the SBG was Bill Hughes who launched the idea for Scottish Enterprise while chairman of the Confederation of British Industry in Scotland and who later became vice-chairman of the Scottish Conservative Party. A symptom of the polarisation of Scottish opinion which the Thatcher years had produced was the presence in the core group of the financier Angus Grossart who in the 1970s had been an advocate of a Scottish assembly.

Bill Hughes was closely associated with the restructuring of the Scottish Conservative Party carried out by the new chairman Michael Forsyth with the aim of bringing in younger, ideologically more militant organisers to pep up Conservative campaigning in the constituencies.

There were only a few other signs of a mobilisation of the Scottish middle class in the Thatcherite cause. The Adam Smith Institute publicised a free-market agenda for Scottish politics, although unfortunately for its political credibility the poll tax was its best known contribution to government policy. The *Sunday Times Scotland* supplement provided a platform for free-market, or at least conservative opinion, most notably through the contributions of novelist Allan Massie. A group of Conservative, if not Thatcherite, ministers and elders was reported in 1989 to be organising within the Church of Scotland to challenge the dominance of the anti-Thatcherites. And there were isolated instances of groups of doctors and hospital managers with government encouragement braving the disapproval of colleagues, unions, Health Councils and local politicians by floating proposals for local hospital 'opt-outs'.

The evidence of middle-class mobilisation to support or oppose Thatcherism is clear enough. But it adds up to something less than a revolution in the public aspirations of the Scottish middle class.

There are few signs that the poll tax is beginning to persuade a wider section of Scottish opinion that the local state needs to be drastically pruned back. Nor is there any evidence to date that a significant number of Scottish parents are likely to take advantage of the 'opting-out' provision in the Conservatives' education reforms. It seems that Scottish opinion has been unimpressed by the Government's attempts at social engineering on the educational front.

Equally, very few doctors and consultants have shown any inclination to follow government exhortations and incentives to take advantage of the new market opportunities in the health field. What little there has been in the way of positive response has been initiated by hospital managers acting with ideologically committed Health Boards or by straightforward commercial interests. Although the *force majeure* of legislation and government economic coercion is affecting a significant change in the balance between private and public sectors in Scotland, the Scottish middle class seems disinclined to discard its collectivist habits in favour of Thatcherite individualism.

Apostles of the market may find more reason to be optimistic about the chances of creating a new generation of business leadership. Certainly Scottish Enterprise has attracted significant support from the business community at both national and local levels. But Scottish Enterprise still has everything to prove. Many of the businessmen who have declared their support for the Local Enterprise Companies would probably not subscribe to the claims Bill Hughes made for the inherent superiority of businessmen over public authorities in economic development and training. Some leading businessmen have expressed doubts about the compatibility of market-led entrepreneurship and public accountability. Others fear that effective power will in any case rest with the public servants transferred from the Training Agency and the Scottish Development Agency and with central government.

In any case, the private sector base on which a new business leadership must be built is very weak. As we have seen, external takeover has reduced Scottish ownership in manufacturing to a minority interest. Scotland has one of the worst records of new firm formation of any region. It is difficult to accept at face value claims for a glorious revival of Scottish business confidence when a spokesman such as Professor Jack Shaw of Scottish Financial Enterprise, representing the most dynamic sector of the Scottish economy, insists that legislative devolution would cripple the Scottish economy, as if political decentralisation had crippled the bankers of Basel and Zurich, Boston and Houston, Frankfurt and Hamburg, Barcelona and Madrid.

There remains an unresolved dilemma at the heart of the free-market evangelism of the Scottish Business Group. Is the full rigour of the market to be applied to Scotland even if that means the final elimination of Scotland's business autonomy in an integrating world? The Adam Smith Institute would argue that the elimination of Scottish ownership and control from the 'mature' sectors of the economy would simply be the prelude to a rebirth of Scottish enterprise on a more competitive and sustainable basis in new sectors. Whether such faith could withstand the rest of a takeover of the Royal Bank of Scotland, Standard Life, Scottish and Newcastle or the Wood Group is doubtful. After the debacle of the Trustee Savings Bank, the loss of Distillers and the failure to secure any clear corporate advantage for Scotland from the sale of Britoil and British Gas, the pressure for political intervention would be intense. It is worth asking whether any significant section of the Scottish business class will maintain its ideological zeal for the market beyond the term of Mrs Thatcher's premiership. With Mrs Thatcher gone, Michael Forsyth and Bill Hughes lose their political base, even their political *raison d'être*. Freed from the bullying of the Scottish Office and Conservative Party headquarters it is not improbable that many businessmen would want to restore, if not old-style Scottish corporatism, at least the sort of collaborative relations with the public sector typical of other European economies.

If the prospect of Scotland being transformed into an 'enterprise' society in the Thatcherite image is remote, there are question marks too over the political significance and staying power of the 'oppositional' middle class activism of the last five years. The only theme obviously common to all the opposition campaigns, from teachers to lawyers, is resistance to the application of market prescriptions to their respective occupational sectors or professional concerns. Constitutional reform does not qualify as a unifying theme. The representative organisation for some of the oppositional groups – school and university teachers, the churches – have declared their support for one form or other of legislative devolution for Scotland. But the professional organisations of the socially more powerful doctors and lawyers have not – and probably will not – take a stance on the issue, however clear their interest in the creation of a Scottish legislature may appear to observers.

The oppositional campaigns are perhaps best understood as part of a syndrome of Scottish resistance to Thatcherism which draws its strength from a combination of mutually supporting factors. One is Scotland's greater dependence on the public sector. Another is the common perception that the liberalisation of markets will handicap rather than benefit Scotland. Another is the widespread belief that Mrs Thatcher was instinctively unsympathetic to Scotland, symbolised for many by her categorical rejection of the case for a Scottish legislature. Yet, another is the higher level of commitment by Scottish opinion to such core social democratic values as a preference for welfare spending over tax cuts, for public rather than private provision of social services, of a belief in collective rather than individual responsibility for unemployment.

None of these factors is immune from change. Mrs Thatcher has gone. As privatisation is extended Scotland's dependence on the public sector will diminish. Social democracy is on the defensive if not in retreat in most parts of Europe. If Scotland remains loyal does that represent a source of radical energy, or is it due to a time lag between developments in Scotland and developments elsewhere? What is clear is that if the oppositional middle class groups do represent a potential source of radical energy, an effective catalyst for their political development and coalescence is still wanting.

The opinion polls in the spring of 1990 suggested that the Labour Party may have been the chief electoral beneficiary in Scotland of middle-class opposition to Tharcherism. But the Labour Party has its own interests to pursue. Whatever the electoral auguries, it is still ideologically on the retreat from Thatcherism and preoccupied with adapting its policies to the interests and values of the voters in the Midlands and South of England. It is more interested in containing than in catalysing Scottish disaffection. By early 1989 the party had declared against a campaign of non-payment of the poll tax, thus surrendering the opportunity simulta-neously of defending the weakest members of Scottish society, inflicting a major defeat on Thatcherism and vindicating Scotland's political claims. By the end of the year Robin Cook, the only senior party spokesman to declare himself a non-payer, was insisting that his stance was purely a personal one and that he would not be urging it on the party – an apt illustration of the Labour Party's disabling effect on Scotland's civic conscience. By early 1990 the Labour Party's Scottish leadership had succeeded in containing the advance of the more radical spirits grouped in Scottish Labour Action. It had won conference approval to reinterpret the *Claim of Right* as little more than a statement of the right of the Scottish people to vote in Westminster elections. It had secured the rejection of the 'dual mandate' reserving the right of the Scottish people to determine their own future in the event of Scotland again voting for Labour while England returned another Conservative majority. The drive for a clear commitment to proportional representation had been diverted into a party study of alternative electoral systems. Thus, the Scottish Labour leadership had secured its political base in preparation for another bid for the ultimate, deceiving, prize of sovereign power at Westminster.

Meanwhile, the SNP had weakened its credentials as a catalysing force by its ill-judged withdrawal from the Scottish Constitutional Convention. Not that the party had shown much inclination to extend its campaigning fronts to respond to the spread of middle-class disaffection. In 1989, despite Jim Sillars's 1988 Govan by-election promise that SNP would promote a broad anti-Thatcher coalition, the party opted for a strategy of polarising anti-Thatcherite opinion on two different axes: payment or non-payment of the poll tax and support or opposition to Scotland's independent membership of the European Community. In these confrontations other issues such as the future of the Health Service, poverty, the environmental crisis, the future of Scottish education, were sidelined. The SNP had lost its capacity to seize the policy initiative except over a very narrow range of issues. Like the Labour Party it failed conspicuously to articulate an alternative to the Thatcherite vision of the 'enterprise' society. Indeed, its uncritical enthusiasm for embrace of the European Community's single internal market suggested an indifference to the effect of closer European integration on the more vulnerable members of Scottish society.

With its radical prospectus and middle-class identity the Scottish Constitutional Convention appeared in its earlier days in 1988 to have potential as a catalysing force for middle class disaffection. But the Convention has been revealed as too much a creature of vested political interests: the Labour Party, the STUC, the Convention of Scottish Local Authorities (COSLA), the churches. To retain political credibility it has had to conform to the electoral strategy and timetable of the Labour Party. Weakened by the SNP withdrawal, it has failed to establish its own political identity. By the end of 1989 it appeared more as a forum for bargaining between political interests - notably the Labour Party and the Liberal Democrats but also the radical elements within the Labour Party – than an independent source of political ideas and action. Crucially, by failing to proclaim its definition of Scotland's right as the moral basis of the poll tax non-payment campaign, it surrendered the opportunity to vindicate the constitutional radicalism of the *Claim of Right* by applying it to the political issue of the moment. The Convention's failure was emblematic of the failure of any prominent middle-class Scots outwith a sprinkling of MPs and Nationalist leaders publicly to proclaim the doctrine of justified defiance of the poll tax legislation.

Scottish developments cannot be judged by events in Eastern or Baltic Europe. But the comparison helps to highlight a major defect in the structure of political dissent in Scotland. In the Eastern European countries the

Communist monopoly of power forced the opposition to create new, informal structures of civic and intellectual dissent which owed no loyalty to the establishment. In Scotland, as the record of the Convention illustrates, political opposition is heavily institutionalised in organisations such as the Labour Party, the STUC and COSLA which have a powerful vested interest in controlling and limiting the growth of dissent. Even if there had been a more powerful moral and intellectual impulse in Scotland towards a radical critique of the political system, these vested interests would have moved quickly to block the formation of independent centres of organisation.

Even so there are some grounds for believing that the Scottish middle class will adopt a more radical political stance in the 1990s. First the events of the 1980s have loosened the social and economic moorings of key sections of the middle class including university teachers, school teachers, doctors and public sector managers and administrators. It seems unlikely that a change of government within the United Kingdom will restore the old 'corporatist' order in Scotland. Important elements of Thatcherism – a belief in consumer rights, a new balance between public and private provision, enhanced concern for 'value for money', greater scope for the contracting out of public services, the liberalisation of the market in professional services – will survive the passing of Thatcherism and reinforce the social impact of longer-term changes in the economic structure.

Second, the infrastructure of middle-class debate outwith the vested political interests has been strengthened. Although the Scottish universities have failed to contribute proportionately to their intellectual resources to the reassessment of Scottish needs and opportunities, their experience in the 1980s has made them more committed to Scotland both politically and intellectually. The Scottish media have diversified and strengthened their contribution with the growth of the Scottish quality press and a more confident presentation of Scottish issues on television. There is now a significant grouping of Scottish 'think-tanks' with varying degrees of independence from political sponsors, from the Nationalist Centre for Social and Economic Research and the Labour John Wheatley Centre at one end of the spectrum to Edinburgh University's Centre for Theology and Public Issues, the Red-Green conferences and the Free University of Glasgow at the other end.

Environmental issues are bound to impinge more and more forcefully on political debate, forcing a reassessment of the conventional political and economic priorities. The infant Scottish Green Party is already exerting an influence on Scottish debate out of all proportion to its numbers. It is the only party which shows any appreciation of the challenge which European integration presents to the ideal of participatory democracy.

The European factor will also have an increasing impact on the Scottish debate. In the shape of the European Community's single internal market it will expose sections of the middle class including Scottish businessmen and professional groups to increased competition. Its free-market bias will create a further obstacle to the restoration of the old 'corporatist' order in Scotland.

European integration within and without the frontiers of the European Community will also increase the economic pressures for a more direct and coherent Scottish response. At one level it will generate support for a direct Scottish voice in the management of European integration on the same basis as other comparably sized member nations. At another, as the discretionary powers of national governments are restricted by the process of integration it will increase pressure for the politically co-ordinated Scottish response in the still unrestricted policy areas to minimise Scotland's disadvantages and maximise her opportunities in the new single market.

But perhaps the most important effect of European integration will be to accelerate the erosion of the 'dual' Scottish-British identity which in the 1970s John P. Mackintosh was championing as a constraint on the growth of Scottish nationalism. Mackintosh's argument was a valuable reminder in the heat of the Nationalist debate of the 1970s that most Scots, particularly middle class Scots, saw themselves as both British and Scottish. But Mackintosh's argument gives insufficient weight to the fact that national identity is a dynamic not a static quantity and that discounts the duty of intellectuals constantly to assess and redefine myths of national identity against the changing needs and opportunities of their national community.

The advance of European integration makes that task more urgent. Integration both increases the incentive to change and secures the opportunity for change without the perceived risks of 'separation'. That may well prove to be the formula which breaks down at least the outer defences of Scottish middle class conservatism. The growth of a positive will to radical action on Scotland's behalf may depend on a more profound Europeanisation of the Scottish imagination in which the Scottish middle class learns to see itself equally with the Scottish working class as the hero and heroine of its own nation's history.

British Inequality and the Nordic Alternative

SNP *Annual Conference, Donaldson Lecture, October 2007*

ISSUES OF POLITICAL CULTURE, the changing components of Scottish identity, the struggle for an autonomous Scottish culture, the limits of independence in a globalising world – grand topics of this sort have usually been the substance of these Donaldson Lectures.

As someone whose academic background is in philosophy and theories of international society, I have appreciated those contributions as much as anyone. But today I want to take a more practical policy focus. Specifically, I want to look at the relationship between the economic case for independence and the social challenges Scotland faces.

The most striking feature of Scotland's situation today is the size of the gap between the reality of life for many Scots and Scotland's potential. I can think of no other democracy of a comparable size and stage of economic development which suffers a similarly sized gap between its potential and the reality of life as experienced by a substantial portion of its population. I can think of another country of far greater size and wealth which also suffers from a conspicuous gap between reality and potential: the United States of America. Its social problems are if anything greater than Scotland's. The USA is a case to which I will return.

In the SNP we are accustomed to illustrating the independence 'deficit' by comparing Scotland's economic performance within the United Kingdom with the performance of small, neighbouring independent countries. It is a telling comparison which is at last beginning to win an audience beyond the ranks of committed Nationalists. It shows that in recent decades Scotland has endured a rate of economic growth very roughly half that of its most obvious comparators – the small democracies of Western Europe. And that comparison is all the more telling when we add in the unrealised potential for growth represented by Scotland's North Sea oil. That potential is usually expressed in terms of the value of the public revenues Scottish oil has pumped into the London Treasury over the last 30 years – approximately £220bn.

But, of course, the lost potential cannot adequately be expressed in revenue terms. Even more important is the accumulated loss of economic development opportunities which Scotland has suffered because of its lack of control over North Sea resources – including the loss of three decades of investment in the development of the alternative energy technologies so critical to the 21st century.

But if Scotland's economic performance has been at best mediocre over the last several decades, what can we say of Scotland's social record? Mediocre doesn't begin to describe it. Disappointing, downright poor, disastrous, catastrophic – the appropriate term certainly lies at the latter end of this spectrum. The facts have been well enough publicised and many of them will be familiar to you. Here is a selection:

- On life expectancy Scotland ranks in the lowest quartile of 22 countries for both men and women, along with Poland, Turkey and Mexico

- On infant mortality Scotland is at the bottom of the third quartile of 26 countries

- Among the European Union's 15 member states, Scotland has the poorest performance on premature death, low birth weight, infant mortality, underage pregnancies and drug misuse, while achieving the average on long term illness and dental health

- Compared to England on the same indicators, Scotland's rate of premature death is 30 per cent higher, of long-term illness 20 per cent higher, of dental ill health 80 per cent higher, and drug misuse 40 per cent higher

- Scotland has a suicide rate higher than most of its developed country peers and nearly twice as high as the UK average

- The proportion of Scots self-reporting as being dissatisfied with life is higher than for the British population overall

- Our levels of alcohol misuse continue to increase from levels which already exceeded UK levels. The proportion of Scots smoking excessively (more than 20 cigarettes a day) is also above the British level though that was before the ban on smoking in public venues

- Scotland's reputation for having one of the highest levels of drug addiction among Western European countries is supported by a death rate from drug dependence and abuse 25 per cent above the British average

The cheerful statistics keep coming – who doesn't know by now that Scotland has the second highest proportion of obese children after the United States? Many of you will have read a recent UNICEF report which found that, with the exception of the US, among the world's richest countries the UK offered the poorest prospects for children.

Facts like these challenge everyone who lives in Scotland or professes concern for Scotland. But they are a particular challenge to those of us who champion the cause of Scottish independence.

Independence can be argued on many different grounds: as a fundamental right, as a duty of self-responsibility, as the key to more representative and more effective governance, as a way to maximise the contribution we could make on the great global issues of climate change or international peace. When we make the case for independence we all probably use a changing mixture of these arguments depending on the audience and the context. Individually or severally, they can constitute a rational and convincing case for independence.

But to my mind the truly compelling case for independence will include an explanation of how it will help to improve the prospects of the more than one in five Scots represented by all those gloomy statistics on poverty and chronic ill health. There is a principle at stake here which is at least as important as the principled grounds on which we usually argue the case for independence. It might be called the principle of maximising advantage for the least advantaged members of the community.

Some of you may detect a distorted echo here of the American political philosopher John Rawls' 'Difference Principle', which asserts that economic and social inequalities can be justified only in so far as they improve the lot of the least advantaged. My crude variation of Rawls' principle is that in developed countries in which a majority of the population enjoys a good standard of living, the case for radical constitutional change – with its inevitable uncertainties and risks – needs to demonstrate how it will improve the conditions of the most disadvantaged groups of the population. Of course, the principle of maximum advantage for the least advantaged does not trump all other considerations – how could it when climate change and nuclear proliferation threaten global survival? And the comfortable majority have their own claims for a better life. But an argument for independence which does not have this question at its core seems to me be morally compromised.

Traditionally, public debate around independence has focused on the economics of independence, and with good reason. Historically, the greatest obstacle to winning public support for independence was a widespread fear among the public that independence would lead to economic meltdown, with cuts in public services and lower living standards all round. That fear still lurks in the shadows but, with the help first of North Sea oil and then of a relative improvement in Scotland's economic performance from the low points of the 1960 and '80s, the debate has moved on.

Opponents have now downgraded their argument from claims of economic collapse to the claim that there would be no clear economic gain for Scotland – that is if they make an economic case at all. Our chief opponent (who is of course Gordon Brown not Wendy Alexander) now gives more time to a different argument altogether: a politico-cultural case for subsuming Scottish identity within a Greater British identity. So far he's not finding many subscribers, even among his main target constituency of middle England.

The fundamentals of the economic case for independence are now well established. It may be impossible in strict terms to *prove* that independence will increase Scotland's rate of economic growth. But the links between independence and an improved economic performance are well supported by the record of other small Western European countries – not just by the bare facts of their sustained higher growth but also by the historical detail of *how*, over decades, they have used their political independence to maximise their economic welfare. And this appeal to the international record is supported by the many specific examples of London government failing to maximise Scotland's economic benefit-failures over North Sea oil, the electronics industry, fishing, alternative energy, transport, fiscal regimes and, most recently, agriculture. Put these two fields of evidence together and they create a strong probability that independence would bring major economic benefit to Scotland.

But if we can be confident in arguing that independence will improve

Scotland's economic performance, can we have the same confidence that independence will secure any major improvement in Scotland's social condition?

The relationship between economic success and social wellbeing has never been straightforward. We know that economic change always produces losers as well as winners. We know that national economic growth does not translate automatically into reduced poverty. We know that, above a certain threshold of national wealth, further increases produce diminishing returns in social progress and wellbeing. Other factors come into play too. Professor Richard Wilkinson in his 2005 book *The Impact of Inequality: how to make sick societies healthier* identified a clear correlation between the degree of economic inequality in society and the incidence of its social problems, irrespective of an absolute level of wealth. The US was his prime exhibit and the UK not very far behind. This summer a team from Dundee University reported a strong relationship between the level of income inequality and infant mortality in the 24 richest OECD countries, with the US and the UK – followed by Australia, New Zealand and Ireland – again as the leading illustrations.

So we cannot simply assume that the improved rate of economic growth which independence can be expected to produce will translate into a steady decrease in the number of Scots living below the conventional poverty line – 60 per cent of the median household income. Ireland stands as a warning here. As the Celtic Tiger, Ireland has famously enjoyed a rate of economic growth in recent decades twice or in some periods three times that achieved by Scotland yet, along with Scotland, the rest of the United Kingdom and the United States, it has one of the highest rates of relative poverty – for both children and adults – among developed countries.

We should not be surprised at this disjunction between economic prosperity and social progress. Economic growth has never guaranteed a fair distribution of its fruits. Today globalisation adds a further distortion by intensifying external competition to which the weakest members of society are most vulnerable. There is a global trend not just for the highest incomes but also average incomes to grow more quickly than the incomes of the lowest earners.

But globalisation is only one of the causes of the increasing economic inequality which many societies are now experiencing. Another more powerful cause is found in the advance of neo-liberalism since the 1970s and the greater autonomy which that doctrine awards to economic markets. Again the US pulled the UK and a foot dragging Scotland along in its wake.

But there is an alternative to the Anglo-American model of free-market capitalism available to us. The record of the Nordic welfare democracies – Norway, Sweden, Finland, Iceland and Denmark – in combining consistent economic growth with high levels of welfare and low levels of inequality and poverty is simply unmatched in the world. And they are now adding enlightened environmental policies to their premium mix of policies.

Independence will allow Scotland to share in some of the structural strengths of the Nordic countries: their advantages of scale; short lines of political communication and feedback; flexibility in building a national consensus about how to respond to external change even within an interdependent world (and in the face of the centralising tendencies of the European Union). Like the Nordic countries, independent Scotland will be able to make the best of its natural assets and of the opportunities which come its way in a shifting world.

We can also look forward to sharing in some of the intellectual and moral advantages they enjoy as small independent countries: their awareness that they have no alibis for failure; their knowledge that in confronting their problems and exploiting their opportunities independence insists they look first and last to their own resources of intelligence and imagination and courage; their knowledge that no one will subsidise their failures except at the cost of their freedom; their confidence that, because of independence, the experience and achievements of each generation will accrue through a fully developed range of national institutions to the benefit of succeeding generations.

Nations are *sui generis*. Scotland will enter on independence with a very different social legacy from the Nordic states. Historians stress how distinctive Scotland's social experience has been. In the modern age, Scotland has experienced the successive traumas of rapid industrialisation and deindustrialisation, of a long, sustained high level of net emigration, of the disproportionate blood sacrifice in British wars – all compounded by 300 years of displaced government. We cannot underestimate the severity of our social legacy from these passages of our history. Scotland's social problems are both extensive and intensive – their extension measured by the fact that one in five Scots still lives in relative poverty, their intensity by the several hundred thousand Scots who experience multiple disadvantages – economic, health, environmental, educational – which produce the terrible 11 or 12 year difference in life expectancy between neighbouring parts of Glasgow. But we need to remember that all countries have their narratives of epic change and challenge, no less the Nordic countries with their modern histories of grinding rural poverty and mass emigration, of military occupation, resistance and civil war, of swiftly changing global markets. Where they differ from Scotland – so far – is that they chose, and continue to insist on, political independence as the indispensable condition of an effective response.

The other condition of the Nordic countries' social success has been their faith in social democracy. Scotland shares much of the Nordic bias towards social democracy. Of course we will have to work out our own version to suit our peculiar legacy and the particular global circumstances in which independence is finally achieved. But, given the scale and intensity of our social problems, I find it difficult to conceive of an effective response which is not based on the social democratic fundamentals of an active state committed to egalitarian outcomes through universal public services and a redistributive tax and welfare system. How we combine those fundamentals with the contemporary expectation of individual autonomy, social and cultural pluralism and civil empowerment is our greatest challenge.

There are models out there to instruct and inspire us, and with independence we will have a resource of far greater value than North Sea oil or renewable energy: the means to apply the full resources of our own intelligence and the will to achieve our own vision of the public good. We will need every ounce of those qualities if we are to make independence work for all the people of Scotland.

Social Justice and the SNP

The Modern SNP: From Protest to Power
(ed. Gerry Hassan, Edinburgh), 2009

THE SNP WAS FOUNDED, and remains, a party whose overriding purpose is the achievement of independence for Scotland. That is the source and the target of its strongest impulses. Its second strongest impulse, sourced in the desperate economic conditions of the inter-war years which saw the party's foundation, is the improvement of Scotland's economic performance. Perhaps its third strongest impulse is opposition to the nuclearisation of Scotland, focused with a particular intensity on the use of Scottish territory as a base for the UK's nuclear weapons capacity. Only then comes the impulse for social justice.

This ranking is supported by a 2007 survey of SNP members' first priority for the powers they would like to see transferred to the Scottish Parliament. Economic and taxation powers came first with 55.7 per cent, defence and foreign affairs second with 12.6 per cent and social security pensions third with 6.7 per cent (Aberdeen and Strathclyde Universities 2007). This is consistent with my personal judgement based on decades of membership and observation of the party. The ranking is offered here in support of the proposition that while independence, economic development and opposition to nuclear weapons are in the SNP's political DNA, a politically relevant sense of social justice has had to be learned.

The Origins of SNP Social Policy Thinking

The leaders of the SNP in the immediate aftermath of the Second World War were drawn mainly from the professions and small business. The first historian of modern Scottish nationalism, H. J. Hanham, presents them as small-town democrats (Hanham, 1969). While their Presbyterian heritage gave them a strong sense of the fundamental equality of all men and women, as well as a robust ethic of social responsibility, it was at best ambiguous towards economic and social equality and distanced from the pervasive sense of class which characterised so much of Scotland.

These limitations are evident in the party's 1946 *Statement of Aims and Policy*, which had plenty to say about a Scottish constitution, about local government, planning and economic development, but rather less to say about Scotland's social future. It advised that medical and other health services must be provided 'free, if necessary, by the state where they do not exist or do not reach a reasonable standard', while insisting that state intervention must not transform the medical profession into a state monopoly. While it identified housing as one of Scotland's most urgent problems and called for national building standards and planning, it said nothing about who should fund and own the new stock.

It declared that economic democracy was the basis of political freedom without any reference to industrial democracy or to the security and welfare of workers. It offered an economic policy aimed at maximising Scotland's economic potential as a precondition of providing a 'decent standard of living and not of a bare subsistence' for those unable to work, to be funded by a contributory social insurance scheme paying benefits 'without recourse to the humiliation of means test'. It stated that there should be no 'great inequalities' in individual wealth or income, but offered no suggestions as to how any redistribution should be effected.

Overall it was a limited and ambivalent response to the social and economic challenges which had generated a political mandate for the creation of the British welfare state (SNP, 1946). From this limited base the SNP's sense of social justice has been shaped by three main factors – its electoral rivalry with the Labour Party, the impact of Thatcherism and the creation of the Scottish Parliament.

Electoral Rivalry

Of these three, electoral rivalry with the Labour Party is the most important and, from the February and October 1974 elections onward, the SNP called itself 'social democratic'. That this was more than a handy piece of camouflage was made clear by the direction of the SNP's policy development. Under Billy Wolfe's leadership the party's 'It's Scotland's Oil' campaign was promoted nationally through posters featuring, documentary style, the faces of four deprived Scots – a pensioner, an unemployed industrial worker, a child in poverty, a harassed housewife – above statistics describing the extent of Scotland's social problems and the punchline, 'It's his oil

... It's her oil'. This directed the SNP's attack at the heart of Labour's traditional claim to be the champion of social justice for Scotland's working class.

The SNP followed this up by adopting at its 1974 conference a strategy to combat poverty. Where previous SNP conferences had tended to treat poverty through isolated resolutions, the 'War on Poverty' policy took a more comprehensive approach, drawing on the policy packages – raising of tax thresholds, increased child benefits, guaranteed minimum income – publicised by UK campaigning bodies such as the Child Poverty Action Group (SNP, 'War on Poverty', 1974). Labour's sensitivity to this new emphasis was displayed by its furious denial of a subsequent SNP claim that 5,000 elderly Scots were dying from hypothermia each year in oil-rich Scotland, a dispute which resolved around the distinction between deaths by hypothermia and deaths from cold-related diseases (Maxwell, 1987).

The movement in the SNP's understanding of social justice towards mainstream social democracy was also influenced by increasing reference to Norway amid other Scandinavian models. Norway was already popular with SNP activists because it provided the example of a small country successfully pursuing nationally oriented strategies on both oil and fisheries while, in the SNP's eyes, Scotland's oil and fisheries were being sacrificed to UK priorities. But the Scandinavian welfare model was also increasingly recommended as the solution, with the help of oil revenues, to Scotland's intractable social problems.

Distance Travelled

The distance the SNP had travelled from 1946 was measured by its 1978 policy summary, *Return to Nationhood*, which looked confidently forward to the following year's referendum on a Scottish assembly. Rather than concentrating on the SNP's classic claim for Scottish sovereignty, it proclaimed that the party fought elections on its proposals for 'social and economic justice for the people of Scotland'. Based on the Universal Declaration of Human Rights, its policies would eventually eradicate 'society's damaging divisions without resort to the extremes of outdated class politics' (SNP, 1978). Those policies included raising the tax threshold for low-income families, the replacement of tax allowances by tax credits guaranteeing a universal minimum income, the replacement of rates with a redistributive local income tax, an uprated universal child benefit, a comprehensive system of allowances for disabled people, opposition to any incomes policy which further eroded living standards, the index linking of main benefits to average earnings, the extension of care 'in the community' rather than in institutions and an assisted home-buying scheme for council house tenants where the public housing stock was equal to the demand.

Of course it is the prerogative of opposition parties – particularly parties as distant from government as the SNP then was – to adopt populist policies without too much regard for their practicality. But the cursory attention SNP policy decision bodies gave to complex social policy issues reflected some features peculiar to the party. One was the paucity of social policy expertise within the party membership and the lack of any special-ist policy staff beyond oil and economic development. What expertise existed within the party's active membership was usually conscripted into the policy committee charged with developing policy and so was likely to be *parti pris* before the wider party membership was engaged. Among the party's MPs only Margaret Bain majored on social policy issues, though Gordon Wilson was a forceful campaigner for a cold climate allowance in the 1979–87 parliaments. Nor did the SNP have an associated think tank which could make up the deficits. A further factor was the widespread confidence within the party by the mid-1970s that North Sea oil revenues would cover the costs of whatever policy commitment the party chose to make.

The Thatcher Effect

The consolidation of the SNP's left-of-centre position on social issues was completed by Margaret Thatcher. Her imposition of a poll tax in Scotland in 1987 was received as a gross injustice by almost as many of the middle Scots who stood to gain from the tax as of the working-class Scots who stood to lose, a sentiment which the SNP enthusiastically encouraged by its campaign of non-payment. But it was the social consequences in Scotland of her flagship policies on the economy and welfare reform – Scottish unemployment and poverty levels both peaked in the later 1980s at more than double the 1979 levels – that had the deepest impact. The offence caused to Scotland's sense of moral identity strengthened the SNP's commitment to democracy as the Scottish alternative to what was widely seen as Mrs Thatcher's denial of social solidarity and even social compassion.

But while Mrs Thatcher's perceived social ethic was firmly rejected by the SNP, her promotion of a liberalised market as an indispensable source of economic dynamism struck a chord with sections of the party leadership looking for ways of injecting new vitality into the Scottish economy. The SNP's embrace of the single European market through its 'Independence in Europe' policy went part of the way to meeting the need while the emergence of Ireland as Europe's tiger economy provided a model of small-state economic success without the Nordic ambivalence towards the EU.

A New Testing Ground

The establishment of the Scottish Parliament forced social issues to the forefront of Scottish politics. Scotland's designated First Minister, Donald Dewar, raised the stakes for the new Parliament in 1998 in a preview of its main challenges:

> We have a proud tradition [in Scotland] of working to tackle social division... Devolution is an end in itself: but it is a means to other ends, and none more important than the creation of a socially cohesive Scotland.
>
> The Herald, 3 February 1998

While there is room to challenge Dewar's confidence that the Holyrood Parliament had the capacity for effective action on the most important factors behind Scotland's social problems, there is no doubt that the Parliament has made social policy the main front of Scottish politics. The first, Labour-led executive took up the challenge by appointing a Minister for Social Justice committed to Annual Social Justice reports, established a Scottish Social Exclusion (soon amended to Inclusion) Network recruited from civil society as an advisory forum, and part-funded a Centre for Research on Social Justice based at Glasgow University.

The SNP faced a particular challenge. Having built a social democratic platform against poverty which assumed independence, it now confronted the reality that its credibility on social issues would be judged on the more immediate and certainly no less complex social issues devolved to Edinburgh. It would no longer be able simply to counterpoint any Westminster failures on social justice issues with its own pristine commitments to more radical action. While UK issues would continue to exert a strong influence on Scottish electoral preferences, the Scottish Parliament had created a new testing ground for the party's credibility on social policy.

If some opponents of the SNP hoped that the extended social challenge presented by the Scottish Parliament would expose deep tensions and divisions in what they continued to see as a 'one issue' party, they were disappointed. Building on the devolution referendum's endorsement of a tax-varying power for the Parliament, the SNP campaigned in the 1999 elections on the theme of 'A Penny for Scotland'. This was a bold affirmation of its social priorities, detailing the social and educational projects on which the SNP would spend the £670 million additional income generated over three years by a 1p 'tartan' tax supplement.

The struggle with Labour and the challenge of Thatcherism had helped to educate and stabilise the SNP's sense of social justice around a policy platform which proved well matched to the politics of devolved Scotland. In the parliament the SNP was part of a regular parliamentary majority with Labour and the Lib Dems, and later the Greens and the Scottish Socialists, which embraced free personal care, radical homelessness legislation, abolition of Section 28, charity law reform, social inclusion programmes, new rights for mental health patients, the recognition of civil partnerships, opposition to top-up fees for students, the abolition of poinding and warrant sales, new safeguards for the rights of people with learning difficulties and a ban on smoking in public places.

The rights agenda was advanced by the extension of freedom of information and the creation of a public services complaints ombudsman and new arm's length service inspectorates. Supported by large increases in public spending, the expansion of health and education within the public sector also enjoyed majority support, though the SNP became progressively more critical of the use of PFI as a major source of funding. Housing and council tax were other areas where the SNP broke with the consensus, criticising the Glasgow Housing Association (GHA) model as the vehicle for the transfer of Glasgow's housing stock and opposing the council tax as an inflexible and regressive form of local taxation.

Public and Party Opinion

In its adoption of a pragmatic left-of-centre position on social policy the Parliament was in tune with Scottish public opinion. Successive opinion surveys have shown Scottish public opinion as being to the left of English opinion on a range of attitude tests. Election surveys from 1979 to 1997 show the proportion of Scots favouring more redistribution of income and wealth varying from between 14 per cent and six per cent higher than English voters. The Scottish Parliament Election Survey of 1999 indicated a 25 per cent gap, with 61 per cent of Scots respondents in favour as against 36 per cent of English respondents. The differences on other indicators were much smaller. More Scots than English agreed that income inequality in Britain was too high, fewer Scots believed that benefits were too high, and most Scots agreed that government was mainly responsible for providing health care, support to retired people, disabled people and low-income parents and residential care. The only measure on which Scots were to the right of the English respondents, albeit narrowly, was (rather perversely) on whether government should increase taxes to spend more on health and other support (Paterson *et al*, 2001: 126–7).

Evidence from the 2005 British Social Attitudes Survey shows more muted results, with 51 per cent of Scots agreeing with the proposition that benefits were too generous compared to 50 per cent of English respondents (Sinclair *et al*, 2009). On the other hand, a 2008 poll revealed that 61 per cent of Scots said that they would be more inclined to support a political party that took serious measures against poverty, compared to an average of 51 per cent across Great Britain (Maxwell, 2009).

The 2007 survey of SNP members suggests that in its social values, if not its constitutional aims, the party membership is aligned with the values of the country. 45 per cent agreed that there is one law for the rich and one for the poor against 15 per cent who disagreed, while no less than 71 per cent disagreed with the proposition that the government should cut spending in order to cut tax. On the more challenging proposition that it is not government's responsibility to provide a job for everyone who wants one, 47 per cent agreed against 35 per cent who disagreed (Aberdeen and Strathclyde Universities, 2007).

Most commentators maintain that these differences in surveyed social values between England and Scotland are too small and variable to serve by themselves as the political foundation for a distinctive Scottish social politics (Paterson *et al*, 2001; Sinclair *et al*, 2009). This of course leaves the leftist bias of the Parliament's actual social record to be explained. One explanation is that the values of the elected MSPs are to the left of the Scottish voters while remaining within the voters' margin of tolerance.

A more structured explanation looks to the particular conditions of the Scottish constitutional settlement – the devolution of spending power, principally social spending, to a legislature elected by a form of proportional representation but without any substantial tax-raising power. While the lack of fiscal responsibility biases the Parliament towards populist spending, the electoral system ensures that the party most disposed to challenge the bias, the Conservative Party, struggles to escape from its minority status in the Parliament.

This explanation is at best partial. While the electoral system does indeed make it difficult for a single party to achieve an overall majority by comparison with the Westminster system, by the same token it provides more opportunity to other parties critical of the Parliament's bias in favour of spending to gain representation. The more representative a voting system, the less credible it is to dismiss the role of voters' preferences.

The Challenge of Government

If the arrival of the Scottish Parliament created a new testing ground for SNP social policy, the party's move into government following the 2007 election added a new dimension to the challenge. The inclusion in the party's election manifesto of ambitious targets for raising Scotland's rate of sustainable economic growth was entirely expected, as were commitments to reducing Scotland's levels of poverty and welfare dependence. Rather less expected was the focus on inequality. The manifesto identified Scotland as having one of the highest levels of income inequality in Europe, attributing it to 'serious political and economic failure'. The SNP's response was to promise that, as part of its economic growth strategy, it would set specific targets to increase the proportion of national wealth held by *each of the* lowest *six income deciles* of the population.

This must be one of the most radical commitments to redistribution made by any UK political party since the founding of the welfare state. To increase significantly the share of national income of each of the six lowest deciles would require a major transfer of income from the top 40 per cent of Scottish earners, going well beyond a common-sense interpretation of the warrant provided by the margin of Scottish over English support for redistribution in opinion surveys. A cynic might claim that its inclusion in the manifesto was a symptom of the rather casual way in which the SNP's policy making process treated social issues. It is not surprising that the SNP government's subsequent social strategy papers have carried a much reduced, though still significant, commitment to reduce income inequality.

In government the SNP has strengthened rather than diluted its commitment to social democracy. While the major economic policy strategy paper, *The Government Economic Strategy* (GES), defined the government's single overriding purpose as being 'to increase sustainable economic growth – to which all else in government is directed and contributes' (Scottish Government, 2007), for a statement of economic strategy it has an unusual amount to say about the social dimensions of economic growth. Its economic objectives are to be consistent with 'golden rules' ranking solidarity and cohesion alongside sustainability. While cohesion is presented as equity between geographical area, solidarity is presented in terms of equity between income groups, with Scotland's inequality levels compared unfavourably, though with minimal differentiation, with those in the 'arc of prosperity countries' (Ireland and selected Nordic countries). The radical manifesto commitment to reducing income inequality between each of the six lowest deciles and the top four is replaced by a more sober, but still challenging, commitment to increase the share of the *three* lowest deciles as a *group*. At the same time Ireland is commended for using the 'opportunity of globalisation' to achieve high rates of economic growth through large-scale infrastructure investment and low corporation tax with only the most fleeting reference to its poor record on poverty and inequality.

The GES was followed by *Taking Forward the Government Economic Strategy: A Discussion Paper on tackling Poverty, Inequality and Disadvantage* (Scottish Government, 2008a). In contrast to the GES, *Taking Forward* is clear about the lack of any automatic transfer from economic growth to reductions in poverty and inequality. It carries a table showing that Ireland's high growth rate had been accompanied by rates of poverty and inequality among the worst in the developed world alongside the US and UK. The table also showed that even the Nordic countries with their long commitment to egalitarian welfare had not been able to prevent some increase in poverty during the 1995–2005 period, albeit from levels half or more lower than in Ireland, the US and UK. As a discussion paper it focused more on questions and issues than solutions and so left many loose ends, but it stretched the horizons of the Scottish policy debate farther than they had been pushed before under either Westminster or devolution.

The Scottish government's record of executive decisions during its first two years in office reveals the politically pragmatic side of the party's convergence on social democracy. Among the government's earliest actions was the decision to halt the closure of the A&E departments at hospitals in Ayr and Airdrie, which had been the target of vigorous local opposition. It abolished some hospital car-parking fees and began the phased abolition of prescription charges. It announced that the £850 million bill for the new Southern General Hospital in Glasgow would be funded publicly and not through PPP. While it retreated from its election promise to write off student debt, it went ahead with its promise to abolish the graduate endowment and to establish a fund for the support of part-time learners. It piloted free school meals and committed to rolling them out across primary and secondary schools. It abolished the right to buy for new social housing and made £25 million available for the building of new council houses for rent. It uprated payments for residential care and continued to meet the rising bill for free social care.

Some of these measures have invited charges of populism and opportunism from the SNP's opponents. But they fit into a consistent trend in SNP policy of challenging some of the more controversial Labour Party policies introduced by the Blair and Brown administrations and adopted with varying degrees of enthusiasm by their Scottish colleagues.

A New Dawn?

The impression of a party comfortable presenting itself as a champion of a pre-Blairite, if not 'Old Labour', understanding of social democracy is reinforced by the Scottish government's latest social policy statements, *Equally Well* (Scottish Governmnent, 2008), outlining the Government's proposals to tackle Scotland's health inequalities, *Achieving our Potential: A Framework to Tackle Poverty and Income Inequality in Scotland* (Scottish Government, 2008c) and *The Early Years Framework* (Scottish Government 2009).

Early Years, the most recent of the three, claims that taken together the statements represent 'a new dawn in social policy' for Scotland. If the claim can be justified it is less because of their shared promise of a 'coordinated approach to early years, health inequalities and poverty at national and local levels' than because of the consistency of the focus on inequality. *Achieving our Potential* firmly identifies inequality as a cause and not just a symptom of poverty. It restates *Taking Forward*'s modification of the manifesto's commitment to reduce income inequality as a commitment to increase the share of national income enjoyed by the three income lowest deciles.

The excision of any references to Ireland and Iceland gives a monopoly to the core Nordic countries, though no analysis is offered of the reasons for their superior record on poverty and inequality. Alongside reminders of actions already taken, it reaffirms its commitment to a fairer and more redistributive system of local taxation and extends its strategic horizons by promising a study of the scope for action on public pay, as well as a joint campaign with the STUC and the voluntary sector to raise awareness of workers' rights on pay and leave entitlements. It also reaffirms its intention to engage with the UK government on the interaction of the benefits system with employability programmes, as well as on the case for devolving benefits along with tax to the Scottish Parliament.

The claims of the health and early years documents to be social policy path-breakers rest principally on three elements. One is their emphasis on the need to combat the effects of generational inequality by shifting the focus of services from crisis intervention to prevention by 'anticipatory' intervention. The government's approach is described as being to provide a high level of universal services with additional support provided at the earliest possible opportunity to the most vulnerable, to prevent their vulnerabilities developing into major social or health problems. The third element is a focus on the 'engagement and empowerment of children, families and communities' in the services they receive. Though no attribution is offered, these three elements – early intervention to support and engage the most vulnerable from a baseline of high-quality universal services – could serve as a summary of the best practice in the Nordic welfare states.

Omissions and Limitations

How coherent and how adequate to the challenges facing Scotland is the understanding of social justice at which the SNP has now arrived? First, gaps should be noted. There are very few references in either party or government documents to inequality of wealth as a cause of poverty and other social ills and, notoriously, the SNP's proposals for a local income tax excluded unearned income (Mooney and Wright, 2009). After three decades of increasing inequality of wealth, the paucity of reference seems significant.

Second, the government fails to provide targets for reducing income inequality or to specify which of the many policies described in its policy documents do the heavy lifting in achieving the desired reduction. It gives no indication of what share of national income the three lowest deciles should enjoy, nor how that share should be distributed between them. The relative roles of paid employment, fiscal redistribution and public services in achieving the reduction are never explained. The government seems to be relying on higher rate of economic growth and the better coordination of public services though council-led Community Planning Partnerships to make a major contribution in defiance of recent experience and medium-term prospects.

Another neglected area is sexual equality. While the importance of the equalities agenda in general is acknowledged, the SNP seems content with the rather modest role of women in Scottish public life beyond the economy. Despite Norway's favoured status as a model, there is no public evidence of SNP interest in Scotland emulating Norway's highly effective initiatives on boosting the role of women in its business and political life. This indifference may reflect the complacency with which the SNP appears to regard the modest representation of women among the party's elected representatives, its members, and even in recent years among its voters (Aberdeen and Strathclyde Universities, 2007).

The implementation of the SNP's 2007 manifesto commitment to engage and empower individuals and communities has been selective. While the government has extended the discretionary spending power of councils by reducing ring-fencing, the freezing of council tax has increased councils' financial dependence on central government, an effect which would have been reinforced had its local income tax proposals been implemented. Direct elections to health boards have been provided for and the intention to legislate for patients' rights reaffirmed, but promises to pilot measures directly empowering local communities have been ignored, perhaps as the price of securing the concordat with local councils, and little has been done to fulfil commitments to promote direct payments.

Policy Dualism: the Economic Head and the Social Heart

While some of these omissions may be attributable to the inevitable attrition of government and others to tactical compromises on a longer road to social democracy, some – notably the exclusion of wealth from the strategy to reduce inequality, the absence of targets for that reduction and the vagueness about the main policy instruments – may reveal a persistent ambivalence about the social democratic model itself. Over the last decade, as the SNP's social heart has become more attached to social democracy, its economic head has inclined to neo-liberalism. The dualism is most evident in the SNP government's social policy documents. *Taking Forward* compares the poverty records of neo-liberal Ireland and the social democratic Nordic countries statistically, much to the former's disadvantage. But even though it is presented as a 'taking forward of the government's economic strategy' to tackle Scotland's poverty and inequality, it ignores the conflict between its preferred social model and the government's preferred economic model. In some political parties such tensions would be the stuff of major debate if not ideological division – but the SNP has always shied away from ideological contention. *Achieving our Potential* and two companion statements continue the Nelsonian strategy.

That the tension has not created division or significant debate within the party may be due in part to the way the dualism seems to run through SNP leaders rather than between them. Alex Salmond has been the chief cheerleader for the Irish low-tax model even while claiming it, by virtue of its high level of investment in education and infrastructure and its social partnership, as an example of social democracy (Salmond, 2004). In one of only two published attempts by any SNP leader to resolve the tension, Justice Minister Kenny MacAskill acknowledges strengths in both the Irish and the Scandinavian models on his way to asserting that 'competitive business taxation is not inconsistent with social justice and quality public services'. But his supporting argument swings wildly between recommending the Scandinavian model for Scotland and declaring that the Swedish social welfare model is no longer an option in an interdependent global economy, while completely ignoring Ireland's poor social record and the fact that after 2000 low taxation in Ireland spread from the corporations to personal incomes (MacAskill, 2004).

Minister for Culture, External Affairs and the Constitution Michael Russell's recent assessment of Scotland's options aspires to be more radical, but is not much more coherent. He proposes cutting Scotland's public spending/GDP ratio by half to the Irish level and abolishing universalism in public service provision. Yet at the same time he acknowledges the economic (though not the social) success of the Nordic countries, even with their much higher public expenditure/GDP ratios, and warns against losing any of the 'guarantees of essential services which are the hallmark of a modern and civilised society'. Like MacAskill, he omits any reference to Ireland's social record (MacLeod and Russell, 2006).

Further symptoms of dualism may be found in the SNP's response to the impact on Scotland of the crisis in financial services and of the global recession. On the one hand, the Scottish government has campaigned for a sustained public expenditure-led response to the economic crisis. On the other hand, it has offered no policy response to the collapse of the greater part of the Scottish banking system. None of its economic spokespersons – neither Salmond, Finance Secretary John Swinney or Industry Minister Jim Mather – has made any public statement about the lessons to be drawn for the future shape and regulation of Scotland's financial services, except for vague murmurings that it must be consistent with reform of the international system. This may be a tactical silence intended to avoid drawing public attention to a general Scottish embarrassment or to the First Minster's connections to leading figures in Scotland's financial sector. Or it may derive from a strategic judgement that SNP talk of tighter regulation would frighten off potential supporters in the financial and business world in the run-up to an independence referendum and a Westminster general election. Or again it may be because the SNP leadership, or at least the sections of it in charge of economic strategy, continue to favour light-touch regulation as an essential ingredient along with low corporation tax and low wealth taxes for a dynamic Scottish economy under independence capable of achieving the government's single overriding purpose of a higher rate of sustainable economic growth.

Resolution

It is difficult to be sure how, or whether, this dualism will be resolved. The SNP has a strong aversion to ideological debate, as the left wing '79 Group discovered between 1979 and 1981. The establishment of the Scottish Parliament shifted policy initiative further from the party's elected policy-making bodies – the National Council and the Annual Conference – to the leadership in the Parliament and its paid staff. The SNP's move into government has centralised policy initiative even further. SNP members are in any case traditionally loyal to the party leadership and the party's recent electoral record and its move into government have cemented that. If the tension between the party's social heart and its economic head is to find resolution, the initiative will have to come from within the party's leadership, or at least from within the ranks of its MSPS and MPS.

It is tempting to assume that the ministers responsible for the 'new dawn' in social policy – Health and Wellbeing Ministers Nicola Sturgeon and Shona Robison, and Early Years Minister Adam Ingram – will be most sensitive to the tension between their social democratic strategy and the neo-liberalism underpinning their party's economic strategy, and that their perspective would be shared by the two ministers publicly identified as of the left, Housing Minister Alex Neil and Environment Minister Roseanna Cunningham. It might also be supposed that MPS and MSPS with a demonstrated interest in social issues, for example Glasgow East MP John Mason (the first SNP MP to serve on a Westminster Bill Committee for a welfare reform issue) and MSP John Wilson, a former director of the Scottish Low Pay Unit, would be alert to the tension. But given the absence of public comment by any of the ministers or backbenchers and the general opacity of the party's policy process, this remains supposition.

As always it is external pressures which will force change, in this case the exceptional pressures generated by the multi-layered global crisis. Neo-liberalism was the first victim of the global financial and economic crisis, though its demise has so far been acknowledged by the SNP only by its prompt exclusion of Ireland from its list of small-state exemplars. The cost of the crisis to Scotland is not just the destruction of what remained of a Scottish-led banking sector, but increased levels of unemployment and poverty and an intensification of the chronic social problems which the government's new social policies were designed to combat. The third wave of the crisis, the public-spending crunch, will condemn many of those policies to survive only as paper promises.

What price the government's commitment to universalism in public services caught between the relentless rise in public demand and a reducing public budget? The signs so far are that SNP will try to persevere with the policy pragmatism which has brought, or at least accompanied, the relative electoral success the party has enjoyed over the last two decades, in the hope that things will return eventually to pre-recession normality. But overshadowing these dire medium-term economic prospects is the fundamental challenge of environmental degradation with its own imperatives of radical economic and social adaptation. The inescapable challenge for the SNP is to integrate its case for Scottish independence with the transformational social and economic policies which our multiple global crises demand.

Scotland's Economic Options in the Global Crisis

A Nation Again: *why independence will be good for Scotland (and England too)* *(ed. P.H. Scott, Luath)*, 2011

WHERE DOES THE economic case for Scotland's independence stand after the drama of the banking crisis?

'When the facts change, I change my mind. What do you do, sir?' asked Keynes. He must have known that such a straightforward principle does not apply in politics, where changed facts are more likely to change arguments than conclusions.

Unionists argue that the collapse of Ireland's economy and the need of Scotland's two largest banks and private sector employers to be rescued by the UK Treasury have exposed the unreality of the SNP's case for Scottish independence. Supporters of independence argue that Scotland's exposure within the Union to the failures of UK economic and regulatory policies reinforce the case for independence. Service as usual.

The Unionists promote two lines of argument. The most common is that an independent Scotland could not have afforded to bail out its own banks and would have had to follow Ireland in accepting an EU and IMF bail-out with the loss of sovereignty and all the economic and social damage that entails. The second is that, were Scotland to become independent in future, Scots taxpayers would have to carry by themselves the cost of the UK's £470bn financial salvage of the Scottish banks.

These claims provide Unionists with handy debating points but they unravel on analysis.

The first claim – that Scotland would have followed Ireland's path to financial ruin – rests on a long trail of assumptions. Its plausibility depends on the supposition that Scotland became independent on the very eve of the banking crisis burdened with the uncorrected legacy of its preceding decades of misgovernment by the UK. Even in its own terms this ignores important facts. First, the rest of the UK would have been seriously exposed to the collapse of the Scottish banks by virtue of the sizeable proportion of their liabilities and staff located in the rest of the UK (rUK), principally England. In effect RBS and HBOS had ceased to be Scottish except by the location of their registered headquarters. They were products of the Big Bang deregulation of the UK's financial sector in 1986 and were integrated with the rest of the UK's financial sector. In its own interest the rUK would have been impelled to share the costs of rescuing the Scottish banks.

Second, unlike Ireland, even a newly independent Scotland would have possessed its own insurance fund in the form of its North Sea oil reserves worth wholesale anything between £600bn and £1trillion. While the two Scottish banks' total liabilities were several times the value of Scotland's annual GDP they also had large stocks of sound assets, particularly RBS. The Treasury projected RBS capital losses at £60bn out of £282bn of assets placed by RBS in the government's Asset Protection Scheme. By September 2009 actual losses amounted to £37bn (National Audit Office, 2010). So even on this extreme hypothesis an independent Scotland would have been able to avoid Ireland's fate.

The assumption that Scotland became independent on the eve of the UK's banking crisis is just a piece of rhetorical self-serving. An alternative scenario could have located the moment of independence in, say, 1980 at the beginning of Scotland's role as a major oil producer. But Unionists would then have needed to deploy even more extravagant assumptions. Firstly, that through three decades of independence Scotland had followed the same path to banking crisis as the UK and Ireland. In this scenario Scotland would have squandered its oil wealth rather than used it to diversify Scotland's economy (as urged by the SNP at the time and endorsed by the then Chief Economic Adviser to the Scottish Office, Gavin McCrone, in his secret 1974 memorandum) in the process reducing the relative weight of financial services in the Scottish economy (Scottish Office, 1975). Secondly, that from 1997 Scotland would have followed the example of Gordon Brown's light touch regulation of the banks rather than the stricter regimes introduced by the Nordic countries following their financial crises in the late 1980s and early 1990s.

The second Unionist claim is that if Scotland were to become independent before the banks were free of the life support provided by the UK Government, Scottish taxpayers would have to shoulder the full cost of the UK's investment in and guarantees to the Scottish banks, estimated at £470bn (Scottish Parliament, 2010). The liability is of course a possible cost: the real current cost is a fraction of the principal. This argument ignores the logic of the Union. Whatever the root causes of the banking crisis in the UK the public liability rests with the political authority with responsibility for regulating and supervising the banks. The responsible authorities were the UK Parliament and government. Even the new leaders of the Labour Party have now acknowledged their government's failure to regulate the banks adequately. Without any formal responsibility, Scotland's responsibility is as part of the UK. Based on Scotland's shares of the UK's population or GDP, between 8–9 per cent, her share of the UK's liabilities might be £40bn. Such a sum would be an unwelcome addition to Scotland's legacy of national debt from the UK, currently around £80bn, but the cost would be manageable. In any case, short of a total collapse of the financial system, it remains hypothetical.

It is not surprising that financial crisis on the scale now facing many western economies has pushed the issue of risk to the forefront of the debate on Scotland's future. A more sophisticated Unionist interpretation of the financial collapse of Ireland and Iceland than the empty speculations peddled by the Unionist parties claims that the collapse demonstrates that under globalisation an independent Scottish economy would be exposed to an unacceptable level of financial risk.

But the relationship between the size of an economy and its exposure to risk of financial or broader economic collapse is not at all clear. True, the larger a country's territory the more opportunities it might be expected to have to diversify its economy – but the link is weak. In practice the exposure of any particular economy to risk depends on how well its people use their particular resources and opportunities. Well into the industrial age Finland and Norway were regarded as countries with limited economic prospects, but using what resources they had they have developed into highly successful post-industrial states. They have had their share of crises and disasters along the way, but so have much larger states. It needs to be remembered that notwithstanding their current troubles, both Ireland and Iceland have enjoyed periods of great prosperity as independent states. Even in 2010 their per capita GDP was higher than the UK's (CIA World Factbook, 2011). Small economies may have a smaller margin for error in their economic and political decisions than larger states, but would anyone seriously argue that Ireland would have done better to remain under Westminster control or Iceland under Danish control, let alone that Norway would have done better under Swedish authority or Denmark as part of the German Confederation?

The chief executive of Ireland's Central Bank, Patrick Honohan, has seized on the collapse of the Irish banks as confirmation of his view that small countries should have foreign owners for their banks (Reuters, 24 November 2010). Given the way in which Ireland's bid to establish herself as a friendly offshore tax haven for foreign banks unravelled, most spectacularly with the collapse of Germany's Hypo Real Estates Irish arm DEPFA in 2008, perhaps Dr Honohan should not be dumping all the blame on Irish controlled banks. His view condemns Ireland to be a perpetual dependant of global neo-liberalism. Like most small developed countries, the Nordic countries prefer to maintain nationally or jointly owned banks as the foundation of their banking system.

Dr Honohan must be gratified by the situation in Scotland, where the combined effects of Mrs Thatcher's 1986 Big Bang liberalisation of financial services and two decades of light touch regulation has left the Airdrie Savings Bank, with eight local branches in its home region of Lanarkshire and a capital base of £130m, as the sole independent survivor of a once diverse and vigorous Scottish retail banking system. He will take further encouragement from the fact that no Scottish political party, not even the SNP, has shown any interest in rebuilding an independent Scottish banking system. The best that Scottish politicians appear to hope for is that new banks such as Tesco Bank and Virgin, along with foreign based newcomers such as Santander, will inject fresh competition into a Scottish market which since the restructuring of 2008 has been dominated by RBS and Lloyds TSB. On current policies if political nationalism makes further progress Scotland could be the only European country in the modern age to approach independence without any nationally owned banks.

In Honohan's globalist vision this need not matter. In the absence of its own national banking system a small country can still have a central bank. If a member of the Eurozone, it can have its own seat at the European Central Bank as well as at international forums for banking regulation. Currently, Scotland lacks not only independent Scottish commercial banks but also, unlike most other developed economies, local savings banks, public pension backed regional banks specialising in infrastructure investment, mutual banks or charitable banks of significant size, or even, thanks to Treasury obstruction, a bond issuing agency for public infrastructure projects such as the originally conceived Scottish Futures Trust or a functioning state development bank. The result is a lack of competition in mainstream banking, a chronic scarcity of patient investment capital, an uncertain supply of venture capital and a dearth of development funding for small businesses, the third sector and communities, all contributing to a narrow and unstable Scottish financial base.

The apparent indifference of Scottish political opinion to the hollowing out of Scotland's financial system raises the question of how an independent Scotland would position itself in a globalised world in which neo-liberalism is the dominant ideology. While the crisis was a product of neo-liberalism the response of the West's political leaders has turned it into a crisis of social democracy. The money needed to bail out the banks is being found from cuts in the public services which are part of the foundations of social democracy. In the US, a resurgent Republican right is challenging Obama's progressivism. In the UK a new centre right government is imposing cuts in public budgets worse than Mrs Thatcher's. Centre right governments rule in Germany and France. In Spain and Greece socialist Prime Ministers are bleeding the public sector to satisfy their international creditors and in last year's election even Sweden swung decisively to the right. Meanwhile, the bankers who caused the crisis are escaping with their bonuses barely dented and their 'too-big-to-fail' banks intact. One Scottish commentator judges that social democracy is 'in tatters and retreat across the Western world' and concludes: 'Scotland cannot buck this development. We cannot be the land where time stood still' (Hassan, *Scotsman*, 24 January 2011).

Yet in planning its future as an independent state it would be perverse for Scotland to opt for the neo-liberal alternative which is the cause of the present crisis. The key principle of social democracy – that a democratic state has a responsibility to provide security and welfare for all its citizens – is more necessary than ever in a world buffeted by global market forces. The record of the Nordic countries in the last three decades shows that far from being a handicap in a globalised economy, social democracy offers the best chance for economic stability and social welfare. Even Sweden, the Nordic country which has shown the greatest tendency to challenge social democratic orthodoxy, has in its taxing and spending policies remained loyal to the Nordic model as against the liberal Anglo-American model represented by the USA, the UK and Ireland (OECD, 2010).

This does not mean that social democracy, which devolved Scotland inherited from the United Kingdom, is an adequate foundation for an independent Scotland. It was too heavily imprinted with the centralising corporatism of Old Labour as well as being corrupted by New Labour's excessive deference to markets (Maxwell, 2007). While the first decade of devolution has improved the legacy in some important ways – easier public access to policy making, the introduction of STV for local elections, first steps towards direct community empowerment, setting boundaries to the role of markets in public services – it has failed to seize the potential for a second phase of devolution focused on the democratic empowerment of Scottish communities and civil society.

While more could have been achieved under devolution, the continuation of the Union undermines the political and social base for more radical reforms. For the second time in a generation Scotland is being forced by a UK government – which Scots voters emphatically rejected at the polls – to inflict large cuts on the social democratic settlement favoured by the Scottish majority. Mrs Thatcher doubled Scottish unemployment and poverty. Whether David Cameron's even deeper cuts will wreak destruction on a comparable scale remains to be seen, but the economic cost to Scotland in the form of lagging investment in Scotland's economic potential, particularly in renewables, is already accumulating. As long as Scotland is exposed to the fickleness of middle England's political moods she will struggle to maintain the levels of capital and social investment necessary to repair the injuries inflicted by her history of industrialisation and deindustrialisation compounded by centuries of misgovernment from London. Even more damagingly, the economic and social effects of the cycles of right wing government from England erode the confidence of Scots voters, fuelling those defensive reflexes which have regularly pushed them back to a Unionist Labour Party.

If the development of a bespoke version of social democracy balancing a strong national framework for economic development and social welfare with civil empowerment and the decentralisation of the management of public services is Scotland's best hope for the future, where is the space in a volatile global economy for such a project? The Union with England is evidently counterproductive. An enlarged European Union offers one option but, even before the banking crisis, the EU had begun to trim the disproportionate power small states enjoyed in the Union's decision making in response to enlargement. The Euro crisis is now directing the EU towards closer central control of the economies of Eurozone members. Like the Nordic countries, an independent Scotland could probably satisfy any strengthened economic criteria for Eurozone membership, at least after a transitional period. But it is doubtful whether membership of the Euro would best match Scotland's opportunities for national development. It is significant that of the four mainland Nordic countries only Finland is a member of the Eurozone. Assuming that the rUK remains outside the Euro, if the crisis forces the EU towards a two tier structure with membership of a more centralised Eurozone the dividing line between inner and outer circles, Scotland's best option would be in the outer circle allowing her to remain competitive with the rUK while providing maximum scope for developing her links with the Nordic countries. Whether Scotland then adopts sterling or, bolstered by rising world energy prices, opts for a separate Scottish currency would be a pragmatic judgement. Even if the rUK were to join the Eurozone, remaining outside the Euro, or even like Norway outside the European Union altogether, might offer Scotland more scope for the development of its social democratic project.

Ill Fares the Land, the valedictory message of the late Tony Judt, the pre-eminent interpreter of Europe's post-war history, offers two key judgements: that after three decades of retreat in the face of globalisation the nation state is poised to reclaim a dominant role and that, in confronting the current crisis, nation states should look to social democracy as their route map, not because it represents an ideal future, even less an ideal past, but because it is better than anything else to hand. It is a message which should at once hearten and inspire the movement for Scottish independence.

Socialism in Democracy

Scottish Left Review 67,
November / December 2011

THE LEFT WING CASE for Scotland's independence starts with democracy. For 27 of the first 65 post-war years (1945 to 2010) Scotland was governed from Westminster by governments which it had rejected at the polls. In the 2010 general election, the two parties that formed the coalition government gained only 36 per cent of the Scottish vote against a combined SNP and Labour vote of 63 per cent. If the coalition survives to the end of its five year term Scotland will have been governed from Westminster by parties it rejected for 32 of 70 post-war years. That will mean that for almost half the post-War period the tax, welfare, industrial, energy and labour market policies applied in Scotland will have been decided by governments Scottish voters did not vote for. How can a country expect to flourish if it is ruled for long periods by governments it doesn't want?

When those governments are ideologically hostile to the politics of the 'rejectionist' country they rule, the malign effects will be magnified. That has been the case with the Westminster governments rejected by Scottish voters since Alex Douglas-Home's 1964 government, through to the governments of Heath, Thatcher, Major and now Cameron. From Heath on, these governments have been progressively more hostile to Scotland's social democracy. The growing divergence between Scottish and English voting patterns has cost Scotland 21 years of social democratic government it could ill afford to lose with another four lost years in prospect under the existing coalition.

Mrs Thatcher's governments exacted a particularly high price. Scottish manufacturing employment declined by 30 per cent while poverty and unemployment rates doubled. Adding to the injury, Mrs Thatcher enjoyed a massive £160bn (2008 prices) inflow of oil revenues, principally from Scotland's North Sea territory, to spend on her failed experiments with monetarism and selling council houses at grossly discounted prices.

But the cuts in public expenditure on which the coalition government is now embarked exceed anything which Mrs Thatcher aimed for, let alone achieved. Contrary to the pro-market commentators intent on using the failure of the West's banking system to persuade Scots voters that their welfare state is no longer affordable, Scotland does not have a disproportionately large public sector by the standards of most advanced democracies, particularly when North Sea oil production is counted as part of Scotland's national output as it should be. Yet the Independent Budget Report on Scotland's budgetary prospects from 2011 estimated that between 2011 and 2026, £42bn would be stripped from Scotland's spending budget. It failed to note that on conservative projections of oil production and price levels Scotland could send twice that sum in oil revenues to the UK Treasury over the same period.

That does not mean that an independent Scotland in control of the revenues could escape all the effects of the world's worst financial crisis since the 1930s ('or possibly ever', in Mervyn King's opinion). But it does signal that it would have more opportunities to pursue social democratic policies than are likely to be available as part of the United Kingdom.

It is not that the rest of the UK does not have the financial resources to pursue progressive policies on its own account. When balanced against higher Scottish per capita expenditure, Scotland's North Sea revenues make a net contribution of less than one per cent to the UK's total public revenues. The rest of the UK could easily absorb the loss of the £7–8bn of Scottish North Sea revenues it stands to draw annually over the next two decades under the status quo if it chose to diversify its revenue sources and reassess its political priorities. About £70bn a year is lost to the UK Treasury by tax avoidance or evasion, while under the UK tax system capital wealth, so much of which is concentrated in London and the south east, goes virtually tax free. And then there is the enticing possibility of raising revenue from some form of Tobin Tax on financial transactions.

If these options are excluded by the veto power of the City of London, there are more accessible options. The Iraq War cost about £9bn. The UK's nuclear deterrent costs over £1bn a year, with a further £1bn in preparatory costs for the Trident replacement now added each year. From the 2015 decision deadline for the Trident replacement, further sums from the estimated £25bn cost of the replacement will be added. These all contribute to the UK's status as the world's fourth largest spender on defence at 2.5 per cent of GDP, second only to the United States among NATO members.

Government Expenditure and Revenue Scotland (GERS) 2009 – ten identifies Scotland's contribution to the UK defence budget at £3.2bn. If an independent Scotland spent the same 1.5 per cent of its GDP that Norway spends as a non-nuclear member of NATO, its annual defence budget would be around £1.8bn releasing £1.4bn for promoting alternatives to the UK defence jobs that would be lost to Scotland and for spending on maintaining and improving public services. More radical defence strategies would save even more.

But the security case for independence offers another benefit: Scotland's insistence on the removal of the UK's nuclear submarines from Faslane could act as the catalyst for the abolition of the deterrent altogether. The financial costs to the UK of providing an alternative to the base facilities on the Clyde would run to several billion pounds. Even more problematic would be the willingness of voters in areas identified as possible sites on the coast of England, or even Wales or Northern Ireland, to accept in their locality an operational nuclear base for four missile-carrying submarines and probably up to ten other nuclear powered submarines. It is more likely that an English public increasingly sceptical of the case for the Trident replacement would finally call a halt to the UK's nuclear obsession.

Meanwhile, the mooted alternatives to independence such as full fiscal autonomy or 'independence-lite' would, among other disadvantages, deny Scotland the substantial economic dividend to be won by going non-nuclear which, depending on the defence policy pursued by an independent Scotland, could be up to £1bn a year. Scotland's options for alternative economic development and for social reforms would be more limited as a result.

Defenders of the Union will look for salvation from two possible sources. First they will hope for a revival of the Labour Party's electoral fortunes in England to reconcile Scottish social democrats to the continuation of the Union. But the prospects for this are uncertain at best. It is not just that the Labour Party has a hard route back to power in the face of the loss of public trust in its economic competence and its near wipe out in southern England. The more fundamental problem is the public's confusion over what a Labour Party – which, under Tony Blair, opened the door to many of the market reforms of the welfare state the coalition government is now developing – actually stands for any more. Even if Ed Miliband and his colleagues are able to develop a coherent vision capable of dispelling that uncertainty, Scottish voters may choose to stay with the more familiar versions of social democracy on offer on their home turf.

The current pleas by senior Scottish Labour figures, most recently Douglas Alexander, for Labour to regain the leadership of a Scottish agenda for change suggests that few of its Scottish activists are content to rely on the possibility of a UK-wide revival of Labour's fortunes. But defining that Scottish agenda in ways consistent with the stability of the Union is no easy task. How far is Labour willing to champion more radical versions of devolution than the Calman-inspired Scotland Bill currently before Parliament? Will they support the devolution of corporation tax, of energy policy and oil taxation, of the welfare budget? Once started on this road unionists might be excused for feeling that they are out of control on Tam Dalyell's slippery slope.

While delivering government consistently in accord with the social democratic preferences of Scottish voters provides the foundation of the left wing case for independence, it offers no guarantees of a long future of progressive reforms under independence. The current limited form of devolution does not provide a serious test of Scottish social democracy's capacity to generate serious changes to the distribution of power and wealth, least of all in the midst of financial crisis. The devolved Parliament has legislated some significant reforms, of which the introduction of STV for local government and the Climate Change Act are probably the most significant, and Holyrood governments have championed some progressive policies such as free social care and the defence of an integrated health service. But no Scottish political party is offering the Scottish public a developed and comprehensive programme of social democratic reform. And since the credit crunch in 2007/8, the most conspicuous feature of Scottish public life has been the absence of any ideological response to the seismic changes in Scotland's economic and political environment, to which the apparent consensus to ignore the implications of the final disappearance of a Scottish banking system stands as inglorious testament.

So, Scottish Left-wingers will have to be patient: independence is unlikely to spark an instant Scottish Spring of radical reform. But it can be expected to increase the level of activity and urgency in those state and civil institutions which sustain public debate and prepare the way for change. It will sharpen Scots' sense of responsibility for their own future. It will help them to counter the neo-liberal influence of Anglo-America with the practical social democracy of the Nordic countries. It should raise the expectations Scots have of their governments. By raising the stakes for Scottish decision-taking it should stimulate Scottish civil society – its voluntary organisations and think tanks, its unions and Churches – to become more active in developing and promoting their various claims. It will necessarily generate debate around what sort of constitution Scotland should have, how power should be distributed between central government and parliament, local government, communities and the general public. It will encourage people to question how well Scotland is served by its institutional legacy from the UK, from its media and the banks to its welfare state and its monarchy. Not least, by setting Scots the everyday challenge of running their own society, independence may induce them to discard some of their more tiresome cultural tics such as agonising over whether they suffer a 'crisis of confidence' condemning them to stick for ever in their same auld groove.

Arguing for Independence

Stephen Maxwell

ISBN 978-1-908373-33-5 PBK £9.99

With the referendum on Scottish independence almost certain to be held in October 2014, *Arguing for Independence* challenges the currently accepted style of arguing for and against Scottish independence.

Acknowledging the complexity and conditional character of political argument, this book marks the beginning of the real debate on independence as the author goes beyond referendum wrestling and tendentious headlines.

Looking at the consequences of independence for particular areas of Scottish life usually considered in isolation, the book draws on a diversity of sources characteristic of political debate.

Controversially, the author includes criticisms of leading Scottish members of the last Labour government and the current coalition government over attitudes to economic and banking issues.

Extensive 'Aye but...' section.

On his death [Stephen Maxwell] left as his testament a compelling, deeply informed and meticulously argued book, Arguing for Independence, *which succinctly encapsulated his final thoughts on the vital questions to which he had devoted his politically committed life.*

JOHN HERDMAN, Another Country

A Model Constitution for Scotland

W. Elliot Bulmer

ISBN 978-1-908373-13-7 PBK £9.99

Scotland is a free, sovereign and independent commonwealth. Its form of government is a parliamentary democracy based upon the sovereignty of the people, social justice, solidarity and respect for human rights...

A Model Constitution for Scotland sets out a workable model for Scotland's future and includes detailed constitutional proposals together with informed discussion on the topic.

The independence debate has to break out of political elites and address the 'after independence' question. Elliot Bulmer's book is an important contribution to this, exploring how we make Scotland constitutionally literate, and how we shape our politics in a way which reflects who we are and what we aspire to be. Bulmer rightly argues that independence has to aspire to more than abolishing reserved powers, Holyrood becoming a mini-Westminster, and nothing else changing. A must read for independentistas, thoughtful unionists and democrats.

GERRY HASSAN, author and broadcaster

Bulmer deals with fundamental rights and freedoms in a broad-minded and incisive fashion.

NEWSNET SCOTLAND

A Nation Again: Why Independence will be good for Scotland (and England too)

Edited by Paul Henderson Scott
ISBN 978-1906817-67-1 PBK £7.99

If you believe in the Case for Independence, this book will provide you with a stirring endorsement of your view. If you are sceptical, it might well persuade you to convert to the cause. If you are downright hostile, this book could be dangerous – it could prompt you to rethink.

Suddenly Scottish Independence is within grasp. Is this a frivolous pipedream, a romantic illusion? Or is it, as the writers of this dynamic and positive collection of essays insist, an authentic political option, feasible and beneficial?

As the Scottish people prepare for their biggest ever collective decision, this book forcefully sets out the Case for Independence. The distinguished authors, from a variety of different perspectives, argue the case for the Imperative of Independence.

Radical Scotland: Arguments for Self-Determination

Edited by Gerry Hassan and Rosie Ilett
ISBN 978-1906817-94-7 PBK £12.99

Scotland believes it is a radical, egalitarian, inclusive nation. It was hoped that the establishment of the Scottish Parliament was going to give expression to this. Instead, we have witnessed a minimal, unattractive politics with little to choose between the main parties. This might be adequate in the good times, but no more. *Radical Scotland* explores how we can go beyond the limited politics we have experienced and makes the case for shifting from self-government politically to self-determination as a society and a nation. It asks how do we shake up institutional Scotland? How do we shift power and give people voice?

The editors Gerry Hassan and Rosie Ilett have brought together in one volume some of the most original thinkers in our nation making the case for a very different politics and society. It includes conversations with leading global figures on some of the key issues facing the world which impact on Scotland.

Building a Nation: Post Devolution Nationalism in Scotland

Kenny MacAskill

ISBN 978-1842820-81-0 PBK £4.99

 Where stands Scotland post Devolution and what is the future for Nationalism in a devolved Parliament? Is the Scottish Parliament a Unionist dead end or a Nationalist highway to Independence? Has Devolution killed the SNP stone dead or given it a platform to build from? These are questions that need to be answered as Scotland begins to come to terms with Devolution and decides where to go next.

In this book, Kenny MacAskill searches for the answers to these questions, which are vital to the future of Scotland. He makes the case for a distinctive Scottish version of social democracy that can balance a vibrant economy with quality public services, and believes that Post Devolution Nationalism is about Building a Nation to be proud of.

A manifesto to inspire and infuriate; pacey, intelligent and accessible. Like all good political pamphlets it is best enjoyed when read out loud.

SCOTTISH REVIEW OF BOOKS, VOL I

Agenda for a New Scotland: Visions of Scotland 2020

Kenny MacAskill

ISBN 978-1905222-00-1 PBK £9.99

 *The campaign for a Scottish Parliament was ongoing for centuries. Lamented in prose and championed in print. Petitioned for, marched in support of and voted upon. Dear to the hearts of many and whose absence broke the hearts of a few.* From Kenny MacAskill's Introduction to *Agenda for a New Scotland*

It has now reconvened after nearly 300 years. A Devolved Legislature but a Parliament all the same. Unable to address all issues but able to make a difference in many areas. It is for the Scottish Parliament to shape and mould the future of Scotland. But, what should that future be?

This is a series of contributed articles from politicians, academics and Civic Scotland. They outline opportunities and future directions for Scotland across a range of areas socially, economically and politically. This is an *Agenda for a New Scotland*. Visions of what Scotland can be by 2020.

Scotland: Land and Power – agenda for land reform

Andy Wightman

ISBN 978-0946487-70-7 PBK £5.00

Land reform campaigner Andy Wightman delivers a hard-hitting critique of the oppressive absurdities of Scotland's antiquated land laws. His is by no means a purely negative analysis – here are thought-through proposals for reforms which he argues would free both country and urban Scots from the shackles of land laws that are feudal and oppressive.

Andy Wightman's views are controversial, but he doesn't mind a good argument. He is an influential figure in Scottish political life these days. Those who don't agree with his views do pay attention to them, and his contribution to one of the hottest debates of the new millennium is well respected.

Writers like Andy Wightman are determined to make sure the hurt of the last century is not compounded by a rushed solution in the next. This accessible, comprehensive but passionately argued book is quite simply essential reading and perfectly timed – here's hoping Scotland's legislators agree.

LESLEY RIDDOCH

Scotland: The Growing Divide

Henry McLeish

ISBN: 978-1-908373-45-8 PBK £11.99

Is there a growing divide between Holyrood and Westminster? What does this mean for the people of Scotland, and for England?

In 2007, *Scotland: The Road Divides* posed a provocative political question:

Had the SNP victory at Holyrood changed forever the mindset of Scottish politics?

As a Scottish Independence referendum fast approaches, *Scotland: The Growing Divide* returns to answer this question and more with a hard-hitting, incisive and informed look at where the devolution journey has taken us – from the heady days of the new Blair government in 1997 to the Independence referendum in 2014. It poses new questions about the issues facing Scottish politics:

How has devolution altered Scotland's national perception of itself?

Is there a fusion of identity and nationality politics with traditional politics and priorities taking place in Scotland? Is this creating a serious realignment of political thinking and ideas and the possible demise of the old politics of both the UK and Scotland?

Arguing that the Union must adapt to survive, former First Minister Henry McLeish contends that the devolution referendum paved the way for a bold new constitutional settlement. A contentious and pertinent commentary, this book maintains that many politicians have yet to come to terms with these dramatic changes and do not appear to understand the 'new politics', or the new Union.

Details of these and other books published by Luath Press can be found at:
www.luath.co.uk

Luath Press Limited
committed to publishing well written books worth reading

LUATH PRESS takes its name from Robert Burns, whose little collie Luath (*Gael.*, swift or nimble) tripped up Jean Armour at a wedding and gave him the chance to speak to the woman who was to be his wife and the abiding love of his life. Burns called one of 'The Twa Dogs' Luath after Cuchullin's hunting dog in Ossian's *Fingal*. Luath Press was established in 1981 in the heart of Burns country, and now resides a few steps up the road from Burns' first lodgings on Edinburgh's Royal Mile.
Luath offers you distinctive writing with a hint of unexpected pleasures.

Most bookshops in the UK, the US, Canada, Australia, New Zealand and parts of Europe either carry our books in stock or can order them for you. To order direct from us, please send a £sterling cheque, postal order, international money order or your credit card details (number, address of cardholder and expiry date) to us at the address below. Please add post and packing as follows: UK – £1.00 per delivery address; overseas surface mail – £2.50 per delivery address; overseas airmail – £3.50 for the first book to each delivery address, plus £1.00 for each additional book by airmail to the same address. If your order is a gift, we will happily enclose your card or message at no extra charge.

ILLUSTRATION: IAN KELLAS

Luath Press Limited
543/2 Castlehill
The Royal Mile
Edinburgh EH1 2ND
Scotland
Telephone: 0131 225 4326 (24 hours)
Fax: 0131 225 4324
email: sales@luath.co.uk
Website: www.luath.co.uk